The Wines of South Africa

James Seely was born in Nottinghamshire in 1940. He entered the wine trade in 1960, having served two years in the Merchant Navy. He worked for Harveys of Bristol, and started his own wine merchant and shipping business in 1973.

His first book, *Great Bordeaux Wines*, was published in 1985, followed by *The Loire Valley and its Wines* in 1987, since when he has been a regular contributor to *Decanter* and other magazines.

He lives in a farmhouse in Essex, where he continues to run his merchant business, as well as organizing luxury wine tours to the vineyards of the world.

THE WINES OF SOUTH AFRICA

JAMES SEELY

faber and faber

LONDON · BOSTON

First published in 1997
by Faber and Faber Limited
3 Queen Square London WC1N 3AU

Phototypeset by Intype London Ltd
Printed in England by Clays Ltd, St Ives plc

A CIP record for this book
is available from the British Library

ISBN 0–571–17645–3

2 4 6 8 10 9 7 5 3 1

Contents

CONTENTS

CONTENTS

CONTENTS

List of Maps

Key to Map Pages

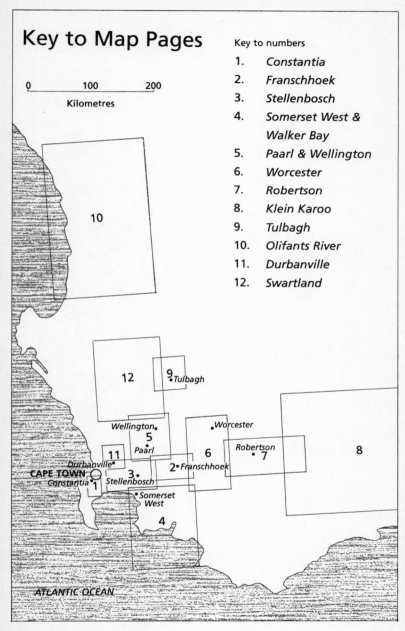

Key to numbers

1. *Constantia*
2. *Franschhoek*
3. *Stellenbosch*
4. *Somerset West & Walker Bay*
5. *Paarl & Wellington*
6. *Worcester*
7. *Robertson*
8. *Klein Karoo*
9. *Tulbagh*
10. *Olifants River*
11. *Durbanville*
12. *Swartland*

Key to Map Pages

Acknowledgements

If I were to list all the people who gave so much time and help during my long stay in South Africa, this section would be longer than the book itself. Everywhere I went, I was treated with a warmth and welcome that simply could not have been feigned for a visiting wine writer. I would ask all whom I met, and those whom space does not allow me to mention, to accept my very sincere thanks.

For generous hospitality, help and advice, I would particularly like to thank Julian Ogilvie Thompson of Anglo-American Farms and his wife Tessa, as well as Keith Hosking, Don Tooth and Margaret Leroy of Anglo-American; not only was I given Rhodes Cottage on the Boschendal estate for an initial week-long reconnaissance trip – as well as two weeks in the Boschendal student accommodation, and free use of their office telephone and fax – but these last three gave me invaluable help in planning my main research visit. This they did by introducing me to a number of key figures in the industry, who, in their different capacities, did much to help me unravel the mysteries of the Cape wine scene. I thank this group for their help, namely Dr Jannie Retief of the KWV, Sydney Back of Backsberg, Jacob Deist and Kobus Joubert.

Tim Hamilton Russell of Hamilton Russell Vineyards was extremely kind and helpful, and gave me much sound advice, not only on my research trip for this book, but also back in 1988, when I first became interested in writing about South African wines. Hans Joachim Schreiber of Neethlingshof generously allowed me the use of the lovely apartment at Stellenzicht Mountain Winery for the greater part of my stay in the Cape, without which my researches would have been far more expensive, and proportionately less enjoyable. My very first visit was to the Clos

Cabrière Estate in Franschhoek, where Achim von Arnim set the tone of the whole trip with his enthusiastic vitality and the warmth of the welcome that both he and his wife Hildegard extended to me. I was well fed, watered, wined and informed on more than one occasion by Stan Ratcliffe and his Bordeaux-trained, Canadian-born wife and winemaker, 'Storming' Norma. Of the other leading winemakers whom I remember for their special help and welcome, I would like to thank especially Etienne le Riche of Rustenberg, Kevin Arnold of Rust-en-Vrede, Jan 'Boland' Coetzee of Vriesenhof, Beyers Truter of Kanonkop, Abey Beukers of Lievland, Giorgio Dalla Cia of Meerlust, Herman Kirschbaum of Buitenverwachting and Lowell Jooste and winemaker Ross Gower of Klein Constantia.

During my trek through Robertson and the Klein Karoo, I was warmly received, fed and lodged by Abrie Bruwer at Springfield Estate, Pieter Ferreira of Graham Beck's Madeba Winery, Danie de Wet of de Wetshof, Paul and Cuckoo de Wet of Zandvliet, Andri van Zyl of van Zylshof, and Swepie le Roux at Domein Doornkraal.

John Platter, doyen of South African wine writers, was both encouraging and helpful in every way. The 1996 edition of his handbook, *South African Wines*, the sixteenth since 1980, was an indispensable vade-mecum; it gives not only all the important names, telephone and fax numbers, and vital statistics for all the producers and their wines, but also a mass of useful information, maps of all the regions, and details of restaurants and hotels. I am also indebted to Phyllis Hands, co-author with Dave Hughes and John Kench of the handsome, illustrated work, also titled *South African Wines*; she was, like so many wine writers I have met, most helpful and encouraging to a newcomer on her patch, as was Cape Wine Master Christine Rudman, author of *A Guide to the Winelands of the Cape*.

Through the kind offices of Michael Fridjhon and the generosity of South African Airways, I was given a free return flight from London to Cape Town, and I thank them both.

Thanks are due to Marius de Burgh of the Toyota dealers in Stellenbosch; he is a very kind man, and helped me to secure a good car-hire deal, as well as generously giving me a free tank of petrol every week.

Two people in South Africa merit a very special expression of my appreciation and gratitude. Both are gifted winemakers, princes among men, and have become lifelong friends. The first of these is François Naudé, winemaker at Marc Wiehe's L'Avenir in Stellenbosch; an unassuming, self-taught winemaker of great flair, François, and his wife Magda, opened their hearts and their home to me, and I hope that some day in some way I will be able to repay them for all they did for me. The second, though equal in my affection, is André van Rensburg, the crazy, brilliant winemaker at Hans Joachim Schreiber's Stellenzicht Mountain Winery; although young, he has already forgotten more about winemaking than I shall ever know. He led me into all manner of enjoyable trouble and was, and will remain, a staunch friend and guide.

A special note of thanks is due to Lowell Jooste who provided the photograph of Klein Constantia for the cover of the book.

On the home front, I would like to thank Diana Makgill for her kind introductions to her friends in the Cape. Special thanks are due once more to my elder son Christian, who lent me the lap-top computer on which this book was written, and gave me his usual patient and understanding initiation into the mysteries of word-processing. Both he and my younger son, Johnny, have given me an unbelievable amount of help and support through some very dark days during the writing of the book, and I salute and thank them with pride and love.

I am particularly grateful to Julian Jeffs, who edited this book with patience, tact and great skill. A final and deserved thank-you is due to my assistant, Amanda Butler. She kept my somewhat eccentric business affairs running during my long absence in South Africa. Without her loyal and consistently cheerful help, as they always say during the Oscar awards, this book would never have been written.

Apologia

Sadly, time and resources did not allow me to visit every single producer in the Cape. I hope that I have chosen a representative selection of all the different types of winemaking establishment. I apologize to the many fine estates, co-operatives and wineries that are not covered, and trust that they will understand that, although pruning is necessary, many of the finest bunches must perforce be sacrificed. I have tried to include a list of those who have been so shamefully neglected at the end of each section.

Introduction

THE INDUSTRY TODAY

The South African wine industry is currently at the most exciting point in its three-hundred-year history. Apart from the noble dessert wine of Constantia, production of fine table wine in the Cape was relatively limited for the first two hundred and fifty years after the first vines were planted by the early Dutch settlers. There are three reasons. First, the original purpose of making wine in the Cape was to victual the fleets of the Dutch East India Company on their long trading voyages to the Far East, and the demand was mainly for brandy and fortified wines, which could withstand the conditions of many months at sea, often in great heat. Second, the taste of white South Africans has always been more for brandies, 'port', 'sherry' and sweet fortified wines than for natural table wines. Third, sales during this period were largely restricted to the domestic market, due to the sheer physical difficulties and distances involved in export.

In the early part of this century, as the Cape vineyards recovered from the ravages of phylloxera, growers became more interested in making table wines. The First World War left the European wine producers in disarray and, with faster shipping, export became viable. The Second World War brought another five-year gap in export trade for French, German and Spanish wines, opening up yet more opportunities for the wine farmers of South Africa. Until this time, one of the Cape's biggest problems in the making of table wines, particularly whites, had been the hot weather experienced in January and February which made temperature control during fermentation difficult. For white wine production, which accounted for the huge majority of the total table-wine crop, a solution arrived with the newly developed cold fermentation process. The reason for the preponderance of white wine at this time was mainly that white varieties had always predominated for the making of fortified wines, sherries and brandy, and government restrictions on the import of plant material were even stricter than they are today. In addition, there was a tendency for young winemakers to study in Germany rather than in France – the language posed fewer problems for Afrikaans speakers than did French – so that their expertise was in the making of whites rather than reds. Although there have always been certain estates making good red wine, the huge expansion in this field did not really come about until the 1970s and 1980s.

Whilst great strides in vinification and viticulture have continued over the past twenty years, exports were brought to a virtual standstill in the 1980s by the moral and economic sanctions applied by potential importers against the South African government. In the very short time since the ending of apartheid, wine consumers worldwide have become keenly interested in the wines of the Cape, and demand, especially for the wines at the top end of the quality spectrum, exceeds supply for the first time this century.

As in other wine-producing countries around the world, there is a new generation of keen, energetic and highly qualified winemakers in South Africa today, and they are responding, to the best of their ability, to the boom in demand for quality wines from the Cape. Whereas in the past winemakers tended to work in isolation, jealously guarding the secrets of their craft, today's industry is far more open, and there is a tremendous spirit of co-operation in the winelands of South Africa. Evidence of this is clearly demonstrated by the establishment of associations of certain groups of winemakers in an effort to promote and improve the quality of the wines that they make. For example, there are two such organizations for the makers of 'port' and sparkling wines, and the latest to be formed is the Pinotage Association.

THE PRODUCERS

At the time of writing there was a total of 102,625 hectares under vines in South Africa, of which 93,680 were planted with grapes for making wine and brandy; the rest were mainly table grapes. The

1995 crop yielded 9.5 million hectolitres, of which a massive 5.87 million hectolitres, equivalent to over 65 million cases, were made into wine.

There are over 4,700 wine producers in South Africa today, and these fall into five categories. By far the biggest group are the farmers who supply grapes to the 70 co-operatives; these account for 85% of total production. Then there are the co-operatives themselves, which vary in size from as few as five members handling 1,000 tons of grapes, up to the giant Vredendal Co-operative, which has 158 members, and processes more grapes than the whole of New Zealand. The co-operatives sell the majority of their production in bulk for distillation to the wholesaler/producers for use in their blends, or on the export market for bottling overseas. There is a growing tendency, however, for the co-operatives to bottle a small proportion of their output for marketing under their own labels.

Next in terms of volume are the wholesaler/producers. The largest of these are Stellenbosch Farmers' Winery, Distillers Corporation and Douglas Green Bellingham. Typically, wholesaler/producers will have their own flagship estates or wineries and large production, blending and bottling units, where they will blend, age and bottle the wines that they buy in from the co-operatives and other growers. They are also wholesalers with their own marketing and distribution network throughout South Africa and the rest of the continent, as well as being major exporters of their own estate and blended wines.

The other two groups are the estates and private growers. The difference between these two is that those properties registered as estates may only sell wine under the estate label, provided that the grapes used for that wine come exclusively from the estate's own vines. Like the private growers who are not registered estates, they may buy in grapes from other sources, but wine made from these grapes must be sold under a different label.

THE VINEYARDS

The winelands of South Africa lie in a strip of territory at the southern tip of the African continent. The western boundary is a line of about 120 kilometres from just north of Latitude 33 South to just below Latitude 34 South, with the northern end at the top of the Olifants River vineyards, running down to below Constantia. The eastern limit is about 350 kilometres away, running between the same latitudes just east of Oudsthoorn. This is a wine-producing region of spectacular scenic beauty, dominated by towering mountain ranges and fertile green valleys, bounded to the south and west by the lovely coastlines of the Indian and Atlantic oceans, and dotted with hundreds of beautiful old Cape Dutch homesteads set about with mature trees, planted hundreds of years ago for shade.

The majority of the quality table wines come from the vineyards of Constantia, Stellenbosch, Franschhoek, Paarl, Tulbagh, Somerset West and around Hermanus in Walker Bay. These areas lie in the south-western corner of the wine-producing region, where all the classic grape varieties thrive on the decomposed granite soils of the lower mountain slopes, and benefit from the cooling sea breezes.

The regions that lie further to the north, at the western end of the winelands, like Swartland and the Olifants River, are far hotter and have less rainfall, which makes them better suited to growing grapes for blending by the wholesaler/producers, for the making of sweet fortified wines and for distillation. The same is true of the more easterly regions, from Wellington and Worcester, through Robertson to the arid, semi-desert of the Klein Karoo. In all of these hotter regions, there are exceptions, where good winemakers are producing fine wine from isolated pockets of the right soil with the right micro-climates. The white wines of Danie de Wet and the reds of Paul de Wet, both in Robertson, are good examples, and in the Klein Karoo, at the far eastern extremity of the winelands, good table wines and superb 'ports' are made by the Nels at Boplaas and Die Krans.

THE GRAPES

The wine farms of South Africa differ from other wine-producing areas around the world in that, with a very few exceptions, there is a tendency to plant a large number of varieties, rather than specializing in one or two. This is largely because the estates are generally far bigger than in Europe, and they have a greater variation in soil and micro-climate. Moreover, growers have been dependent over the last two or three decades on the domestic market, and particularly on passing trade. Thus, it has obviously been expedient to produce a whole range of different wines, so that their regular clients can fulfil all their wine needs in one stop.

Chenin Blanc is the notably predominant white variety grown now, as for the last three hundred years. Although planting is now decreasing, the Chenin, or Steen as it was originally called in the Cape, still accounts for nearly a third of all the vineyards. It is a heavy cropper, and historically was planted mainly for brandy production. A large quantity of Chenin table wine of mediocre quality is produced, but some of the new-generation winemakers are beginning to recognize the potential of this very versatile grape.

Colombar is the second most-grown white grape. Although mainly used for brandy and for blending, there are some good single-varietal wines made, especially in Robertson.

Hanepoot, the local name for Muscat d'Alexandrie, is widely grown, and its main use is in the making of a sweet, fortified wine; the same is true of the white **Muscadel**.

Two **Rieslings** are found. The Cape Riesling, also known as Crouchen Blanc, is mainly vinified as a dry wine, and the best come from Stellenbosch and Paarl. The **Rhine**, or **Weisser Riesling**, is the grape from Germany, and some good, mainly medium-dry wines are made, again in the south-western regions.

Rapidly gaining ground throughout the South African vineyards are the classic white cultivars, Sauvignon Blanc, Chardonnay, Sémillon and a little Gewürztraminer.

The best **Sauvignon Blanc** single-grape wines come from Constantia and Stellenbosch. Unwooded versions are the most common, and generally the best, though a few growers vinify a proportion of their crop in oak, when the wine usually carries the word Fumé on the label.

Chardonnay is more widely planted, and examples of varying styles can be found in almost every region. The use of oak casks for fermentation and ageing is the subject of much experimentation, and fine wooded Chardonnays are making their appearance from Constantia to Robertson. The Chardonnay is also widely used in conjunction with Pinot Noir for the making of 'Cap Classique' sparkling wine.

Sémillon was one of the first cultivars to be planted in the Cape, when it was known as the Green Grape, and was used mainly for distillation and blending. Until recently it had lost much of its popularity with growers, mainly due to poor plant material, but is now making a comeback with the availability of better, virus-free clones, and some lovely single-varietal wines are beginning to appear.

Gewürztraminer is less widely grown, and is usually vinified as a medium-sweet to sweet wine.

Red varieties represent a far smaller proportion of grapes grown for wine than white, though they are very much on the increase in tune with growing demand for South African reds.

Cinsaut has always been grown in quantity, and is usually used in blended red wines. This grape came from the Rhône valley in France, and used to be known as the Hermitage. In the 1920s, Professor Abraham Perold of Stellenbosch University crossed it with the Pinot Noir, giving birth to South Africa's own Pinotage.

For years the **Pinotage** was not highly regarded, and was mostly used as a wine for blending, but it is now enjoying a renaissance. This has been largely due to the efforts of Beyers Truter, winemaker at Kanonkop in Stellenbosch, who has proved beyond doubt that the Pinotage, when treated with due respect, can produce a red wine of extraordinary quality.

Cabernet Sauvignon is a major player and, although traditionally made as a single-grape wine, is now appearing more often in 'Bordeaux' blends, with Merlot and sometimes a little Cabernet Franc, which also appear as single-cultivar wines.

Pinot Noir is a difficult grape to vinify as red wine, though it has been established in the Cape for some time, mainly for making into sparkling 'Cap Classique'. Valiant and increasingly successful efforts are being made to make red wine from the Pinot Noir, Hamilton-Russell in Walker Bay, and Clos Cabrière in Franschhoek being among the best.

Shiraz, the French Syrah, can be very successful here, and thrives better in the hotter regions than other red varieties; the example made at Stellenzicht is definitely one to keep an eye on for the future.

South Africa has always been a big producer and consumer of 'port'. In the past, before the importation of plant material became easier, these wines were made from Cinsaut, Shiraz and some

Tinta Barocca. Today the traditional Portuguese varieties are on the increase, and serious producers are planting Touriga Nacional, Sousao, Tinta Roriz and many others.

THE WINES

South Africa probably produces more different types and styles of wine than any other country in the world. Innumerable blended table wines, both red and white, are made from countless combinations of varieties, which range from the predictable to the unimaginable. These are produced right across the winelands by the co-operatives, the wholesaler/producers, the estates and private wineries, as well as by the KWV (see Chapter Two).

Single-grape table wines – red, white and rosé – from all the classic varieties, in every conceivable style, abound at every level of quality and price. The best of these are of exceptional merit, and tend to come from estates and private wineries, mainly in the south-western regions like Constantia, Stellenbosch, Franschhoek, Paarl and Walker Bay – but some fine examples are beginning to emerge from the hotter, more difficult regions.

Some really fine sweet, unfortified wines are made, and these are called Special Late Harvest and Noble Late Harvest, terms peculiar to South Africa. The former must have a residual sugar level of between 20 and 50 g/l (grammes per litre), and the latter over 50, though they usually have in excess of 100, and a far higher content of botrytized grapes.

Sparkling Wines produced range from tank-fermented bubbly to fine bottle-fermented Méthode Cap Classiques made from the Champagne varieties. They are finding their way on to the export market, where they compare very favourably with sparklers from other countries in terms of quality and price.

'Port' and 'sherry' of good quality are made, though world demand for sherry has declined to such an extent that even the Spanish have halved the area of production in Andalucia. The 'port' industry in the Cape is thriving, however, and the styles most commonly found are ruby and vintage. The word 'port' is disappearing from labels to allow export access to European Community countries, and is being replaced by 'Cape Ruby', 'Cape Vintage' and so on. South African 'port' has always tended to be sweeter than the Portuguese wine, but there is a leaning now towards a higher alcoholic degree and a consequently drier finish. J. P. Bredell and Overgaauw Estate, both in Stellenbosch, are making excellent 'port', but the capital of 'port' in the Cape is definitely Calitzdorp, where the Nels at Boplaas and Die Krans are the masters.

The style most peculiar to South Africa is that of the sweet, fortified wine. These are found throughout the wine country, though the best examples seem to come from Worcester, Paarl, Robertson and the Klein Karoo. The fortification of wines with brandy probably originates from the days when heat caused problems in both vinification and conservation. Now, with the advent of cold fermentation techniques, it is much easier to make natural table wines, but old habits die hard, and these fortified wines are still consumed in prodigious quantities on the home market. They are most commonly sold under the name of the grape, either Hanepoot or Muscadel, both of which may be either red or white. The style is rich, honeyed and raisiny, and the residual sugar level must be between 75 and 160 g/l, and alcohol between 16.5% and 22%. Jerepigo, variously spelled Jerepiko and Jerepico, is unfermented grape must with alcohol added; it is usually made from Hanepoot or Muscadel, and has a minimum of 160 g/l of sugar. The name comes from the Portuguese Geropiga or Jeropiga, which is an alcoholic syrup, made in exactly this way, and used for sweetening 'port'. They are very sweet and relatively inexpensive, usually sold in screw-top bottles.

PROMOTION, PUBLICITY, FESTIVALS AND COMPETITIONS

South African Airways' commitment to the promotion of the wines of the Cape goes a lot further than selling a few small bottles of wine with in-flight meals. The importance of the country's airline as an airborne international shop window for Cape wines was first recognized by the late wine impresario and expert, Peter Devereux. Under his influence, competition for inclusion on the airline's list has become fierce, and every month there is a selection of two Wines of the Month, a red and a white, for service in the front of each aircraft. In addition SAA has shown a commitment to wine education for the less privileged members of the community. An entry fee of R150 for each wine submitted for inclusion in the SAA list goes towards providing bursaries to Stellenbosch University and Elsenberg Agricultural College; in the first year this raised R64,000, a sum that SAA doubled straight away.

On the death of Peter Devereux, his mantle was assumed by Michael Fridjhon, a distinguished man of many vinous parts – importer, writer, journalist and consultant. Since he took over in 1994, SAA has taken a selection of award-winning wines to be tasted with South African foods at events staged in London, New York, Hong Kong and Bangkok. At Michael's instigation, SAA sponsored the first of what is to become an annual international wine challenge, by organizing a 'Wine Test Match' between South Africa and Australia. Each country put up 100 wines, spread over eleven categories, which were tasted by a panel consisting of three tasters from each country and three international experts. The wines were tasted blind, and marked with 3, 2 and 1 points – denoting first, second and third in each category – the highest aggregate score winning the match. Not surprisingly Australia romped home, having had far more exposure to market trends than South Africa, who nevertheless managed to win several categories. In a few years the result may be very different.

Wine shows in the form of competitions play an important role in promotion and the improvement of quality. The most prestigious of these are the SA National Young Wine Show, organized by the KWV in a different region each year in July or August, and the SA National Bottled Wine Show, on the results of which the coveted Veritas Double Gold, Gold, Silver and Bronze awards are given to the best wines. Local wine shows are also held annually in Stellenbosch, Robertson, Paarl, Worcester, Olifants River and Klein Karoo during October and November. Stellenbosch and Robertson also take their show wines on a sort of roadshow to Johannesburg, Pretoria and Durban, where the public are offered the wines to taste.

There are a large number of wine festivals held each year, starting with the Paarl Nouveau Festival in April. Other regional events include the Muscadel Festival held in Montagu in April or May; the Calitzdorp Port Festival in July; the Robertson Wine and Food Festival and the Stellenbosch Wine and Food Festival in October; and the Mossel Bay/Klein Karoo Food and Wine Festival, the final event of the year in December. At all of these events the public can, for a small fee, taste, discuss and buy the wines and produce of each region. Major festivals held outside the winelands include one held in Grahamstown in the Eastern Cape; the Business Day Festival held over a week in July in Johannesburg; and two held by the Natal Mercury in July and the Natal Witness in August. Two other newspaper-sponsored events are the Argus Waterfront Wine Festival in September/October, and one run by Die Burger in November. Both of these are held in Cape Town.

Wine auctions play a big part in the selling and promotion of South Africa's wines, and the biggest and oldest is the annual Nederburg auction, held at the farm just outside Paarl. This is one of the major items on the Cape social calendar, and full details are given in the Nederburg article in the chapter on Paarl. Sale of wine by public auction was prohibited until the first Nederburg event in 1975. But there are now general auctions organized by Stephan Welz – a former associate of Sotheby's, who was also instrumental in starting the Cape Independent Winemakers' Guild auctions – which take place every year on the first Saturday in September. The CIWG was formed in 1983, and its members are the best winemakers of the Cape like Beyers Truter, Jan Boland Coetzee, Norma Ratcliffe, Gyles Webb, Kevin Arnold, Jacques Kruger, Jean Daneel, Achim von Arnim and many others. The CIWG auction offers the young wines made by its members, and is open to private customers as well as to the trade, unlike the Nederburg sales which are exclusively for licensed liquor outlets and importers from abroad.

Visits and tastings are exceptionally well organized in South Africa's winelands. All the regions have 'Wine Routes' to help tourist and buyer alike. Most of these produce brochures, listing participating estates, wineries and co-operatives with details of tastings, times of visits, charges where applicable, and other services offered. Many producers have restaurants, some provide picnic hampers, and facilities for *braais* (South African for barbecues) are frequently offered. Maps of the Wine Routes are provided, and each Wine Route member is clearly indicated by roadside signposts. I was impressed by the open, friendly welcome that is extended among all the wine producers, which is in sharp contrast to some parts of the European wine regions.

WINE EDUCATION

For the professionals, Stellenbosch University's Department of Agriculture offers graduate courses in Oenology and Viticulture, and the Elsenburg Agricultural College, 11 kilometres north of Stellenbosch, includes an excellent winemaking course on its curriculum.

For interested amateurs, Stellenbosch Farmers' Winery, through the Cape Wine Academy, and the KWV, through its Wine Foundation, run wine courses for the general public. These range from basic wine appreciation courses, with tastings and lectures, to advanced diploma courses. The most sophisticated and gruelling of these courses is the Cape Wine Master's Diploma, which is akin to the standard achieved by British Masters of Wine. These courses are well supported, and over 30,000 students have participated since their inception.

I

History

The story of South Africa's wine industry is so interwoven with that of each estate, winery and co-operative, whose histories I have sketched in their respective chapters, that only a brief outline is needed here.

There is a tendency to lump the Cape in with the so-called New World wines of California, Australia, New Zealand and Chile. This is an error, for the story begins when the Médoc in Bordeaux was still a marsh. When the first Dutch settlers landed at the Cape in 1652, they were under the command of Jan van Riebeeck. He had been sent by his masters, the Dutch East India Company, not to found a new colony, but to establish a halfway house on the long voyage to the important trading posts of the East Indies, where the Company's fleets could put in to re-victual, take on fresh water, and effect repairs.

Within a short time a settlement was established. A simple mud fort was erected against the depredations of wild animals and the curious, marauding bands of Hottentots. Cattle and sheep pens were built, and gardens established for the planting of vegetables which they had brought with them. Although the soil appeared poor, the settlers' gardener, Hendrik Boom, was soon able to report to van Riebeeck that the vegetables had taken and were flourishing. Having observed the natives eating berries from a species of vine, van Riebeeck began to wonder if the grape vine could also be planted in the new land. It was with some hesitation that he wrote to the Secretary, asking if some vine cuttings could be sent on the next available ship, as the Company always suspected that any special request was for the purpose of enriching its servants. He finally prevailed by using the known fact that a regular ration of wine taken during a voyage reduced the incidence of scurvy, a disease that had cost the Company dear in loss of life on many an expedition.

The first vine cuttings arrived, but had been over-zealously watered, and had rotted to pulp. In 1656 the first healthy cuttings arrived, packed in earth. Much research and guesswork has been expended in trying to determine what these grapes were, but it seems most likely that they were French, and probably both Muscat d'Alexandrie, later known as Hanepoot, and Chenin Blanc, known as Steen in the Cape, were amongst them.

The vines, planted by Boom and his assistant, an ancestor of the Cloetes of Constantia, flourished and bore fruit. That they did is a tribute both to the hardiness of the vine and the Cape's suitability for their cultivation, for neither gardener had the remotest idea of their care, apart from some tips from a passing German sailor from the Rhineland. Jan van Riebeeck was clearly very excited, continually asking for more cuttings to be sent out, and finding more and more places to plant them.

The first proper Company farm was established near the source of the Amstel river, named after the river that flows through Amsterdam, later renamed the Kiesbeek. At first the farm was called Wijnberg, later Bosheuvel, and large plantations of vines soon flourished. Van Riebeeck realized that the farms run by the Company would not be sufficient to furnish the needs of the set- tlers, let alone those of the Company's ships. With the permission of the Lords XVII (governing body of the Company) he started to offer selected settlers the option of discharge from the Company's service, and a grant of land on which to set up their own farms.

It was a tough life for those who accepted the offer, and many found the challenge too hard, either returning to the safety of the Company's employ, or sometimes joining visiting ships and running off to sea. Those who stuck it out were given help with stock and planting material, but they were simple folk, and their farms were limited to the growing of vegetables and wheat and the raising of sheep and cattle – vines were something foreign to them, and at first they showed no inclination to grow them. Gradually this began to change, however, as they were encouraged by van Riebeeck's enthusiasm, by the apparent hardiness of the vine, and by the success of the Bosheuvel vineyard.

With the establishment of the free burghers' farming community, there was soon a shortage of labour. The solution was found with the arrival of the first shipment of slaves, 200 of whom arrived in 1658. They were from other parts of Africa, Madagascar and the Far East, and their cross-breeding was probably the basis of the 'Coloured' population of the Cape today. Slavery was still, in general, a morally unquestioned practice – and it was certainly deemed necessary for the survival of the struggling new colony. At first the slaves all belonged to the Company, who set up a school for them, giving them religious instruction, a rudimentary education, and a daily ration of brandy and tobacco. The slaves who did not run away either stayed in the Company's service, or were given or sold to the free burghers.

On 2 February 1659, Jan van Riebeeck recorded in his journal: 'Today, praise be to God, wine was pressed for the first time from Cape grapes, and from the virgin must, fresh from the vat, a sample taken, pressed from the three young vines that have been growing here for 2 years yielding 12 mengels must from French and Muscadel grapes, the Hanepoot Spain not yet ripe.'

No comment is offered on the quality of the wine, but one can hazard a guess that it was not wonderful. Birds and the raiding Hottentots were a menace, and the grapes were doubtless picked well before they were ripe just so that there were enough to press. In addition, the settlers were Dutch and had no experience of winemaking techniques, so vinification must have been a combination of guesswork and luck rather than of judgement.

The colony grew rapidly, and parties were sent further afield to find good farming land. Tulbagh was actually discovered by one of van Riebeeck's expeditions, but at that time was judged infertile. The most important figure for the wine industry was Simon van der Stel, the first Governor of the Cape, who arrived there in 1679. He continued the expansion of the farmlands, founding Stellenbosch as the centre of the rural community within a year of his arrival. He was responsible for many innovations beneficial to the wine industry, including the setting up of a committee, whose responsibility it was to inspect farmers' grapes for ripeness; a hefty fine was imposed on any farmer who picked before maturity. He also introduced both the Muscat de Frontignan and Pontac grapes, stressed the importance of cleanliness of cellar and casks, and instructed fining with egg whites and isinglass. His own rather dubiously acquired estate at Constantia was to serve as a model wine farm.

Around this time Louis XIV revoked the Edict of Nantes, which had freed French Protestants from religious persecution. Between 1688 and 1690 some two hundred of these dispossessed Huguenots were sent out to settle in the Cape by the Dutch East India Company, to whom they had appealed in their hour of need. The Lords XVII, never ones to look a gift horse in the mouth, immediately saw the advantages that could derive from this transfusion of skilled families, especially those experienced in weaving and winemaking. Among the many Huguenot families, most of whom were settled by van der Stel in the Olifantshoek valley, later called Franschhoek, were three brothers bearing letters from the Lords XVII, recommending them for their skill in winemaking. They were Pierre, Abraham and Jacob de Villiers, who founded one of the leading wine dynasties in the Cape.

By the end of the eighteenth century the Cape wine farmers were enjoying undreamed of prosperity, which stemmed largely from the wars between the English and the French. This had cut off the export of French wines, and the British, a nation of heavy consumers, especially of ports, sherries and sweet wines, had become major importers.

The second occupation of the Cape by the British in 1806 marked the start of less happy times for the industry. The ending of the Napoleonic wars freed French wines once more and, following the boom of the eighteenth century, the quality of wines produced had slipped, as demand had been so great that many wine producers had allowed their standards to drop. The British administration did what they could to help, and in 1811 Sir John Cradock appointed one W. Caldwell as an official taster and adviser, and the imposition of heavy duties on the newly freed French wines in 1825 proved of considerable help.

A major blow to the farmers of the Cape came in 1834 with the emancipation of the slaves. As much because of the disruption to their way of life as because of any direct labour problems that it caused, this action resulted in the Great Trek. Many Boer families simply upped sticks and headed north to settle in places like the Transvaal, where they would be free of the British.

In 1861 Palmerston negotiated a commercial treaty with the French, resulting in drastic reductions in the tariffs on French wines, and this spelt the end of the already dwindling exports to England. As if this were not enough, the Cape vineyards were to suffer two further misfortunes in the ensuing years: the onset of the crippling oidium, followed swiftly by the fatal ravages of the phylloxera aphid.

Those wine farmers who managed to survive the financial hardships brought about by forty years of problems, and re-established their vineyards on American rootstocks, found export no easier. The early twentieth century then saw a period of mammoth overproduction, resulting in a wine lake of huge proportions, and further extreme distress for the already hard-pressed farmers. This brought about the foundation of the KWV, which is discussed in more detail in the next chapter.

The fact that the South African wine industry has survived at all is a tribute to the tenacity and endurance of the Afrikaner wine farmers, coupled with a self-sufficiency and a belief in their ability to survive, completely independent of the world outside.

This is not a political book, but the history of any Cape industry would be incomplete without mention of the problems caused by the apartheid regime. For the entire period of its existence, sanctions, either enforced or moral, created a virtual vacuum for export business. It is one of life's ironies that the current boom in export of South African wine, and the consequent astonishing strides in quality, can be ascribed to the new government, headed by a man who suffered 27 years' incarceration at the hands of the regime that brought about those sanctions.

Boom-time is certainly here again for South Africa's wine industry, and it is responding in no uncertain manner. Orders are pouring in, and the main problem is finding enough wine to satisfy world demand and curiosity. The upward quality curve is quite amazing in the comparatively short time since the ANC came to power. The country is in desperate need of overseas capital, and happily this is already forthcoming in the wine industry, though there is certainly room for more. Provided that political stability can be maintained, winemakers – and drinkers – can expect a very bright future.

2

The KWV

The role played by the KWV in the South African wine industry today has changed considerably since its early days. At the beginning of the twentieth century, the wine farmers of the Cape were experiencing dire problems for a variety of reasons. From the mid-nineteenth century onwards, the main difficulties stemmed from the onset of oidium tuckeri in the 1860s, to the harsher depredations of the phylloxera aphid in the 1880s and '90s. This pest, for which there was initially no solution, completely laid waste the vineyards of South Africa, as well as those of Europe. The answer was eventually found in the grafting of vines on to phylloxera-resistant American rootstocks – but the re-establishment of the vineyards was a lengthy business, and many farmers, deprived of their livelihood for years, went to the wall.

For those who survived the phylloxera plague, life was slow to improve. Export trade virtually stopped following the Anglo-Boer war, and the re-established vineyards were over-producing in a dramatic fashion. With huge volumes of wine lying unsold, prices for wine were pathetically low, and this led in 1905 to the birth of the co-operative movement. This was instigated by a government commission, appointed that year to look into the problems of the ailing wine and brandy producers. It recommended the creation of the first co-operatives, giving member farmers the strength of numbers to negotiate prices, instead of competing with one another. Co-operative farming also gave members considerable cost savings, in that investment in machinery, especially costly winemaking equipment, could be pooled by using a central winery for the vinification of the members' crops.

The government put up a sum of £50,000 for the establishment of the initial co-ops, a large sum in today's terms, and the first

was at Tulbagh, the Drostdy, which survives to this day. This was
followed by Helderberg, Helderfontein, Groot Drakenstein, Paarl,
Wellington, Bovlei and Over Hex. These were run by committees
of member farmers, usually under the chairmanship of the member
who supplied the premises or the land for the winery. Prices continued to fall, however, reaching a low in 1909 of £1.15.6d a
leaguer (577 litres), and of the first co-operatives, only four survived. Curiously enough, a number of farmers owed their
continuing existence to the boom in ostrich-farming, especially in
the Oudsthoorn and Breede river valley. The huge demand and
high prices paid for the plumage of these birds, however, died
suddenly with the outbreak of the First World War, and the coming
of the motor car (for which feathered clothing was not suitable
attire).

In 1918 there were an estimated 56,000,000 litres of unsaleable
wine in farmers' cellars, but survival still seemed possible through
the co-operative movement, organized on a grander, more national
scale. The Ko-operative Wijnbouwers Vereiniging (KWV) van Suid-
Afrika Beperkt was formed, under the chairmanship of Charles W.
H. Kohler. The stated objective was 'so to direct, control and
regulate the sale and disposal by its members of their produce,
being that of the grape, as shall secure for them a continuously
adequate return for such produce'.

The newly formed KWV was an instant success. Ninety-five per
cent of all wine farmers joined the movement, giving them collec-
tive power over the merchants, and prices increased dramatically
and immediately. There were huge crops in 1921 and 1923, and
prices fell away once more – 52,500,000 litres of wine were
dumped in the Eerste river. Disillusioned members started to resign
from the KWV, and sell their wines direct to merchants at prices
lower than those laid down by the movement.

In 1924 the Smuts government moved in to ratify the powers of
the KWV by the passing of Act 5, the Wine and Spirit Control
Act. This empowered the KWV to set the minimum price each year
for the sale of distilling-wine and as a direct result many merchants
disappeared. The price of 'good wine', or wine that was destined
for sale as fortified or table wines, was not covered by this act, as
the authorities imagined that the price control on distilling-wine
would also have a beneficial knock-on effect on 'good wine' prices.

Unfortunately this was not the case, and it became necessary to pass further legislation in the form of Act 23 in 1940.

It was this new act that gave the KWV the total control of the wine and spirits industry which remains unbroken, including powers over producers, wholesalers, retailers and importers. It not only gave the additional fixed price control over 'good wine', but also stipulated that no deal could be done between growers and merchants without KWV approval, and all payments henceforth had to be made via the KWV. It also stated that no wine could be made without a KWV permit, and that these would only be issued provided that the growers' vineyards and vinification met with the standards laid down by the KWV. The act also gave the KWV the power to determine on an annual basis the quantity of unsaleable wine lying with each grower, which was known as the 'surplus'; this had to be delivered to the KWV cellars without payment, where it would be turned into brandy or wine. Although these powers may seem draconian, limiting the freedom of the growers, it should be remembered that the KWV is a co-operative movement, and that all profits and benefits ultimately devolve to the members – the wine growers of South Africa.

Over-production increased in the 1950s, and the power of the big wholesalers grew in parallel with those of the KWV. The quota system was introduced, empowering the KWV to limit the number of vines on any property, based on 1957 levels of planting. The legislation stated that the quota and surplus systems applied to all growers, whether members of the KWV or not. All these regulations remained in force until 1992, when the quota system was removed.

Overall the influence of the KWV has been of inestimable benefit to South Africa's wine and spirit industry, indeed it could easily have sunk without trace in the 1920s in its absence. Today, however, its role is ambivalent. Producers of bulk wines owe their prosperity to the KWV, but the owners of estates and wineries producing quality table and fortified wines derive little benefit. They find its powers and petty regulations a hindrance to their daily work, often referring, more or less good-humouredly, to its visiting officials as the KGB.

More seriously there is resentment in certain quarters of the fact that the KWV is in direct competition with its members at the quality end of the market. The KWV has a 50% shareholding with

Anton Rupert's Rembrandt Group in Rembrandt KWV Investments, which owns 60% of the shares in both Distillers Corporation and Stellenbosch Farmers' Winery, the two biggest wholesalers in South Africa. Moreover, the recently launched KWV International is a fierce competitor in the fine wine export market. This could be described as running with the hare and hunting with the hounds or, to give it a more South African analogy, refereeing a rugby game and playing on both sides as well. The KWV's answer is that, in addition to all the research conducted into every aspect of the industry, all of which is available to any wine grower, any profit accruing from their sales and marketing activities is also for the ultimate benefit of every member.

The KWV produces an immense range of wines, fortified wines, brandy, 'port' and 'sherry'. In addition they are marketing several branded table wines for the export market, such as the Cathedral Cellar, Springbok, Cape Country and Paarl ranges. They also have an excellent estate, Laborie, which is situated just across the road from their headquarters in Paarl.

Useful Information

Production Manager: Johan Schreuder
Cellar Manager & Fortified Winemaker: Streik de Wet
Red Winemaker: Koosie Müller
White Winemaker: Sakkie Bester
Address: KWV, Box 528, Suider-Paarl 7624
Telephone: 02211.73911 *Fax*: 02211.73000

Tastings and Cellar Tours: Afrikaans and English (German and French by request), Mon to Sat, booking essential on 02211.73008/7
Brandy Cellar, Worcester: Monday–Friday all year, Saturdays November to April, booking essential on 0231.20255
Laborie Estate: Tastings at KWV
Restaurant: 02211.73095

3
Constantia

Constantia was where the making of fine wine in South Africa began. The first Governor of the Cape, Simon van der Stel, in addition to being an able administrator, was no fool when it came to picking a good site for his personal estate and vineyards. Apart from its great natural beauty, the soil, exposure and micro-climate of Constantia combine to make it one of the best areas in the Cape for growing wine grapes. The vineyards are situated high on the slopes of the mountains, and are cooled by sea breezes from False Bay to the south, and from the Atlantic to the west, which gives slower ripening and consequent improvement in flavour and structure in the wines.

The inevitable encroachment of suburban Cape Town has left us with only the four estates described below, plus 60 hectares belonging to Constantia Uitsig, from which wine is made at Buitenverwachting, and is largely used in the excellent Constantia Uitsig restaurant.

The production of Constantia consists almost entirely of fine red and white table wines from classic grape varieties, although Groot Constantia also makes a range of cheaper table wines, as the Trust feels that a national monument of this importance should make wines that are affordable to all South Africans. The Klein Constantia estate has led the way in returning to the production of the wine that made Constantia famous in the eighteenth century, a luscious dessert wine of great delicacy and complexity. They have christened it Vin de Constance, and Groot Constantia plan to follow suit in the near future.

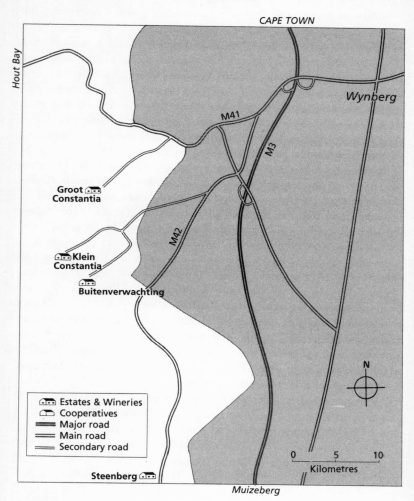

Constantia

GROOT CONSTANTIA

It is fitting that this work should begin with Groot Constantia, for this estate is the cradle of the South African wine story and it is therefore appropriate to take a more detailed look at its history.

Simon van der Stel, the Cape settlement's first Governor, took up his appointment in 1679. His father, a servant of the Dutch East India Company, had died in a clash with rebels in Ceylon in 1648. His mother, a Spanish or Portuguese 'mestizo' (or half-caste), called Monica Dacosta, having married again to a ship's captain called Hendrik van Gent, died herself a mere four years later in 1652, leaving Simon an orphan at the tender age of thirteen. Simon had never seen his mother country, having been born at sea in 1639, just before his father landed in the new colony of Mauritius, where he spent the first six years of his life. In 1659 the Company approved his return to Holland to take up his studies. He must have been a good student and prospered during his youth, for in 1663 he married Johanna Jacoba Six, who bore him six children.

We know that van der Stel served with the army before going to the Cape, where he arrived in 1679 with his children but, curiously, without his wife and accompanied by her younger sister Cornelia, who sadly died only two years later in 1681. Simon van der Stel was an ambitious and conscientious governor from the outset, founding the town of Stellenbosch within a year of his arrival. In 1685 he was granted the estate of Constantia by Rijklof van Goens, which was later confirmed by Commissioner van Rheede in the same year. The choice of name has never been satisfactorily explained, and there are numerous theories, but the most probable one is that van Goens had a daughter of that name, and he wanted to show his gratitude.

Constantia has always been a perfect place for the growing of vines, and van der Stel was a keen horticulturist who expended considerable energy in the production of fine wine, and the construction of a fine house. In 1698, Wilhem van Dam, one of the Lords XVII of the Dutch East India Company, wrote to him, saying: 'With the Cape red I drank Your Excellency's health, but the white Frontignac has a better reputation.' The first cask of Constantia wine was exported to Batavia in 1692, and a letter came back saying that the quality was very high, but the quantity too small.

The problem for Constantia, in common with all other wine farms with grants from the Company, was that they were all obliged to sell their crop at a very modest price to the Company, who then sold it on to passing ships at five times that price. This continued until the estate was owned by Hendrik van Cloete, when an agreement on terms more beneficial to the farmer was reached with the Company.

Simon van der Stel prospered mightily, and in 1691 was appointed Councillor and later Governor of India. In 1699 he resigned his position as Governor of the Cape, which left him in a much freer position to acquire more land. At this time, the Constantia lands covered a vast 891 morgen, an area bigger than the whole of contemporary Amsterdam, at a time when the average land grant was only 60. He also acquired other farms nearby, including Steenbergen, Oude Wynberg and Zeekoeyenvallei. In addition he had a fish-house at Kalk Bay from which he supplied fish to the Company, and employed a Chinese to sell fruit and fish for him, as well as running cattle on the lowlands of Steenbergen. As well as all these Constantia-based businesses, he also entered into partnership with Johannes Phyffer, obtaining the monopoly for all the fishing and sealing at Saldanha Bay.

On his resignation as Governor, Simon's son Wilhem Adriaen succeeded him. He was by all accounts a brilliant man, and an innovative agriculturalist, achieving great things at the Vergelegen estate. However, as the saying goes, all power corrupts, and governorship of the Cape gave the holder of the office a great deal of power. Wilhem Adriaen bent the rules too much, and in 1708 the burghers, including Henning Huysing of Meerlust and his nephew, Adam Tas, confronted him with all his misdemeanours. The rebellious burghers, together with Wilhem Adriaen, were recalled to Amsterdam for an inquiry, which resulted in total justification and return to their estates for the burghers, and disgrace and exile for the Governor. The Lords XVII ordered Wilhem Adriaen's properties, including Vergelegen and Constantia, to be divided up and sold. The beautiful Constantia estate, which had by now become an essential stop for any visiting dignitaries, was split into three parts, Klein Constantia, Buitenverwachting and a much reduced Groot Constantia. Klein Constantia was bought by one Pieter de Meyer, but he was only in it for the money. He immediately sold off part of Klein Constantia, which became Bergvliet, for the price he had paid for the whole and, only two months later, on 26 October 1716, sold the remaining 45 hectares for a tidy profit of 1,750 guilders.

The new owner of Klein Constantia was Jan Jurgen Kotze. He was married to Elsabe van Hoff, who became widowed when he died within a year of the purchase. She then married Johannes Colijn, who was to bring much glory to Klein Constantia, improving the quality of the wine, and setting up regular export trade with Batavia and with Holland. Elsabe died in 1720, leaving Johannes in sole charge.

In the meantime, a Swede called Olof Bergh had bought the Groot Constantia part of the estate, and had let the wine go. In 1733 Johannes Colijn bought Groot Constantia, installing his brother-in-law, Johan Jurgen Wieser, as manager. This was a timely and necessary action, as orders were beginning to outstrip production at Klein Constantia. The acquisition of new vineyards enabled him to consolidate his position and double his prices, and he farmed the two properties together until his death in 1743. This left his widow, Johanna Appel, in sole charge. With six children to look after, she lost no time in finding herself a new husband, and in 1745 married Lambertus Myburgh, doubtless a member of the Meerlust family.

Johan Wieser at Groot Constantia died in 1759, leaving the farm to his stepson, Jacobus van der Spuy. Jacobus was not a farmer, and for the next eleven years the partnership between him and Myburgh drifted along on the previous reputation of the wines, but quality at both estates began to fall off. When Myburgh died in 1771, Johanna Appel passed Klein Constantia to her youngest son, Johannes Nicolaas Colijn, and the name of the farm was changed on the deed to Hoop-op Constantia.

In 1778 Jacobus van der Spuy sold Groot Constantia to one Jan Serrurier, who in turn sold it to Hendrik Cloete, a substantial wine farmer at Nooitgedacht in Stellenbosch. He owned several farms, including Weltevrede and Zandvliet in Robertson, and under his able and energetic ownership Groot Constantia was to reach its zenith in terms of its wines, fame and legendary hospitality. The new cellar was built, possibly using the great Thibault as architect, with its famous triangular pediment adorned by the sculptor Anreith. The vineyards were put into order, and the house was greatly extended, converting the open gallery into a dining-room, raising the roof and adding the end gables, resulting in a house very much in the stately form of today.

Under Cloete's direction, the luscious dessert wines of Groot Constantia became one of the world's most sought after delicacies, and were drunk regularly at the tables of the crowned heads of

Europe. The Tsars of Russia, the king of Prussia and the English Court were among Constantia's devotees, and even Napoleon had the wine delivered to him in exile on St Helena. The estate had become a centre of hospitality. Nobody who was anybody came to Cape Town without a visit and tasting, and the archives are full of letters from travellers from all over the world, extolling the beauty of the house, gardens and vineyards, as well as the high quality of the wines.

All this popularity was causing problems for Hendrik Cloete, however, since the Company were demanding more and more wine at a low fixed price in order to satisfy the insatiable demand. In 1793 Hendrik made an approach to the Company, and it was in view of his considerable investments that Commissioners Nederburgh and Frykenius drew up the agreement mentioned above, in order that he might recoup some of his expenditure. By the terms of this, both Groot and Klein Constantia were obliged to supply the Company with fifteen aums of 135 litres each of red and white – chosen by the Company's representative at a tasting to ensure that they got the best – at a fixed price of 150 guilders per aum in good casks provided by the estate. The rest of the crop of each estate could then be sold on the open market at the best price they could get. This brought relief in the short term, but caused problems later because the price for the 30 aums that had to be supplied to the Company was fixed in perpetuity.

Hendrik's wife died in 1794, and he retired to Nooitgedacht with one of his sons where he died in 1799, having passed over the reins to Hendrik Junior. Young Hendrik was a captain in the Stellenbosch burgher cavalry and fought against the English, to whom the Cape surrendered in 1795. He resigned his commission with the Stellenbosch cavalry, having no wish to serve under the British, and returned to Groot Constantia.

Cloete was optimistic about the future under the British, as he fondly imagined that he was now free from the tiresome and costly restrictions imposed upon his commerce by the Company. Unfortunately the British administration did not see it this way, and insisted that the same conditions should apply to the new government, and a long list of officials was drawn up to whom Cloete had to supply his liquid sunshine at the same miserly rate. In spite of all these irritations, Hendrik Junior prospered both socially and financially in the early part of the new century. He died in 1818, and his death was followed shortly by the death of Lambertus Johannes Colijn at Hoop-op Constantia, marking the end of palmy days for both estates.

The 1830s were difficult times for wine farmers in the Cape. French wines were now available once more, Cape wines were heavily taxed, and the emancipation of slaves caused horrendous problems, especially for Groot and Klein Constantia, which were both highly labour-intensive. Then oidium hit the vines in 1859, followed by the dreaded phylloxera in 1866. Hendrik Junior's son, Jacob Pieter Cloete, died insolvent in 1875, and Groot Constantia was eventually sold in 1885 for £5,275 to the Cape government, who turned it into a model, experimental research farm, with particular emphasis on the growing of phylloxera-resistant American rootstocks. There followed a chequered history beset with difficulties and bureaucratic wrangling. In 1899 phylloxera attacked the Groot Constantia vines for the first time, and virtually all the old vines were replaced with grafted Cabernet Sauvignon, Hermitage, Riesling, White French (sic) and Steen, or Chenin Blanc, spelling the temporary end of the sweet, dessert wines for which the estate and the area had gained such renown. Students were taken on to learn viticulture and vinification, and the objective was for the farm to be self-supporting, but it consistently lost money. The dubious benefit of the students is recorded by a visitor, who witnessed the student sulphur races, in which students took a row of vines each, and then proceeded with sulphur backpacks and sprays to race each other along the rows, the efficacy of the spraying being more than doubtful. Twice moves were made to rid the government of this costly encumbrance, firstly to sell it outright, and secondly to turn it into an official residence for the Governor. Both moves were thwarted thanks to the intercession of Eustace Pillans, who held the grandiose title of Agricultural Assistant and Inspecting Officer of Groot Constantia.

The First World War brought a virtual halt to exports, and in 1925 disaster struck. A fire broke out in the homestead, completely gutting it. This was the last straw, and the government decided to lease the farmlands of Groot Constantia, which lasted until 1957, when the lessees did not renew, and the Department of Agriculture under Minister Paul Sauer took the land back in hand with the objective of once more running it as a model farm. This continued under the Groot Constantia Advisory Committee from 1958 until

1963, when the estate passed into the control of Agricultural Technical Services.

During this period Professor Theuron, a member of the Committee, played a key role, remodelling the cellars and replanting the vineyards, concentrating on Pinotage, Cabernet and Shiraz. A policy was made of keeping the wines for maturation in bottle before issuing them for sale, and the first Groot Constantia wine offered in 1967 was the Shiraz 1963. Sales were only from the cellars, and the first offering was taken up so enthusiastically that sales were limited to Wednesdays only. The wines were well received, and the Shiraz was followed by the 1964 Cabernet. By 1969 sales had risen from 280 dozen to 1,181 dozen. In 1975 the committee was replaced by the Groot Constantia Control Board, which remained effective until 1993.

After the 1925 fire, the government recognized the importance of the old homestead as a national monument, and it was decided to rebuild it to the standard and form of Hendrik Cloete's house. The architect appointed was Sir Herbert Baker, who included in his plans the installation of a 'brandsolder' as a ceiling to the ground floor. This was correct for the time of Hendrik Cloete, and consisted of interwoven reeds, coated on the upper side with a layer of clay, intended as a protection against fire for the downstairs rooms. Sadly Cloete had not had the foresight to employ this relatively simple protection, with the result that the entire contents of the house were lost in the blaze. The only exceptions were some kitchen utensils, together with Cloete's desk, which was fortunately in the cellar at the time of the fire. Apart from these items, there was no furniture of suitable antiquity and type with which to fill what was destined to be an important museum.

To the rescue came a white knight in the form of shipping millionaire A. A. de Pass. He had settled in England in 1900, and became a noted collector of art. On returning to the Cape during the English winter of 1926 and learning of the Constantia fire, he immediately offered to furnish the house with suitable antiques and pictures. The museum opened to the public in 1927, and has remained so ever since. The number of visitors has increased from 1,445 in 1934 to 400,000 a year today. Except for the desk and kitchen utensils, all the beautiful furnishings that the visitor to Groot Constantia's homestead sees are the gift of this generous benefactor.

In 1993 the government conferred company status to the Groot Constantia complex of museum, buildings and farm. The Groot Constantia Trust Company is now administered by a board of twelve directors, including the Managing Director of Nederburg, representatives from the KWV, the Monuments Commission and other civic bodies, none of whom draw any directors' emoluments. The profits are all ploughed back into the improvement and maintenance of this historic and beautiful reminder of the birth, history and abiding beauty of South Africa's winelands.

Now, general management is in the hands of Danie Appel, and the winemaker is Martin Moore, who works closely with vineyard manager Gary Probst. The quality at the upper end of Groot Constantia's wines is improving by leaps and bounds, and in a year or two we should see the renaissance of the dessert wine that made the estate famous, thanks to new plantings of Muscat de Frontignan, both red and white. Danie Appel explained to me, however, that while the Trust is dedicated to producing wines of a quality befitting the Cape's most prestigious estate, the Directors are also committed to making a range of Groot Constantia wines that are affordable to all South Africans as part of their heritage. To fill this requirement there is a Blanc de Blancs dry white at R9.00, a slightly sweeter white called Bouquet Blanc at R7.50, and a Constantia Rood at R10.50.

Tasting Notes

Blanc de Blancs 1995 (70% Chardonnay, 20% Chenin Blanc, 8% Pinot Gris and 2% Riesling): Mid-gold colour; clean fruit bouquet; easy-drinking with nice fruit, a touch of sweetness.

Sauvignon Blanc 1995: Pale straw; up-front Sauvignon nose; New-World style, elegant, racy fruit with a bit of weight to it.

Chardonnay 1995 (25% from old vines barrel-fermented, 75% tank-fermented): Greeny gold; citrussy fruit aromas; pleasant, easy-drinking Chardonnay.

Chardonnay Reserve 1995 (75% barrel-fermented, rest in tank): Darker colour; fat Chardonnay fruit with oaky whiffs; fat, buttery fruit, wood quite strong but starting to blend.

Weisser Riesling 1995 (some botrytized grapes included): Medium deep gold; complex nose with some noble rot; off-dry, rich and very long with green backbone, lovely.

Shiraz/Merlot 1991: Fine ruby colour; Shiraz dominates the bouquet; rounded, ripe fruit with some nice soft tannin and a bit of structure.

Shiraz 1991 (aged in 2nd-fill casks, but from '93 will have 20% new wood): Deep red; nose more Rhôney and powerful than the blended wine; a good Shiraz, with lots of mouth-filling fruit, full-bodied with backbone.

Merlot 1992: Medium deep colour; nice black fruit nose; some nice soft fruit there, but some slightly green tannins are dominant at the moment.

Cabernet Sauvignon 1992 (old clones): Good, medium deep red; cassis nose; soft, blackcurrant fruit with good non-aggressive tannins and some structure – a good Cabernet.

Heerenrood 1989 (37% Shiraz, 37% Cabernet Franc, 18% Cabernet Sauvignon, 8% Merlot): Deep red; ripe fruit bouquet; a lovely mouthful of rich, ripe fruit, very long.

Gouverneur's Reserve 1992 (71% Cabernet Sauvignon, 19% Cabernet Franc, 10% Merlot): Deep, dense colour; intense nose of ripe blackcurrants; excellent Cabernet fruit with soft tannins and enough spine to keep it going for several years; very good Bordeaux blend, well worth the Veritas Double Gold.

'Port': Deep plummy colour; rich, raisiny bouquet; a light ruby 'port' of fine quality.

Technical Notes

Area under vines: 101 hectares

Average production: 580 tons, will increase to 900, 41,000 cases bottled wines

Cultivars planted
WHITE: Sauvignon Blanc, Chardonnay, Chenin Blanc, Pinot Gris, Weisser Riesling, Gewürztraminer, Furmint

RED: Cabernet Sauvignon, Cabernet Franc, Merlot, Shiraz, Pinotage, Tinta Barocca

Wines produced
WHITE: Blanc de Blancs, Sauvignon Blanc, Chardonnay, Chardonnay Reserve, Weisser Riesling, Gewürztraminer, Bouquet Blanc, Natural Sweet, Noble Late Harvest
RED: Heerenrood, Constantia Rood, Merlot, Shiraz, Pinotage, Cabernet Sauvignon, Gouverneur's Reserve
'PORT'

Useful Information

Owners: Groot Constantia Trust Company Limited
General Manager: Danie Appel
Winemaker: Martin Moore
Vineyard Manager: Gary Probst
Address: Groot Constantia State Estate, Private Bag, Constantia 7848
Telephone: 021.7945128 *Fax*: 021.7941999

Tasting/Sales: Open every day except Christmas Day, Good Friday 10.00 to 17.00, Fridays Dec to May until 18.00
Facilities: Cellar Tours 11.00 and 15.00, Homestead Museum, Art Gallery, Curio Shops
Restaurants: Jonkershuis 09.00 to 17.00, Telephone 021.7946225; Tavern Restaurant Sun–Tues 10.00 to 18.00, Weds–Sat 10.00 to 22.00, Telephone 021.7941144

KLEIN CONSTANTIA

Since the lands of Klein Constantia formed part of Groot Constantia until 1823, there is no need to dwell on its history before that date. The name of the estate farmed today by the Joostes only dates from that time. The original Klein Constantia, which was one of the sub-divisions of the Constantia estate made by the Dutch East India Company following Wilhem Adriaen van der Stel's disgrace, subsequently had its name changed to Hoop-op Constantia.

In 1823 the widow of Hendrik Cloete partitioned off a section of Groot Constantia (which now forms the estate as we know it)

and passed it to her youngest son, Johan Gerhard, naming it Klein Constantia. In common with the rest of Constantia, the remainder of the nineteenth century was an extremely difficult period for the estate, and Klein Constantia was subject to a number of bankruptcies and changes of ownership that were normal among wine farms at that time.

In spite of his illustrious wine pedigree, Johan Gerhard does not appear to have been either successful or interested in wine. The three farms of Groot, Hoop-op and High Constantia remained the only producers of Constantia wine, and Johan sold up in 1840. A series of owners followed, including various members of the Cloete family, but with the depressed state of the wine industry, capped by the onset of both oidium and phylloxera in the vineyards, nobody could make a go of things.

In 1890 Klein Constantia was bought by millionaire Wilhem Adriaen van der Bijl, owner of Witteboomen and famous for being the only man to have frustrated Cecil Rhodes by refusing to sell him any land for the construction of Rhodes's highway from Groote Schuur to Constantia Nek. He did, however, lease a plot of six hectares of low-lying land on Klein Constantia to Harry Pickstone to start a nursery. Pickstone, an English horticulturist, is an important figure in Cape farming history. Having first seen the potential of South Africa as part of Sir Charles Warren's Bechuanaland expedition in 1885, he returned in 1894, obtaining a grant from Rhodes to start a nursery at Nooitgedacht. He eventually became General Manager of Rhodes Fruit Farms, based around Boschendal, now part of the giant Anglo-America conglomerate. Pickstone's nursery was called Marlbrook, an Afrikaans corruption of Marlborough after the famous Duke. Mrs van der Bijl, widowed in 1898, sold Marlbrook away from Klein Constantia in 1908. It did not become part of the estate again until it was bought back by the new owner, Abraham de Villiers (who had bought Klein Constantia in 1903), in 1918.

Although bearing one of the great names of South African winemaking, 'Braam de Villiers was no farmer. His money came from a successful ladies' fashion business called 'La Mode' in Paarl. On a buying trip to Paris he met, fell in love with, and married millionairess Clare Hussey from Pennsylvania. On their return to the Cape, 'Braam's new bride was much taken with the country and, when Klein Constantia came up for sale, she bought it. 'Braam sold La Mode, and they moved to Constantia. Although Clare de Villiers made Klein Constantia famous for parties and lavish entertaining, there was probably more Champagne consumed than the wines of the estate. There were around 90,000 vines on the property when they arrived, and wine production, mainly red, certainly continued right up to 'Braam's death in 1930, a fair quantity being regularly exported to London. The merry widow Clare de Villiers had no need of money, and the farm was of no interest. Grapes were no longer pressed in the cellar, the vats being broken up and the timber used for repairs to the homestead.

Jan de Villiers, 'Braam's nephew, returned to Klein Constantia on Clare's death in 1955. He did a certain amount of replanting, mainly of Hanepoot to replace table grapes which were not selling well. He also cleared a lot of timber and sold topsoil, although Klein Constantia still has one of the largest areas of indigenous forest in the Western Cape. It is the proud boast of the present owners that the hallowed turf of Newlands rugby pitch grows on Klein Constantia soil. Jan de Villiers retired in 1963, leasing the farm to the Austins, who bought it in 1972.

When the present owner, Duggie Jooste, heir to an old Cape Town-based liquor business, bought Klein Constantia in 1980, there were only 30 of the total 146 hectares planted with vines, and these, like the rest of the farm, were in a sorry state. Naturally he was aware of the history and enormous potential of the farm and, from the outset, his ambition was to produce only the finest wines – above all to try to make a sweet wine as near as possible to the old Constantia dessert wine that set the wine world on fire in previous centuries.

In all of these things the Joostes have succeeded. Of the four wine estates in the region, the best wines are at present undoubtedly coming from the slopes of Klein Constantia. The work started, as with all serious winemakers, in the vineyard. Duggie enlisted the best help in the form of Professor Orffer of Stellenbosch, and Ernst le Roux, chief viticulturist at Nederburg, later to become general manager of Klein Constantia. The estate is blessed with an ideal micro-climate, sheltered by the mountains behind, and enjoying a cooling breeze from the ocean. This allows for a good spread of time for the harvest: the late-ripening varieties like Cabernet Sauvignon on the lower slopes at around 100 metres above sea-level; with Sauvignon Blanc, Chardonnay, Weisser Riesling and a little Pinot Noir being able to reach full maturity 200 metres higher, near the tree-line.

These upper vineyards suffer from a problem that European viticulturists happily lack. Troops of baboons, who tend to be more gourmands than gourmets, descend from time to time from the forest, and strip yards of vines very quickly. The answer was found in the form of electric cattle fencing, but the wily apes soon discovered exactly how long the batteries lasted, and picked their raiding times accordingly. Lowell Jooste, Duggie's son, countered by replacing the batteries with heavy duty ones from tractors, which last longer, bite harder, and need recharging less frequently; the baboons are now thinner, and the grapes more plentiful.

Detailed soil analyses were made, and replanting started in earnest in 1982 at the rate of 15 hectares a year to the present level of 75 hectares. Tremendous emphasis has been placed on the quality of plant material, and clones have been selected with rigorous care. Vines for red wine are Cabernet Sauvignon and Cabernet Franc, Merlot, Shiraz and Pinot Noir, and the white varieties are Chardonnay, Sauvignon Blanc, Rhine Riesling and Muscat de Frontignan, the latter, after detailed research, being the nearest clone that could be found to the vines brought over from France by Jan van Riebeeck in 1656. This, and a great deal more painstaking research, has resulted in the estate's renaissance of the great Constantia dessert wine, Vin de Constance. Tasting and analysis of rare examples of the original wine convinced the Joostes and winemaker Ross Gower that the fabled wine was not fortified, and the eighteenth century practice of twisting the vines when the grapes were ripe to intensify flavour and sugar has been replaced by severe crop limitation through pruning and selection. The first vintage was made in 1986, and the wine is superb.

Ross Gower is a totally dedicated, passionate and gifted winemaker. He joined the team in 1984, after spending seven years at Nederburg and three as chief winemaker at Corbans in New Zealand in time to help with the design of the superb state of the art cellar, which is half underground. His first vintage was also the first for the new owners, and he kicked off with a winner in the Sauvignon Blanc, which was Champion Wine in the SA Show. This was followed in 1987 by the Cabernet Sauvignon being judged best of the show, and the 1988 was overall winner out of 1,700 entries. Prizes and praises follow without ceasing, and there seem to be no peaks of quality that Gower and the Joostes will fail to conquer.

Despite their triumphant progress, Duggie, Lowell and Ross remain modest, kind and warmly hospitable. The only small criticism that I could find lies in the presence of an amiable, and evidently beloved Labrador in the tasting room, whose bouquet lent nothing positive to the fabulous range of wines.

Tasting Notes

Sauvignon Blanc 1995: Palish, greeny gold; huge wafts of elderflower and up-front fruit; clean, crisp and herbaceous, a truly lovely blend of the best New and Old world styles, with great length. One of John Platter's rare 5-star ratings, and rightly so. The K. C. Sauvignon Blanc has been SAA Wine of the Month in three successive vintages.

Chardonnay 1993: Pale straw colour; good Chardonnay nose with vanilla from the wood; full, fat fruit, with oak quite strong, but will balance out.

Chardonnay 1995 (sample from vat): Paler colour than '93; nice fruit showing on bouquet; good fruit in the mouth, clean and lemony, with oak evident, but well balanced and long.

Rhine Riesling 1995 (some botrytis, 12% alcohol): Pale golden colour; rich fruit nose, still quite shy; rich, concentrated and complex fruit, but not sweet or cloying, will make a very good bottle in a couple of years.

Pinot Noir 1994 (maiden vintage, 8 months in new oak): Brilliant red; open ripe fruit nose; good Pinot Noir fruit with some soft tannins and a nice structure. A KC wine to watch for the future.

Pinot Noir 1995 (cask sample): Paler colour than '94; lovely cherry fruit nose; less concentration than previous wine, but more time in cask will improve after bottling, lots of length and beautiful fruit.

Shiraz 1989 (2 years in mostly 2nd-fill casks): Deep colour; earthy, Rhôney bouquet; powerful mouthful of rounded fruit, tannins ripe, but this still needs time and will be super.

Marlbrook 1990 (60% Cabernet Sauvignon, 30% Merlot, 10% Cabernet Franc, 24 months in 2nd-fill casks): Deep, plummy colour; open, blackcurrant fruit nose; nice cassis fruit, soft tannin and good backbone, a good Bordeaux blend, ready now but will train on.

Cabernet Sauvignon 1990 (mixture of 2 clones, 24 months in Nevers casks): Very deep, dense red; nice Cabernet nose, with some mint and a hint of stalkiness, each coming from the different clones; a fine Cabernet with concentrated, slightly minty cassis fruit, soft tannins and plenty of spine for longer keeping. Listed on SAA 1st Class.

Noble Late Harvest Sauvignon Blanc 1992 (a Gower benchmark, this botrytized Sauvignon is barrel raised and aged, and chalks up yet another well-deserved Platter 5 stars): Deep, treacle gold; bouquet rich and honeyed; terrific concentration of rich, luscious and complex fruit, with that green spine so essential to all great dessert wines. A star.

Blanc de Blancs 1987 (95% Sauvignon Blanc, 10% Chenin, some botrytis): Golden colour; delicious bouquet with botrytis hints; concentration of limey fruit, full and luscious, but finishes quite dry.

Vin de Constance 1991 (this is it!): Deep golden colour; wafts of luscious Muscat fruit and honey; wonderful, light and elegant, with super lemon and lime fruit, though rich and honeyed at the same time. A one-off experience, no fortification or botrytis whatsoever, a superb dessert wine.

Technical Notes

Area under vines: 75 hectares

Average production: 500 tons, 30,000 cases in bottle

Cultivars planted
WHITE: Sauvignon Blanc, Chardonnay, Rhine Riesling, Chenin, Muscat de Frontignan
RED: Cabernet Sauvignon, Cabernet Franc, Merlot, Pinot Noir, Shiraz

Wines produced
WHITE: Sauvignon Blanc, Chardonnay, Rhine Riesling, Noble Late Harvest Sauvignon Blanc, Blanc de Blancs, Vin de Constance
RED: Cabernet Sauvignon, Marlbrook, Pinot Noir, Shiraz, Dry Red (1990 only)

Useful Information

Owners: Jooste family
Winemaker: Ross Gower
Address: Klein Constantia Estate, Box 375, Constantia 7848
Telephone: 021.7945188 *Fax*: 021.7942464

Tasting/Sales: Weekdays 09.00 to 17.00, Saturday 09.00 to 13.00

BUITENVERWACHTING

Originally part of Simon van der Stel's vast Constantia estate, Buitenverwachting, unpronounceable to non-Afrikaans speakers – try Bayton-vair-vackt-ung – was sold to Cornelis Brink on the dissolution of the exiled Wilhem Adriaen's properties in 1793. The farm has had sixteen different owners since then, many of them suffering bankruptcy and all the other problems that plagued wine growers of the Cape during the nineteenth century. From 1866 until 1981 it had been in the hands of the Lategan and Louw families, two names well-known in the Cape wine industry. Since 1981 new life has been injected, along with considerable capital investment, by the new German owners, Richard and Christina Muller. Their money has been well spent, and Buitenverwachting is now a model estate, making wines that hold their heads up with pride in the Constantia constellation.

The Mullers had a clean or, more accurately, a rather dirty slate on which to draw up their plans for the future. The vineyards have been almost entirely replanted, a magnificent new cellar created, and the manor-house rebuilt. An immaculate mini-village houses the estate workers, who benefit from a range of perks including a crèche, free schooling, a playground for the children, free medical services, free water and free electricity. The houses are all freshly painted white, and every one has a beautifully tended garden.

Buitenverwachting has been fortunate in its choice of wine-makers, to whom much of the estate's success is due. Initially it was Jean Daneel, currently working in the same capacity at the Morgenhof estate in Stellenbosch. He was replaced by another talented winemaker, Herman Kirschbaum, who is the present incumbent. Careful analyses of soils resulted in plantings of Sau-vignon Blanc, Chardonnay, Rhine Riesling, the two Cabernets, Merlot and a little Gamay; the last was used for several years to make a Nouveau for promotional parties, but now goes into the red blends.

Herman Kirschbaum, as well as being an excellent winemaker, is a thoroughly nice man. He gave me a great deal of his valuable time, and a delicious picnic lunch on the tree-shaded lawn in front of the lovely old manor-house, where he and his family live. This is a facility which visitors can enjoy, in addition to the superb restaurant.

The success of the Buitenverwachting estate, has been a literal translation of the name, 'beyond expectations'. This was clearly demonstrated on the price list in the tasting room: of the ten listed wines, no less than seven had the words SOLD OUT stamped against them. At the moment only around 15% of the production is exported, the rest being sold mainly in Cape Town, Johannesburg and direct from the estate.

Due to the shortage of available wines, I was able to taste only three wines, for which my tasting notes are shown below. I also tried several new wines from the cask, as well as half a dozen with the picnic. As tasting outdoors always presents difficulties for me, to say nothing of juggling with picnic food at the same time, I have not included notes on these wines. A few really stood out, including a 1995 Chardonnay from a cask made by the French cooper, Taransaud, both 1995 and 1994 Sauvignon Blanc and an excellent, ready-to-drink Cabernet Sauvignon 1991.

Tasting Notes

Cap Classique, Brut 1989: Pale straw colour, with persistent small bubbles; fruit and biscuit bouquet; yeasty and creamy on the palate, with quite a dry finish.

Rhine Riesling 1995 (Herman worked the 1995 with a winemaker from Baden-Baden, and admits this has influenced the wine): Lovely pale golden colour; delicious, delicate Riesling fruit bouquet; fresh, grapey fruit, delightful, long and clean; tasted half as dry as the analyzed 10 g/l sugar.

Grand Vin 1990 (70% Cabernet Sauvignon, rest Merlot and Cabernet Franc): Lovely deep red; good blackcurrant nose, with oaky vanilla notes; loads of ripe fruit, oak still a bit dominant, will go on some time.

Technical Notes

Area under vines: 100 hectares

Average production: 800 tons, 48,000 cases bottled

Cultivars planted
WHITE: Sauvignon Blanc, Chardonnay, Rhine Riesling
RED: Cabernet Sauvignon, Cabernet Franc, Merlot, Pinot Noir, Gamay

Wines produced
WHITE: Sauvignon Blanc, Chardonnay, Rhine Riesling, Buiten Blanc, Noblesse
RED: Buiten Keur, Cabernet Sauvignon, Grand Vin, Christine, Pinot Noir, Gamay, Merlot (last made 1991)
SPARKLING: Cap Classique Brut

Useful Information

Owner: Christina Muller
General Manager: Lars Maack
Winemaker: Herman Kirschbaum
Vineyards: François Baard
Address: Buitenverwachting, Klein Constantia Rd., Constantia 7800
Telephone: 021.7945190/1 *Fax*: 021.7941351

Tasting/Sales: 09.00 to 17.00
Facilities: Cellar Tours 11.00 and 15.00; Picnic lunches
Restaurant: Open lunch and dinner weekdays, dinner only Saturday, closed August. Telephone: 021.7943522

STEENBERG

At the time of my research trip, Steenberg was nearing completion. The land, originally known as Swaansweide, was granted in 1688 by Simon van der Stel to one Catharina Ras to 'cultivate, to plough and to sow and also to possess'. Evidently he did not consider the land good enough for his own empire, or doubtless he would have cultivated, ploughed, sown and possessed along with the rest of his huge Constantia estate (although he is on record as having run cattle here). Be that as it may, the land has not been used for the growing of vines in the recent past.

The whole 205 hectare estate was acquired by mining giant Johannesburg Consolidated Investments in 1990. In addition to an eventual 70 hectare vineyard, a leisure complex is planned with residential accommodation, a championship golf-course and a restaurant, and the old Cape Dutch homestead will be restored to its former beauty.

There are already 55 hectares under vines, and ex-Boschendal viticulturist Herman Hanekom, having carefully studied the suitability of different parcels of the vineyard, will have the last vines planted by 1997. His chosen varietals for white wines are Sauvignon Blanc, Chardonnay and Sémillon, and for red he has selected Cabernet Sauvignon, Cabernet Franc, Merlot and the Italian Nebbiolo. He anticipates that they will be in full production by the year 2000, and the volume will be around 40,000 cases.

The first vintage of Sauvignon Blanc was produced in 1995. As the huge new winery is not yet completed, the wine was vinified by winemaker Nicky Versfeld at the Welmoed Co-operative. He has done an excellent job, and the delicate, herbaceous result is a good indicator for future wines.

Eyebrows may have been raised at the appointment of a relatively unknown figure on the Cape scene, Emmanuel Bolliger, as winemaker. However, as a graduate of Stellenbosch, he had acquired extensive experience in Switzerland at Schenk, in France at Château Berliquet in St Emilion, as well as in the Rhône valley and in Gaillac, and has also spent six months at Esk Valley in New Zealand.

Technical Notes

Area under vines: 55 hectares, eventually 70

Cultivars planted
WHITE: Sauvignon Blanc, Sémillon, Chardonnay
RED: Cabernet Sauvignon, Cabernet Franc, Merlot, Nebbiolo

Wines produced (to date)
WHITE: Sauvignon Blanc
RED: Cabernet Sauvignon

Useful Information

Owners: Johannesburg Consolidated Investments (JCI)
Winemaker: Emmanuel Bolliger
Vineyard Manager: Herman Hanekom
Address: Steenberg, Box 224, Steenberg 7947
Telephone: 021.755708/726863 *Fax*: 021.724300

Tasting/Sales: Summer – weekdays 09.30 to 17.00, Saturday
09.00 to 13.00; Winter – weekdays only 10.00 to 16.00

4

Franschhoek

Franschhoek is one of the smallest wine areas in the Cape, but it is historically important. It was here in this beautiful valley to the north-west of Stellenbosch that Simon van der Stel settled 200 Huguenot immigrants between 1688 and 1690. They quickly settled in with the free burghers from Holland, and their influence in viticulture and vinification, brought from their native France, cannot be over-estimated. Their names live on today, not only in Franschhoek, but in every corner of South Africa's winelands – names like de Villiers, Rousseau, du Toit, du Plessis, Joubert, le Roux, and many more. The French origin of those first settlers is also clear from the names of most of the wine farms in Franschhoek – La Motte, l'Ormarins, Clos Cabrière, La Bourgogne, Dieu Donné.

Surrounded and protected by the Drakenstein mountains, the Franschhoek valley enjoys a relatively high annual rainfall of 900 millimetres per year. The vineyards have a wide variety of soils, exposure and micro-climates, some being in the low-lying land along the riverside, and some on the lower slopes of the mountains. This allows the area to produce a correspondingly wide variety of wines – reds and whites from most of the noble varieties, and some excellent Caps Classiques.

BELLINGHAM

The original grant for 37 hectares was to a Gerit van Vuuren in October 1693, since when it has passed through various hands, including the well-known de Villiers family, and has been considerably expanded.

31

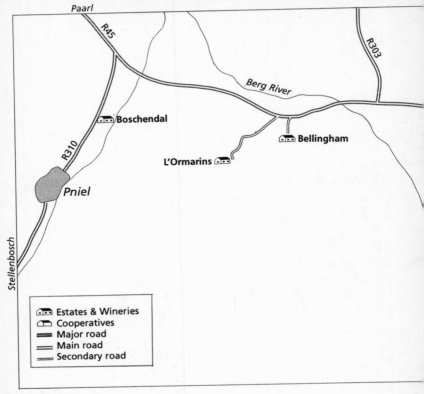

Franschhoek

After the difficult years of the late nineteenth century, followed by the First World War and the economic depression of the twenties, Bellingham was in a state of near-total dereliction. In 1930 the farm was bought by an unlikely winemaker, a Polish immigrant by the name of Bernard Podlashuk. He altogether lacked experience or knowledge of farming, let alone winemaking, and was left with little money after paying the purchase price. Like many of his country's generations, he overcame the odds with sheer determination and enthusiasm. Mortgaging himself to the hilt and beyond, he set about the restoration of the homestead and buildings. He travelled extensively in the winemaking regions of Europe to learn his new trade and returned to Bellingham to replant the vineyards with the right grapes, and set himself to become a winemaker. His

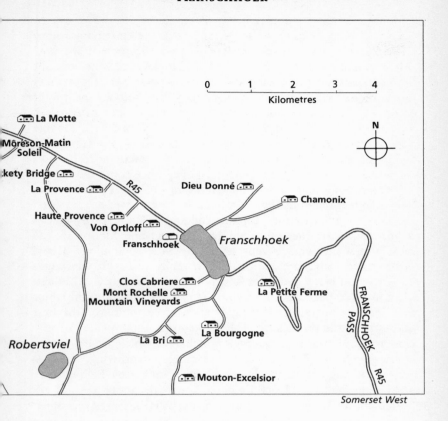

0 1 2 3 4
Kilometres

N

La Motte
Môreson-Matin
Soleil
:kety Bridge
La Provence
R45
Dieu Donné
Chamonix
Haute Provence
Von Ortloff
Franschhoek
Franschhoek
Clos Cabriere
Mont Rochelle
Mountain Vineyards
La Petite Ferme
Robertsviel
La Bri
La Bourgogne
Mouton-Excelsior
FRANSCHHOEK PASS
R45

Somerset West

efforts were well rewarded, as he created two wines that rapidly won the affections of the new South African table wine drinkers. These were the Bellingham Johannisberger and the Premier Grand Cru, which remain big sellers to this day.

In 1970 the farm was bought by Union Wine Limited. Initially, during their ownership the wine was transported to premises in Wellington for maturation, blending and bottling, but new legislation stipulated that wines had to be matured on the property where they were grown. A new cellar had to be built, which was opened in 1985, together with the new reception and tasting room, by Springbok Jan Pickard.

In 1990, coal magnate Graham Beck bought Union Wine, together with Bellingham, and merged the company with Kersaf

Holdings, creating Douglas Green Bellingham. He did, however, annexe Bellingham as his personal property, and so it remains today. One of the first and cleverest moves on the part of the new owner was the appointment of Charles Hopkins as winemaker at Bellingham. Charles is young, dynamic and passionate about wine. He worked at Dry Creek in the Sonoma valley, and has spent a lot of time at Château Fonplegade in St Emilion. Château Ausone is his dream red wine and, having sourced a vineyard with suitable grapes, Pascal Delbeck had better watch out. In 1995, Charles went to New Zealand to learn reductive winemaking techniques for white wines, and so his pursuit of excellence continues.

The successful but rather humdrum range of wines produced by Bellingham at the time of the Graham Beck purchase has now been extended, thanks to the Hopkins influence. A range of six top quality wines are the result. Shiraz, Cabernet and Merlot are the reds, and white wine is represented by Sauvignon Blanc, Chardonnay and Sauvenay, one of the few really successful marriages of Sauvignon Blanc and Chardonnay I have come across. Although there are 110 hectares under vines at Bellingham, the farm is not registered as an estate, leaving Hopkins free to source the best grapes from the prime sites. The throughput of the winery is now close to 2,000 tons in an average year, half of which are bought in.

The demand for Bellingham's wines is huge and growing, and sales and marketing are in the hands of Douglas Green Bellingham's Marketing Director Henry Kempen. Currently about 20% is exported, mostly to the U.K., where Sainsbury's is the largest customer.

Tasting Notes

Sauvenay 1995 (75% Sauvignon, 25% Chardonnay): Very pale colour; lovely fruit nose, mainly Sauvignon; clean and dry, gooseberry fruit of Sauvignon is counterbalanced by weight of Chardonnay, easy drinking, with just the right amount of wood.

Sauvignon Blanc 1995: Very pale straw; great elder-bark and asparagus Sauvignon nose; really good, with crisp clean fruit and perfect acidity, very long, five stars from me.

Chardonnay 1995 (40% barrel-fermented and aged on lees): Pale straw colour; citrus fruit nose; nice and easy, with lemony fruit, definitely New-World style, good.

Merlot 1995 (30% new oak, 30% 2nd-fill, 40% 3rd- and 4th-fill): Deep, dark red; nice black fruits on nose; already soft and fruity, with ripe tannins, St Emilion style.

Shiraz 1995 (new American oak): Excellent deep colour; fruit and vanilla bouquet; rounded and easy, fruit and wood in balance.

Cabernet Sauvignon 1995 (40% new oak, made from 15% old clones, 85% new): Lovely, deep colour; cassis, with mint from new clones on the nose; a good, New-World style Cabernet with a bit of class.

Cabernet Franc 1995 (excellent first vintage): Deep, dense red; great Bordeaux Right Bank whiffs of ripe blackberry fruit; lovely, mouth-filling, with balance of oak and fruit right.

Technical Notes

Area under vines: 110 hectares, plus 1,000 tons bought in

Wines produced
WHITE: Chardonnay, Sauvignon Blanc, Sauvenay, Premier Grand Cru, Paarl Riesling, Johannisberger (exported as Cape Gold), Special Late Harvest, Noble Late Harvest
RED: Cabernet Sauvignon, Merlot, Cabernet Franc (New), Shiraz, Classic, Pinotage
ROSÉ: Almeida Rosé, Rosé Sec
SPARKLING: Brut

BOSCHENDAL ESTATE

Originally granted to a Huguenot immigrant named Jean le Long in 1685, the owner gave it the name of 'Bossendaal', or 'trees and dales'. Only 30 years later it passed into the hands of another Huguenot family, the de Villiers, who were to become one of the leading wine families of South Africa, and who held Boschendal for 164 years. The manor-house, which holds the estate's offices today, was built for Anna Susana Louw, wife of Paul de Villiers, in 1812. Sadly, due to the long period of economic difficulties in the mid-nineteenth century, capped by the onset of oidium, the de Villiers were forced to sell Boschendal in 1879. Paul de Villiers managed to cling on to his Landskroon farm, and there is still a Paul de Villiers owning and running that estate today.

Things went from bad to worse for the beleaguered wine farmers with the new plague of phylloxera, which devastated the vineyards of the Cape. It was in 1902 that Cecil Rhodes bought the estate, incorporating it into the newly formed Rhodes Fruit Farms. This move was supposed to save the skins of the many nearly destitute wine farmers who had lost their livelihood to the ravages of phylloxera. There are those, however, who ascribe more devious, political motives to the empire-building Rhodes, saying that he was in sore need of some good publicity following the ill-fated Jameson Raid. Whatever his motives, the advent of refrigerated shipping showed an excellent return on Rhodes's vast investment. He did not live to see the success of his venture, as he died in the year that the company was formed. His work was carried on by his manager, Harry Pickstone who, as well as being a highly competent fruit farmer, did much for the rebuilding of the wine industry after the solution to phylloxera was found (in the grafting of vines on to aphid-resistant American rootstocks).

After Rhodes's death Rhodes Fruit Farms, including Boschendal, was controlled by de Beers, the diamond mining giant. In 1936 they sold the property to Sir Abe Bailey, on whose death in 1941 it was acquired by a syndicate of four businessmen. In 1969 the syndicate approached de Beers and the Anglo-American Corporation, inviting them to buy a majority interest, and to assume responsibility for the management of the company. As a result Boschendal is part of Anglo-American Farms, a subsidiary of the parent company.

There were doubtless many wine farmers who thought that the acquisition of a good wine property by a huge corporate body would lead to a drop in the quality of the wines. How, they would have asked, can wine be made according to the decisions of a board of directors in far-off Johannesburg, who have as much knowledge of winemaking as they have of brain surgery? This sentiment has been echoed more recently in Bordeaux, where many of the great Châteaux have been acquired by large companies. The answer is the same in both countries.

As long as the running of the estates is put into the best hands available – winemakers and viticulturists who know the area – the combination of these people and the financial backing of the large corporations ensures not only the maintenance, but also the improvement of both property and produce. This has certainly been the case at Boschendal, and at their other showpiece estate, Vergelegen in Somerset West. In addition, Anglo-American have shown themselves to be extremely conscious of their inheritance, and their restoration of the beautiful buildings and the construction of the fabulous hill-top winery at Vergelegen have ensured a stream of visitors by the thousand.

The vineyards of Boschendal now cover a vast 600 hectares, and stretch over fourteen kilometres from the Berg river in the Franschhoek valley to the slopes of the Simonsberg. Within this huge area, there are a multitude of soil types, altitudes and micro-climates, allowing flexibility for the planting of many varieties, and the production of a large range of wines, both for the making of single cultivar wines, and for blending. In John Platter's 1996 guide, the tonnage was shown as 3,400, but there are now a further 210 hectares under vines since he went to press. This figure must be increased accordingly as must the volume of bottled wines, shown by him as 230,000 cases.

General management of both Boschendal and Vergelegen is in the extremely capable hands of director Don Tooth. By training Don is an accountant, but since coming to the winelands he has become a wine buff. Through his unassuming approach and his eagerness to learn, he has made many friends among the wine-makers, who generally relate to accountants like spit to hot fat. Farm and cellar management are the responsibility of Gerrie Wagener, who is one of the most highly qualified viticulturists in the industry, as well as being a thoroughly nice man. Margaret Leroy is in charge of sales, with particular responsibility for the export market. Finally, and perhaps most important, the wine-maker is newly appointed Michael Graham, former cellarmaster at the Bergkelder. He is ably assisted by Ronell Wiid, the deter-mined and talented young lady winemaker, who is responsible for the Boschendal reds.

The range of wines produced at Boschendal is somewhat bewil-dering. There are some ten wines in the regular Boschendal range, which are sold on the home market and for export. Then there is the so-called Reserve range of wines, which are largely experi-mental, and consequently made in quantities too limited for general release – they are sold only through the estate's restaurants, both at Boschendal and Vergelegen, or at auction. As well as these two groups, a number of other wines are made that fit into neither group, and are usually special export labels.

Arrangements for visitors are extremely professional. There are two restaurants, the main one being next door to the superbly restored manor-house (a fine museum of early Dutch and Rhodes memorabilia). Here there is a marvellous buffet, from which you can help yourself to a wide selection of hot and cold foods, and a tempting array of salads, with a wonderful wine list of Boschendal's best to choose from. Further along the same low, thatched building is Le Café, where reasonably priced light meals, teas and coffee are served. There are also mouth-watering picnic baskets on offer, which you can eat in the tree-shaded area around the gazebo. If your objective is just to taste and buy, wine tastings are held in the Taphuis, to which you turn right on entering the gate, rather than going left to the manor-house, restaurants and gift shop.

Tasting Notes

Boschendal Brut 1990 (Méthode Cap Classique, formerly known as Méthode Champenoise, 50/50 Chardonnay and Pinot Noir): Light golden colour, fine, long mousse; nice, biscuity Champagne nose; dry, with lots of creamy fruit, and good length.

Sauvignon 1994 (from a single vineyard at 450 metres altitude): Very pale straw; fantastic Sauvignon nose, elderflower and goose-berry; fine fruit, quite herbaceous, good length and perfect acidity.

Grande Cuvée 1995 (export label only, sold as Grand Vin Blanc in SA, 85% Sauvignon Blanc, rest Sémillon and Rhine Riesling, Sauvignon fermented in small oak): Pale straw; nose good, with some oak, but not overly so; lovely palate, with clean, fresh fruit, good length and just the right amount of oakiness.

Pinot Noir/Chardonnay 1995 (80/20 blend, UK only): Very pale, slightly pinky colour; nose has some nice Pinot fruit; full, rounded fruit, just right balance of acidity.

Chardonnay 1994 (lightly oaked, UK only): Pale straw; nice fruit bouquet, oak muted; well-made Chardonnay with a bit of weight and length, oak coming through on the aftertaste.

Chardonnay Reserve 1995: Same pale straw colour; Chardonnay nose with trace of vanilla; more finesse and elegance than the previous wine, oak evidence similar.

Merlot 1993: Fine, deep red; powerful St Emilion bouquet of Merlot; excellent fruit, with non-aggressive tannins, a good effort from young vines.

Merlot/Cabernet, Grande Reserve 1993 (60/40 blend, matured in casks, 65% of which new): Very deep, dense red; powerful whiffs of blackberry fruit, with vanilla tones; a huge, rounded mouthful of ripe black fruit, big, chewy and still very tannic, but will be superb in time.

Shiraz 1993: Good, garnet red; open nose with good fruit; after the Grande Reserve, very easy and drinkable, good now, but will keep a bit.

Technical Notes

Area under vines: 600 hectares

Cultivars planted: You name it, Anglo-American grows it.

Wines produced, regular range
WHITE: Blanc de Noir (first in Cape), Chardonnay, Sauvignon Blanc, Vin d'Or, Blanc de Blancs, Riesling, Chenin Blanc, Le Bouquet
RED: Grand Vin, Lanoy
SPARKLING: Boschendal Brut, Le Grand Pavillon Blanc de Blancs

Wines produced, reserve range
WHITE: Pinot Gris, Chardonnay Reserve, Chardonnay Bins 101, 102 and 103, Sauvignon Blanc Reserve, Sémillon, Gewürztraminer, Chenin Blanc, Pinot Noir/Chardonnay
RED: Merlot, Pinot Noir, Shiraz, Grand Reserve Merlot/Cabernet

Useful Information

Owners: Anglo-American Farms Limited
General Manager: Don Tooth
Farm Manager/Viticulturist: Gerrie Wagener
Winemaker: Michael Graham

Assistant Winemaker: Ronell Wiid
Marketing/Export: Margaret Leroy
Address: Boschendal Estate Winery, Groot Drakenstein 7680
Telephone: 021.874.1031 *Fax*: 021.874.1864

Tasting/Sales: Taphuis open Monday–Saturday 08.30 to 17.00
Facilities: Boschendal Restaurant, Telephone: 021.874.1252; Le Piquenique, Le Café, The Manor-House Museum, Country Shop

CLOS CABRIÈRE

One red-letter visit was to the Clos Cabrière estate in Franschhoek, where the Huguenots settled in the late seventeenth century. The Lords XVII, the governing body of the Dutch East India Company, sent many of these dispossessed Frenchmen to settle in the Cape, particularly if they had skills that were needed. Among these was one Pierre Jourdan, who was granted this farm, which he named after the village of his birth, Cabrière d'Aigues, in 1694.

The present owner of Clos Cabrière, Achim von Arnim, bought the estate in the 1980s, whilst he was still responsible for the winemaking on the Boschendal and Vergelegen estates of Anglo-American Farms. Achim is a colourful and attractive character, passionate about his wines, a firm believer in the importance of *terroir*, and a deeply patriotic South African. He studied oenology at Geisenheim in Germany, where he met his wife, Hildegard. To illustrate his love of South Africa, Hildegard told me that, as soon as he had passed his exams, in spite of having promised her that he would wait until she had made her plans, he married her and whisked her straight back to the Cape on the first available flight.

Although 'Méthode Champenoise', or 'Méthode Cap Classique', as the Champagne makers now insist that it must be called, was already being made in South Africa, von Arnim was the first to make it with only the classic Champagne grape varieties, Chardonnay and Pinot Noir. His excellent range of sparkling wines, all far drier than anything else produced in the Cape and beautifully presented, still represents the essence of everything that von Arnim believes in. However, he has added twenty hectares of vineyard to the original seventeen, all on the western slopes of the valley, known as Haute Cabrière. So I have the impression that we shall see some fairly stunning still Pinot Noir and Chardonnay wines in the Burgundy style from Clos Cabrière in the years to come. Already the 1994 Clos Cabrière Pinot Noir has won prizes in competition with other Pinot Noir aficionados like Anthony Hamilton Russell, and von Arnim is even more excited about his 1995.

My visit coincided with the arrival of some German tourists, which called for a demonstration of *sabrage*, the removal of the top of a bottle of sparkling wine with a sabre. This is a *specialité de la maison*, and although I know it is widely practised in Champagne, I had never witnessed this romantic decapitation before. Achim explained to a German lady that he would show her how to do it and, in the event that she was successful, she would receive a kiss as a reward for her skill. I had always imagined that this was a dashing exhibition of swordsmanship, a blade flashing through the air, neatly removing the cork, followed by a gush of foaming nectar and the wine then being poured into the lady's dainty shoe. Not at all – a sharp tap with the edge of a very blunt sabre against the rim of the top of the bottle is all that is required to remove the top part of the bottle, complete with the cork inside. The lady succeeded, with a little help from Achim, and duly received her kiss. My turn at *sabrage* came with the second wine that we tasted, and I am pleased to report that I upheld British honour with success and a degree of dash, though I declined the award.

Achim then drove me up the road towards Villiersdorp to the Haute Cabrière Restaurant, which is built into the side of the mountain, with the red wine cellar behind and visible through a window to the rear of the restaurant, and fabulous views over the Franschhoek valley in front. We kicked off with no less than three starters, Oysters, Calamari and Gravadlax, washed down by a bottle of Pierre Jourdan, Brut Sauvage. This is a wine without dosage, and is one of the finest non-Champagne sparklers I have tasted: palest straw in colour with a fine, long-lasting mousse, a curious yeasty nose, which is the reason Achim christened the wine Sauvage, bone dry and elegant in the mouth, and a perfect partner to oysters and all delicate seafood. The blend is the same percentage of Chardonnay and Pinot Noir as the Cuvée Brut, but only the first 200 litres of the Cuvée are used to give extra elegance.

The main course – or I should say courses, for there was both fish and lamb – then arrived accompanied by a bottle each of the

41

Pinot Noir 1994 and 1995. The prize-winning 1994 was excellent, and the equal of many a more expensive red Burgundy I have tasted. The 1995 drove Achim into ecstasy: it had been fined recently, but as yet had had no filtration, and was still a little cloudy, but Pinot Noir came wafting up at you even before you picked up the glass. I look forward to tasting this again when it has had some time in bottle.

A message arrived at the table to say that Achim's carton supplier had arrived down at Cabrière, and was waiting to see him. Plenty of time for coffee and a glass of Fine de Jourdan, a brandy distilled in a traditional copper potstill, and aged for three years in casks of Limousin oak. As we were savouring this smooth, pale gold fine, another telephone call announced that the carton manufacturer was less than happy at being kept waiting. We left at once, von Arnim driving down the mountain road at breakneck speed. Achim's life is lived in permanent top gear, but he is a great respecter of nature and tradition. This is evidenced not only by his use of the Pierre Jourdan name for his sparkling wines, but especially by his insistence that the opening of the Haute Cabrière cellars should be completed and celebrated exactly 300 years to the day from the arrival of Pierre Jourdan at Cabrière. The bull-dozers rolled away as the guests arrived.

Tasting Notes

Pierre Jourdan, Cuvée Brut (60% Chardonnay, 40% Pinot Noir – this was the 1992 vintage, but Achim does not put the year on his Cap Classiques): Very pale colour, fine, persistent mousse; fine, delicate nose; creamy and yeasty, with elegant fruit and perfect acidity.

Pierre Jourdan, Blanc de Blancs (100% Chardonnay, 1993 vintage): Same lovely, pale colour, mousse again long-lasting with slightly larger bubbles; nose more biscuity, with pronounced Chardonnay fruit; texture creamier, with fine fruit, a superb sparkler that will get even better with a year or so in bottle.

Pierre Jourdan, Cuvée Belle Rose (100% Pinot Noir, with 5 hours skin-contact for colour): Lovely, salmon pink, fine mousse; delicate Pinot Noir fruit nose; higher dosage gives this a touch more sweetness, fine and elegant with nice fruit and smooth texture.

Pierre Jourdan, Brut Sauvage; Pinot Noir 1994; Pinot Noir 1995; Fine de Jourdan: All tasted at lunch, see text for comments.

Technical Notes

Area under vines: 23 hectares

Cultivars planted
WHITE: Chardonnay
RED: Pinot Noir

Wines produced
WHITE: Chardonnay/Pinot Noir
RED: Pinot Noir
SPARKLING: Petit Jourdan, Pierre Jourdan Brut, Pierre Jourdan Blanc de Blancs, Brut Sauvage, Cuvée Belle Rose

Useful Information

Owner/Winemaker: Achim von Arnim
Address: Clos Cabrière, Box 245, Franschhoek 7690
Telephone: 021.876.2630 *Fax*: 021.876.3390

Tasting/Sales: Weekdays 09.00 to 13.00, Saturday 10.00 to 12.30
Facilities: Tasting and Tour 11.00 by appointment, Saturdays by special arrangement only; Haute Cabrière Restaurant – lunches daily, dinner in season only, telephone to check on 021.876.3688

LA MOTTE

Pierre Joubert was the original Huguenot settler to whom the lands of La Motte were granted. The farm passed through several Huguenot families. Although vines were planted before that time, it did not really become a serious farm until the Joubert family returned here in the shape of Gideon, great-grandson of Pierre, in 1815. He enlarged and improved the farm and the homestead during the 40-odd years that he lived at La Motte. From the middle until the end of the nineteenth century, things were no easier in

THE WINES OF SOUTH AFRICA

Franschhoek than they were for the rest of the Cape's wine farmers. In 1897 Cecil Rhodes bought the property as part of the emerging Rhodes Fruit Farms enterprise.

It was still a fruit farm when Anton Rupert bought the estate in 1970, and remained so until 1984. The beautiful homestead is now lived in by Rupert's daughter, Hanneli, a well-known mezzo-soprano singer, and her husband Paul Neethling. Since 1984, the winemaking has been done by Jacques Borman, a very able graduate of Elsenburg. The accent is on red wine, with Sauvignon Blanc as the chief white variety, and a little Chardonnay is made also, but this is mainly for export. Like brother Antonij's l'Orma-rins down the road, La Motte's marketing is handled by the Bergkelder, though tastings and sales are possible at the farm.

Although traditionally a white wine area, Borman finds that the poorer soils are well-suited to red varietals; pruning and selection are severe, giving yields of only six tons per hectare in the case of Cabernet. Merlot and Shiraz are also planted, plus a little Pinot Noir, a grape, says Borman, that he likes but which needs a lot of time and attention. There are 96 hectares of vineyard, giving an average of 850/900 tons a year, of which only 650 are vinified at the winery. Rarely for Bergkelder members, not only the ageing, but also the bottling of La Motte wines takes place here.

Tasting Notes

Sauvignon Blanc 1995: Pale straw; typical elder-bark and gooseberry nose; clean, crisp Sauvignon fruit, very long.

Blanc Fumé 1994: Slightly deeper colour than the straight Sauvignon; same nice bouquet, but with wood added; fruit and wood nicely balanced, with some breadth and good length.

Schoone Gevel Chardonnay 1994 (100% new wood barrel-fermented, 7 months on lees): Good gold colour; nice fruit with some vanilla on the nose; full, fat Chardonnay with breadth and length, oak just right.

Millennium 1992 (Bordeaux blend of 55% Cabernet Sauvignon, 36% Merlot, rest Cabernet Franc, 16 months in 50% new wood, 50% 2nd-fill): Deep, ruby colour; nose rich, with nice dark cherry

44

fruit; summer fruits and slight pepper in the mouth, good, soft tannins and good backbone.

Shiraz 1991 (18 months in 15% new oak, 85% 2nd- and 3rd-fill): Garnet, turning to brown; nose ripe, with touch of capsicum; flavour meaty, with nice fruit, and good length.

Shiraz 1993 (same wood treatment): Colour also garnet, browning a little; green peppers again, with gamey hints on nose; more fruit, also gamey and leathery, more tannin structure than the '91.

Cabernet Sauvignon 1990 (contains 15% Merlot, normally much less, 16 months in 50% new, 50% 2nd-fill casks): Deep, plummy red; cedar wood and tobacco on nose; lovely ripe cassis fruit, kindly tannin and some structure.

Technical Notes

Area under vines: 96 hectares

Cultivars planted
WHITE: Sauvignon Blanc, Chardonnay
RED: Cabernet Sauvignon, Cabernet Franc, Merlot, Shiraz, Pinot Noir

Useful Information

Owners: Rupert family
Winemaker: Jacques Borman
Marketing: the Bergkelder
Address: La Motte Estate, Box 45, La Motte 7691
Telephone: 021.876.2196 *Fax*: 021.876.3446

Tasting/Sales: Weekdays 09.00 to 16.30, Saturday 09.00 to 12.00

L'ORMARINS

L'Ormarins, beautifully situated in the Franschhoek valley, with the mountains towering behind the lovely Cape Dutch homestead, was acquired by millionaire businessman, Dr Anton Rupert of

Distillers Corporation in 1969. His son Antonij is now the owner, and lives here, running the large and successful wine estate in a very hands-on manner. Quality has always been the order of the day at l'Ormarins: in the early nineteenth century, owner Jacob Marais had 114,000 vines, and was a consistent winner of prizes at all the local wine shows. In the cellar of the old farm, now used only for storage, there is an impressive rank of large oak vats, on which are carved the names of all the original Huguenot settlers. As well as the five families that have owned l'Ormarins – Roi, the first grantee, Joubert, de Villiers, Marais and Rupert – there are many names which are still commonplace in the South African winemaking hierarchy today like Retief, Rousseau (now Roussouw) and many others. Interestingly, there is also a Cordier, a name now more familiar among the Châteaux of Bordeaux.

Today the fruits of heavy investment are abundantly plain for all to see, in the immaculately laid out and maintained buildings and grounds, the high-tech winery and spacious tasting room as well as in the high quality of the wines. Antonij Rupert may be a very rich man, but he takes this farm very seriously. Production has shifted since the Ruperts arrived here in the direction of quality red wines, and there are extensive plantings of Cabernet Sauvignon, Merlot, Shiraz and Pinot Noir, in addition to the classic white varieties, in the 213 hectares of vineyards. In view of the Distillers connection, it is hardly surprising that l'Ormarins is part of the Bergkelder, by whom the wines are marketed. It is also no surprise, in view of the same connection, that they are one of the growing band of member estates that have changed their policy and are now commonly open for visits, tasting and direct sales from the cellar. Antonij Rupert has for some years benefited from the advice of oenological guru Dr Julius Laszlo. He is now in semi-retirement, however, and the torch has been passed to the able and keen Joseph Minkowitch, ex-winemaker from the Bergkelder. Joseph gave me a great deal of his time, and I thank him for his kindness and hospitality.

Tasting Notes

Sauvignon Blanc 1995: Pale straw; good nose of elder and grass; clean, crisp Sauvignon fruit, dry and long.

Blanc Fumé 1995 (30% barrel-fermented, 3/4 months on lees): Greeny gold; nose OK, but slightly cheesy; good fruit and length, oak there, but not too much.

Pinot Gris 1995: Very pale; nice Burgundian nose; pleasing, ripe fruit and nice length.

Grand Vin Blanc 1995 (15% barrel-fermented, 65% Chardonnay, rest Auxerrois and Pinot Gris): Clear, brilliant and very pale colour; nice, clean fruit, wood very evident, long.

Chardonnay 1994 (30% barrel-fermented and 7 months on lees): Pale, greeny gold; lovely white Burgundy bouquet; very nice Chardonnay fruit, but still strong oak.

Rhine Riesling 1995: Pale gold; Riesling fruit nose; grapey Riesling fruit, with a touch of sweetness, long aftertaste.

Shiraz 1989 (18 months barrel age in 2nd- and 3rd-fill casks): Fine, deep red; spicy, smoky nose with ripe fruit; same spicy, ripe fruit on palate, nice ripe tannins and good structure.

Merlot 1989 (same wood, only sold ex-estate): Deep red, brown at edges; bouquet big, ripe and fruity; a big mouthful, lots of backbone and tannin, maybe too much for fruit.

Optima 1990 (same wood, 55% Cabernet Sauvignon, 36% Merlot, 9% Cabernet Franc): Deep, dense red; fine wafts of ripe cassis fruit; ripe blackcurrant and blackberry fruit on palate, all in harmony, with enough soft tannin and spine to age well.

Cabernet Sauvignon 1989 (same wood): Nice mid-red; strong Ribena nose; some good fruit, tannin and structure, but a bit one-dimensional.

Technical Notes

Area under vines: 213 hectares

Cultivars planted
WHITE: Sauvignon Blanc, Chardonnay, Rhine Riesling, Cape Riesling, Pinot Gris, Auxerrois, Gewürztraminer, Muscat d'Ottonel, Bukettraube

RED: Cabernet Sauvignon, Cabernet Franc, Shiraz, Merlot, Pinot Noir, Souzao

Wines produced
WHITE: Sauvignon Blanc, Blanc Fumé, Chardonnay, Grand Vin Blanc, Pinot Gris, Rhine Riesling, Guldenpfennig Guldenlese, Noble Late Harvest, Franschhoek Riesling
RED: Cabernet Sauvignon, Merlot, Optima, Shiraz
'PORT': Vintage, not commercialized – yet

Useful Information

Owner: Antonij Rupert
Consultant: Dr Julius Laszlo
Winemaker: Joseph Minkowitch
Address: L'Ormarins, P/Bag Suider-Paarl 7624
Telephone: 021.874.1026 *Fax:* 021.874.1361

Tasting/Sales: Weekdays 09.00 to 16.30, Saturday 09.00 to 12.30

UNVISITED

Estates and Wineries: Chamonix, Dieu Donné, Haute Provence, La Bourgogne, La Bri, La Petite Ferme, La Provence, Mont Richelle Mountain Vineyards, Moreson-Matin Soleil, Mouton Excelsior, Rickety Bridge Vineyards, Van Ortloff.

Co-operatives: Franschhoek Vineyards Co-operative

5
Stellenbosch

Stellenbosch is generally recognized as the wine capital of South Africa, although Constantia is a little older. Governor Simon van der Stel, after whom the town is named, founded the agricultural settlement of Stellenbosch in 1679. Although the growing of wheat and the raising of sheep and cattle were the main farming activities of the early settlers, wine formed an integral part of the agricultural economy. The object of the foundation of the Cape settlement was the provisioning of the Dutch East India Company's ships on their way to the Far East and, although fresh meat and flour were the staples, wine, quite apart from its pleasurable aspects, was found to keep better than water, and also proved an effective prophylactic against the dreaded scurvy.

Dominated by the high mountain ranges of the Simonsberg to the north-east of the town, the Jonkershoek to the east, and the Hottentots-Holland and Helderberg mountains to the east and south-east, the area is well-suited to the growing of the classic wine varieties. The town is bounded on the western side by the lower hills of the Papegaaiberg and the Stellenbosch Kloof, as well as by the Eerster River, an important source of irrigation. To the south-west the land is lower and less fertile, eventually merging with the sand dunes of the Cape Flats, which run down to the waters of False Bay. Across these low lands blow the cooling sea breezes, which play an important role in keeping summer temperatures down.

The average temperature during the growing season varies greatly from one property to another, depending on exposure to the breezes from the south and south-east, but is normally between 18 and 19 degrees Celsius. Well-aspected vines on the lower mountain slopes tend not to require irrigation, whilst those which benefit

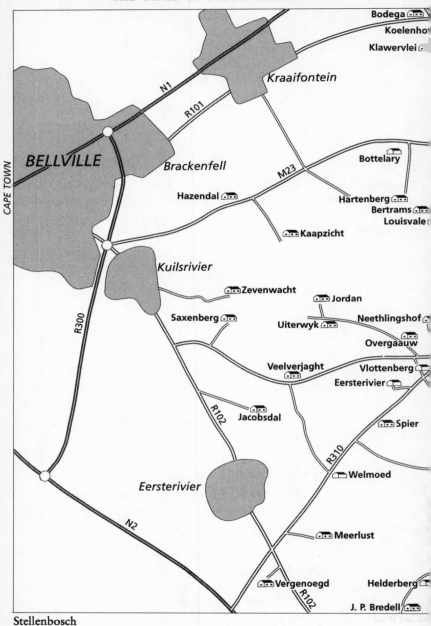

Stellenbosch

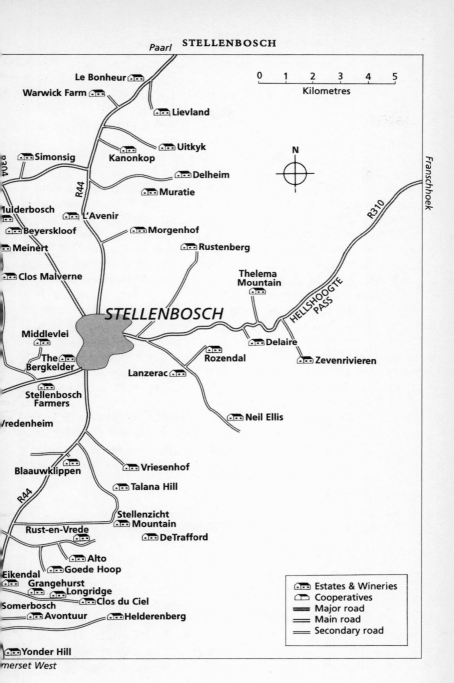

Le Bonheur

Warwick Farm

Lievland

Simonsig

Uitkyk

Kanonkop

Delheim

Muratie

Mulderbosch

L'Avenir

Beyerskloof

Morgenhof

Meinert

Rustenberg

Clos Malverne

Thelema
Mountain

STELLENBOSCH

Middlevlei

Delaire

The
Bergkelder

Rozendal

Zevenrivieren

Lanzerac

Stellenbosch
Farmers

Vredenheim

Neil Ellis

Blaauwklippen

Vriesenhof

Talana Hill

Stellenzicht
Mountain

Rust-en-Vrede

DeTrafford

Alto

Eikendal

Goede Hoop

Grangehurst

Longridge

Clos du Ciel

Somerbosch

Avontuur

Helderenberg

Yonder Hill

Somerset West

0 1 2 3 4 5
Kilometres

N

Franschhoek

R44

R304

R310

HELLSHOOGTE PASS

R44

Estates & Wineries
Cooperatives
Major road
Main road
Secondary road

51

less from the sea breezes, planted on different soils, need supplementary irrigation, particularly in the heat of December and the New Year. The best red wines come from the decomposed granite soils of the lower slopes to the east of Stellenbosch, while the alluvial and sandy soils of Table Mountain sandstone origin to the west are better suited to white varieties.

Stellenbosch itself, a charming town with many fine examples of eighteenth-century architecture, may still be regarded both as the cradle and the capital of the South African wine industry. The town boasts a fine university, with a Department of Viticulture and Oenology. There is also the Nietvoorbij Institute for Viticulture and Oenology at the farm of the same name on the outskirts of the town, as well as the Elsenburg School of Agriculture on the road to Malmesbury. Much important pioneering research work has originated from these institutions, carried out by eminent wine figures like Abraham Perold, father of the Pinotage grape, Chris Theron, Chris Orffer, and many others. The headquarters of the Bergkelder and Stellenbosch Farmers' Winery are also located here.

Of greatest interest, of course, are the numerous famous estates producing quality wines from the classic grape varieties. Virtually every type of wine is made in the Stellenbosch area: reds and whites from all the noble grapes, quality sparkling wines and some excellent 'port'. The making of fine wine is no longer exclusive to Stellenbosch, however. The new generation of innovative and dedicated winemakers, assisted by new technology in the fields of viticulture and vinification, are making better and better wines in the more difficult and hotter regions like Worcester, Robertson and the Klein Karoo.

STELLENBOSCH FARMERS' WINERY

The history of Stellenbosch Farmers' Winery is complex, and inextricably linked with the development of South Africa's wine industry in this century. The founder was William Charles Winshaw, an American adventurer born in Kentucky in 1871. In his youth he served as a Texas Ranger, and then qualified as a doctor, completing his medical studies in New Orleans. His first practice was in New Mexico, where he teamed up with one Lieutenant McGuiness, an entrepreneur who was engaged in supplying mules to the British army in South Africa. Oubaas Winshaw, as he subsequently became known, first set foot in the Cape in 1900, after accompanying four thousand of the animals on their voyage aboard the good ship *Larinaga*. Having delivered the mules to Koelenhof, he joined the British army, and saw active service in the Boer War.

At the end of hostilities, Winshaw turned his hand to farming, and it was at this point that he became interested in growing vines for wine and grape juice. He rented a farm called Patrys Vallei for £6 a month, where he made some good wines, and in 1909 started his first company, the Stellenbosch Grape Juice Works, with a capital of £1,000. The venture prospered, and Winshaw became a highly respected member of the community. The post-war years were very difficult for the Cape wine farmers, however, and in 1921 Winshaw's operations fell victim to insolvency.

It took more than bankruptcy to deter a free spirit like Winshaw, however, and by 1923 he was back in business, having teamed up with G. J. Krige, a Stellenbosch distiller, who also owned the farm known as Oude Libertas. On this land now stands the SFW complex (housing the Cape Wine Academy, a 432-seat amphitheatre, vinotheque, restaurant and offices). An early owner of this farm was Adam Tas, one of the free burghers instrumental in bringing William Adriaen van der Stel to justice. His name is remembered today on many SFW labels – Tasheimer, Oom Tas, Tassenberg and the Taskelder range.

In March 1924, having been released from bankruptcy by the Supreme Court, Winshaw, backed by a friend, bought the Krige business and the farm for £5,000, and established Stellenbosch Farmers' Winery with a capital of £10,000. In the mid-1920s, Winshaw was joined by his son Bill, and later by his younger son Jack, but Oubaas Winshaw remained actively involved in the business, which he always ran with quality as the watchword, until he retired at the age of 92.

In 1950 SFW, in association with V. H. Materson & Son Ltd, was incorporated in the Stellenbosch Farmers' Wine Trust Limited. In order to finance development and new projects, the company did a deal with South African Breweries, whereby two SFW ordinary shares were exchanged for one SAB share, but the Winshaw family remained in charge.

A turning point arrived in 1966 when Monis Wineries, specialists in 'Chianti', 'sherries', 'ports', vermouth and fortified wines, amalgamated with SFW. Perhaps the most significant and beneficial aspect of this merger was Monis's ownership of the prestigious Nederburg estate, a name synonymous with South African quality table wine.

Two years earlier, in 1964, SFW had already seen the way forward in terms of producing quality wine from their own vineyards. They had commissioned young Ronnie Melck, later to become the company's distinguished managing director, to find a suitable property. The farm now known as Plaisir de Merle was acquired for £290,000. Until very recently the wine produced from the huge vineyard was used in SFW's top blends, and later became a supplementary source of wine for Nederburg. Now, with the help of Paul Pontallier of Château Margaux, the estate is producing very fine table wines under its own label.

As a wholesaler/producer, in addition to these two important fine wine properties, SFW buys in wine and grapes from all over the Cape for inclusion in its successful blends, Zonnebloem, Libertas and Sable View, which are familiar to wine consumers all over the world.

Tasting Notes

ZONNEBLOEM RANGE
Premier Grand Cru (Chenin Blanc, Colombar): Nice pale gold good fruit bouquet; clean and dry, with crisp Colombar fruit and good length.

Blanc de Blancs 1995: Pale straw; Sauvignon Blanc evident on nose; some gooseberry and quince fruit, no great length.

Rhine Riesling 1994: Mid-gold; spicy Riesling bouquet; quite full fruit, long aftertaste, will repay keeping.

Chardonnay 1995 (65% wood-fermented and 5 months on lees, 35% in tank): Greeny gold; good fruit, with some faint oakiness on the nose; quite broad and fat, with good fruit – wood not very evident, except on aftertaste.

Sauvignon Blanc/Chardonnay 1995: Pale, greeny gold; curious, slightly cheesy bouquet; herbaceous Sauvignon taste, with some body and oak from Chardonnay, which was 67% barrel-fermented.

Blanc de Noir 1995 (Cabernet Sauvignon): Pale, onion-skin pink; pleasant, boiled-sweet nose; clean, slightly sweet fruit in the mouth.

Noble Late Harvest 1990: Golden syrup colour; rich, fruit-cake nose; glycerol texture, raisins and other dried fruits in the mouth, surprisingly short finish.

Merlot 1992 (2nd- and 3rd-fill casks): Very deep colour; soft, plummy nose; good fruit with length, tannins a bit green.

Pinotage 1992 (all in small wood, some new casks): Deep red; good fruit nose, with oak; a big wine, with ripe fruit, good tannins and some structure.

Shiraz 1991 (mixture of large and small wood): Mid-red colour; ripe fruit and leather on nose; a big mouthful of ripe, strawberry fruit with soft tannins and keeping qualities.

Laureat 1992: Deep colour; good fruit nose; lots of smooth, ripe, black fruit, rounded, with ripe tannins and backbone.

Cabernet Sauvignon 1990: Nice, deep colour; nose quite closed up; summer fruits on palate, tannins to the fore, but will be a good bottle.

SABLE VIEW RANGE

Sauvignon Blanc 1995: Pale straw; some nice wafts of asparagus and gooseberry; crisp, clean fruit, good length, a value-for-money Sauvignon Blanc.

Chardonnay 1995 (very little wood, Zonnebloem barrels sometimes used): Greeny gold; fruit and a touch of vanilla on nose; nice, fat fruit on palate, good length.

Pinotage 1993: Mid-red; open fruit bouquet; easy drinking, strawberries and cherries, a good, marketable red with no complications.

Cabernet Sauvignon 1993: Deep red; cassis nose; blackcurrant fruit in mouth, no woodiness, a little structure, good value.

LIBERTAS RANGE

Chenin Blanc 1995: Pale, greeny gold; quincy, Chenin bouquet; clean, crisp, ripe fruit, a dry, easy quaffer.

Chardonnay 1995: Pale golden; good Chardonnay fruit nose; nice and fat in the mouth, quite buttery, no wood and good value.

Muscat d'Alexandrie 1995: Pale gold; strong Muscat nose; same table grape flavour on palate, with quite a dry finish.

Merlot 1993: Fairly light colour; soft fruit nose; easy, with no complexity, just nice ripe fruit.

Pinotage 1993: Palish red; banana and cherry nose; easy-drinking, with nice fruit.

Cabernet Sauvignon 1993: Deep red; up-front fruit bouquet; will not set the world on fire, but good-value Cabernet.

THE BERGKELDER

The Bergkelder, or 'mountain cellar', in Stellenbosch is part of Dr Anton Rupert's Distillers Corporation. Formed in the 1970s, this was very much Rupert's brainchild. The Bergkelder entered into partnership with some of South Africa's leading wine estates, offering them oenological, viticultural and marketing expertise in return for exclusive distribution rights for the wines of those estates. At the time these partnerships were formed, they seemed in all respects beneficial to the owners. Times were very difficult, and few of them had the necessary contacts, time or ability to market their product. Virtually all they had to do was grow the grapes, make the wine, give it to the Bergkelder for ageing and bottling, and then sit back and wait for the cash to roll in. The problem lies in the terms of the agreement, which in almost all cases stipulates that the owner makes the wine, but that as soon as vinification is complete, the wine must be delivered to the Berg-kelder's cellars – at that point it passes entirely into the control of the Bergkelder.

As far as I am aware, this has never caused any concern to owners from the quality point of view, since the level of competence of the oenologists and cellar staff at the Bergkelder has always been excellent. Difficulties arise, however, should an owner wish to terminate the agreement – if, for instance, he wants to go it alone, or to sell his estate – since the wine of one or two crops, and often large amounts of older bottled vintages are in the Bergkelder's possession. Thus, for at least two years he, or the new owner, has no source of income. Danie de Wet of de Wetshof successfully managed to break away, but his early years were extremely difficult. His cousin, Paul de Wet at Zandvliet, is experiencing similar problems at the moment.

There are currently twelve estate members. L'Ormarins and La Motte, both in Franschhoek, are the personal property of the Rupert family, whilst Uitkyk, Alto and Le Bonheur in Stellenbosch all belong outright to the Bergkelder. The other members are Meerlust, Middlevlei and Jacobsdal in Stellenbosch, Rietvallei in Robertson, Meerendal in Durbanville, Allesverloren in Swartland and Theuniskraal in Tulbagh. Distillers Corporation, through the Bergkelder, are major wholesaler/producers. Only the best wine from member estates is bottled and sold under the estates' labels, the rest of their wine going into Bergkelder leading brands like the Stellenryck Collection, and the Fleur du Cap and Grunberger ranges.

In the past member estates were not permitted to give tastings at their properties, nor to sell wine direct to calling customers. These rules are now being relaxed, however, and it is possible to visit most Bergkelder estates, although some require you to make an appointment. It is possible to taste and buy the wines of the estates at the Bergkelder's premises in Stellenbosch, as well as their excellent blends.

Useful Information

Owner: Distillers Corporation
Production Director: Gerhard Hofmann
Bergkelder Manager: Pierre Marais
Marketing Director: Nico van der Merwe
Vinotheque & Pre-Releases: Jacques Vandewalle
Estates Liaison: Dave Cobbold
Press Liaison: Marliza Tolken
Address: The Bergkelder, Box 184, Stellenbosch 7599
Telephone: 021.887.2440 *Fax*: 021.887.5769

Tasting/Sales: The Bergkelder Wine Shop; Weekdays 08.00 to 17.00, Saturday 09.00 to 13.00

RUST-EN-VREDE

This jewel of a farm with 30 hectares of vines on the lower slopes of the Helderberg mountain, was bought in 1978 by Jannie Engelbrecht, former Springbok rugby player, and current manager of the team. From the start, it was Jannie's ambition to be the leading red wine producer in South Africa. Indeed he was one of the first wine farmers to specialize in red wines, and certainly the first to age all his reds in casks of Nevers oak.

In 1987, Jannie handed over the responsibility for winemaking to Kevin Arnold, South Africa's champion winemaker. This was an excellent move – Kevin is a resolute believer in quality above all else, and follows this objective with total dedication. The future for South Africa's wine industry, he is convinced, lies in making South African wines, and not copies of other countries' styles. The role of *terroir* is paramount in his philosophy, allied to the sacrifice of quantity on the altar of quality. It should be the ultimate aim of every winemaker, he maintains, to produce wines whose place of origin can be recognized in a blind tasting.

The wines of Rust-en-Vrede are currently sold under five labels. Tinta Barocca, a variety that they are gradually eliminating from the vineyard, is at the lower end of the range – a nice, easy-drinking red with a deep colour, somewhat reminiscent of the southern Rhônes. This is followed, in ascending price order, by Merlot, Shiraz, Cabernet Sauvignon, and finally, the jewel in the crown, Rust-en-Vrede Estate Wine, which is a blend of the last three varieties. The ultimate plan is to concentrate on this wine, and to make a second wine, which will be either labelled under varietal names, or sold as a blend under a separate name, from vats that are not considered good enough for inclusion in the Estate Wine. This mirrors the practice of the best Bordeaux châteaux, and will certainly work to the benefit of the 'Grand Vin' of Rust-en-Vrede.

Tasting Notes

Merlot 1994: Good deep bluey red; perfumed fruit bouquet; ripe fruit and soft tannins in the mouth with good length.

Shiraz 1991: Fine, youthful red, with blue at edges; very up-front Rhôney nose; a big mouthful of ripe fruit, with some nice structure and ripe tannins. A very well-made wine with ageing potential.

Cabernet Sauvignon 1991: Again a good deep colour; open nose with ripe blackcurrant and some oak; nice ripe fruit aromas, with plenty of structure and dominant, but not aggressive tannins. This is certainly a wine for laying down for a year or two.

Estate Wine 1991 (60% Cabernet Sauvignon, 30% Shiraz, 10% Merlot): Deep ruby colour; powerful fruit bouquet, with Shiraz to the fore, and some wood; in the mouth there is plenty of good ripe fruit, excellent structure, ripe tannins and good length. Will make a fine bottle in a few years.

Tinta Barocca 1994: Good, bright mid-red; a pleasing, open nose of ripe fruit; easy-drinking red with some nice structure.

Cabernet Sauvignon 1986: Deep colour, no trace of brown; mature fruit nose; a good long mouthful, with plenty of soft tannins to keep it going for some years yet.

Technical Notes

Area under vines: 30 hectares

Varieties planted: Cabernet Sauvignon 47%, Merlot 15%, Shiraz 30%, Tinta Barocca 8%

Average yield: 49 hectolitres/hectare

Average production: 12,000 cases

Vineyard: Deep Hutton and Clovelly soil on slopes of Helderberg mountain. No irrigation. Canopy management for optimum exposure. Green harvest to Merlot if required.

Cellar: 100% New Nevers oak casks for Estate Wine; 60% for

Cabernet Sauvignon; 50% for Shiraz; 2nd- and 3rd-fill casks for Merlot.

Sales: 60% domestic, of which 35% off estate, 65% restaurants, etc. 40% export, mainly Switzerland, Germany and Denmark, with a little to UK through Lay & Wheeler Ltd.

Useful Information

Owner: Jannie Engelbrecht
Winemaker: Kevin Arnold
Address: Rust-en-Vrede, Box 473, Stellenbosch 7600
Telephone: 021.8813881 *Fax*: 021.8813000

Tasting/Direct Sales: Weekdays 08.30 to 12.30 and 13.30 to 16.30, Saturday 09.00 to 13.00

AVONTUUR

Manie Kloppers, Managing Director of this smart winery-cum-stud-farm on the Somerset West road out of Stellenbosch, came here in 1985 after 45 years farming in Zimbabwe, where his principal crops were cereals and tobacco. At that time he was quite ready to retire, but his son-in-law, Tony Taberer, felt that Manie needed more than fishing to keep him occupied in his sunset years, and proposed a partnership in a Cape wine farm.

Manie came down to the Cape to have a look around, and was horrified to see snow on the mountains. The climate would never suit him, and making wine was not really to his liking – not really a man's life for a hands-on farmer. Somewhat reluctantly he went to have a look at Avontuur, where the previous owner, like many wine farmers at that time, was under pressure from the bank. Without much enthusiasm, Manie put in an offer at a third of the asking price, in the firm belief that it had no chance of being accepted. In a matter of days, a telephone call accepting the offer came through and, Manie being a man of his word, the deal was struck.

Now, ten years on, aided by Belgian winemaker, Jean-Luc Sweerts from the Katanga province of Zaire, the Avontuur estate is doing well. Sixty hectares are under vines, and concentration is on three cultivars, Cabernet Sauvignon, Merlot and Chardonnay. The original Avontuur estate was further extended in 1987 by the purchase of neighbouring Stonefield, and virtually the whole vineyard, previously planted almost entirely with Chenin Blanc and Cinsault, has been replanted with the above noble varieties, as well as some Sauvignon Blanc. Some of the old vines, such as Chenin Blanc and Pinotage, have been kept to satisfy the demands of one-stop shoppers.

Winemaker Sweerts, nothing if not an original, studied at the Elsenburg Agricultural College in Stellenbosch, and after his graduation spent some time in France. On his return to South Africa, he went to work at Uitkyk, where he was one of the first winemakers to ferment white cultivars – Chenin Blanc and Cape Riesling – in 225-litre casks. He joined the Avontuur team in 1990, where he is making some excellent, if sometimes rather eccentric wines, including a Chardonnay made in Cabernet Sauvignon casks, giving birth to a pink Chardonnay called 'Le Blush'; and a sweet red, made from Merlot and the unfermented must of Cabernet Sauvignon, sold as Dolcetto. The latter, I was assured by Mevrouw Kloppers, is quite delicious when drunk with a *braavleis*, or South African barbecue, on a very hot day. I decided to take her word for it.

All in all, this is a well-run property making attractive, highly commercial wines. The export market accounts for about half of total sales. Waitrose in the United Kingdom is a substantial customer, taking as much as it can get of Le Chardon, the estate's Chardonnay, and the Cabernet/Merlot blend, sold in South Africa under the name Avon Rouge. The estate, in common with other wine-producers in South Africa, is now finding itself in the unprecedented and frustrating position of not having enough wine to satisfy its growing export market – a situation made doubly irritating when one bears in mind the 15% subsidy on exports.

Tasting Notes

Cabernet Sauvignon 1990: Nice, deep colour; open fruit bouquet with some blackcurrant; good, ripe black fruit on palate, with some nice tannins and backbone.

Cabernet Sauvignon/Merlot (no vintage on SA label, but 1995 for export): Good, deep colour; nice, open fruit on nose; an easy, quaffable red.

Pinotage 1994: Deep red with blue edges; powerful fruit bouquet; a big mouth-filling wine, with loads of ripe fruit.

Merlot 1992: Good ruby colour; ripe fruit on nose; another easy-drinking red, but with some nice tannins.

Dolcetto (blend of Merlot wine and Cabernet must): Ripe, sweet fruit nose; not oversweet on the palate, very grapey; to be served chilled, but not to me!

Chardonnay 1992: Pale, greeny straw; clean, light nose; nice fruit with some weight; a good Chardonnay.

Above Royalty 1995 (a natural sweet wine, mostly Chenin Blanc): Pale colour; very perfumed, grapey bouquet; very sweet, Muscat grape taste; light and elegant.

Technical Notes

Area under vines: 60 hectares

Varieties planted: Cabernet Sauvignon, Merlot, Chardonnay, Sauvignon Blanc, with some Chenin Blanc, Riesling, Pinot Noir, Pinotage and Cabernet Franc

Sales: 50% domestic/50% export

Useful Information

General Manager: Manie Kloppers
Winemaker: Jean-Luc Sweerts
Address: Avontuur Winery, Box 1128, Somerset West 7129
Telephone: 024.553450 *Fax*: 024.554600

Tasting/Sales: Weekdays 09.30 to 16.30, Saturday 09.00 to 13.00

L'AVENIR

Marc Wiehe, a French-speaking Mauritian, is equally fluent in English, having spent years in London trading on the sugar market.

He came to Stellenbosch in the early '90s, with the intention of buying somewhere to live in peaceful retirement and, in 1992, bought this estate, which was very run down. The vineyard, however, was in good heart, although the previous owners had not made their own wine, preferring to sell their grapes under contract to Nederburg, the Stellenbosch Wine Farmers giant.

A businessman to his boots, Marc Wiehe was not content to sit back and do nothing, but decided to make his own wine, and to build a beautiful guesthouse to accommodate the ever-increasing flow of discerning visitors. This is idyllically situated about five kilometres outside Stellenbosch, with views of the majestic Simonsberg mountain and surrounded by some of the most immaculate vineyards I have seen anywhere. There are eight guest rooms, decorated and furnished in impeccable taste, and all have well-appointed bathrooms, colour television, direct-dial telephones, and comfort is the watchword. There is a swimming-pool for the use of guests and, not surprisingly, the food is excellent.

On the wine front, a smiling fate brought François Naudé to L'Avenir. Formerly a pharmacist from Pretoria, François had recently uprooted his family and brought them to live here in the hope that he could make a living from his life's passion – wine. A jack-of-all-trades, he had started a building business, and first met Marc Wiehe when he was asked to build a fireplace at L'Avenir. The two hit it off, and François became the winemaker. This appointment was something of a gamble since, passionate and knowledgeable though he certainly was, François had never made wine in a professional capacity. Through his love of wine, he had made the acquaintance of many of the Cape's best winemakers – especially Beyers Truter of Kanoncop, a red wine expert renowned in South Africa – and learned a great deal. He even made a barrel of wine before he came to L'Avenir through the good offices of one of his winemaker friends who gave him the grapes. François's story of his 'home winemaking' – crushing the grapes with hands and feet, filtering through a laundry-bag – is nothing short of hilarious, but the proof is definitely in the pudding, and an excellent wine was the result.

François's first vintage at L'Avenir was not an easy one. The purchase was not completed until after the grapes had been harvested, which meant that the crop had to be bought, and special permission obtained to vinify the wine elsewhere, as there was no winemaking equipment on site. Problems did not end here. Once the wine was made and put into cask, it had to come back to L'Avenir for ageing, but there was no proper cask cellar, so the 1992 vintage spent much of its cask life in the garage, with all the difficulties of temperature control that this involved. The end result was a credit to François's hard work and dedication, though he soon realized that the use of 100% new oak was an error. Subsequent vintages of Cabernet Sauvignon L'Avenir are only aged in 50% new wood, and are all the better for it.

The first priority at L'Avenir was the construction of a winery and barrel cellar. Marc Wiehe employed a Mauritian friend, Pierre Lagesse, a partner in the London-based architects, Downey and Partners, who consulted closely with François Naudé through all stages of planning and building. The result is a clean, modern and highly practical vathouse, equipped with the best and latest stainless-steel fermenters in varying sizes, and all fitted with built-in temperature-control systems. This was completed in time for the 1994 harvest.

In the vineyard there was less to do, but some old Cinsaut and Cabernet Sauvignon vines have been taken out, and Sauvignon Blanc planted in their place, and some old Pinotage has been replaced with new, virus-free clones.

In addition to three classic wines, Chardonnay, Cabernet Sauvignon and Pinotage, L'Avenir also makes a red and a white at a very reasonable price for ready drinking. The first Dutch Governor of the Cape, Simon van der Stel was, like Marc Wiehe, born in Mauritius. The new owner of L'Avenir drew on this coincidence when naming his two quaffing wines: the red, a 50/50 blend of Cabernet Sauvignon and Merlot, is called L'Ami Simon; while the white, a Colombard/Rhine Riesling cross, is labelled Vin d'Erstelle.

François Naudé is a true winemaker, dedicated and passionate about his wines, and a man of integrity. He and his wife, Magda, are a kind and generous couple, and gave me much of their time, help and a hefty portion of South African hospitality. As long as responsibility for the wines lies in François's hands, L'Avenir, as the name implies, has a great future.

Tasting Notes

Vin d'Erstelle 1994: Pale golden colour; generous nose of fresh grapey fruit; pleasing, easy wine, essentially dry, but with touch of Rhine Riesling fruitiness.

L'Ami Simon 1994: Bright, deep ruby; good red-fruit bouquet; soft, ripe Merlot fruit, but the Cabernet adds a bit of structure.

Chardonnay 1995 (tasted from a vat, 30% of the blend had been fermented in new oak): Pale straw appearance; nice Chardonnay nose; some good, rich fruit, with oak there in just the right amount, but not in any way overpowering.

Pinotage 1994 (50% new oak, 50% 2nd-fill): Very deep, blacky red; nose still very tight, but some nuttiness; a huge mouthful of concentrated fruit, terrific structure and ripe tannins. A fine example of what Pinotage can do with the right treatment – this will last for years, and will make a wonderful bottle.

Cabernet Sauvignon 1993: Very deep colour; good cassis and some oak on nose; a big wine with lots of fruit, soft tannins that dominate at the moment, but will give a fine wine in a year or so.

Cabernet Sauvignon 1992: Dark red; nose redolent of ripe, black fruit and vanilla; oak very pronounced, but given time and patience, all the elements are there to make a fine wine.

Technical Notes

Area under vines: 45 hectares

Varieties planted: Cabernet Sauvignon, Merlot, Pinotage, Chardonnay, Sauvignon Blanc, Rhine Riesling, Cape Riesling, Colombard, Chenin Blanc

Soil: Glenrosa (gravel on decomposed shale) upper slopes; sand and gravel on clay on lower ground

Average yield: 50 hectolitres/hectare

Useful Information

Owner: Marc Wiehe
Winemaker: François Naudé
Address: L'Avenir, Box 1135, Stellenbosch 7599
Telephone: 021.8895001 *Fax*: 021.8897313

Tasting/Sales: 09.00 to 17.00 Monday to Saturday; light lunches
and meals in guesthouse by appointment

MEERLUST

The Meerlust estate is steeped in history. The first recorded owner
of the land was a powerful and ambitious free burgher called
Henning Huysing, who built the homestead around the beginning
of the eighteenth century. His fortune stemmed from the supply of
meat to the passing ships of the Dutch East India Company on
their way to the Far East. Wilhem Adriaen van der Stel, Governor
of the Cape at that time, saw Huysing and his like as threats to
the power of the Company, and to his own ambitions. When the
free burghers rose up against the despotism of the Company, van
der Stel was quick to have Huysing arrested and sent to Holland
to appear before the Lords XVII. The result of the Council hearing
was the exile of the Governor, and Huysing returned to his lands
completely exonerated.

After Huysing's death in 1713 without a successor, the estate
passed through various hands until it was bought in 1756 by
Johannes Albertus Myburgh, and it has remained in the same
family ever since. When the present owner Hannes Myburgh's
father, Nico, inherited the property in 1950, it had sunk a long
way below its eighteenth-century glory. The vineyards were planted
almost entirely with Chenin Blanc and Sémillon for the production
of sweet fortified wines.

Nicolaas Myburgh set about an extensive programme of restoration to both buildings and vineyards, and well before his death
in 1988, the results were there for all to see and to taste. One of
Nico's first projects was the construction of the large dam that lies
on the right of the drive up to the farm, which allows for irrigation
– for the most part only after the vintage – in exceptionally dry

years. The vineyards were gradually replanted, mainly with red varieties, for this was where Nico saw the future for Meerlust.

In 1975 Meerlust became part of the Bergkelder, an organization controlled by the mighty Distillers Corporation. A number of quality wine-producing estates form the Bergkelder, which provides a range of services for owners, from advice on oenological and viticultural problems to marketing. Apart from the many obvious advantages of allying itself to the Bergkelder, this decision was to have a far-reaching additional benefit for Meerlust. Fifteen years ago, the Bergkelder's head winemaker, Giorgio Dalla Cia, an Italian by birth, joined Nico Myburgh as Meerlust's cellarmaster.

The first red wine produced at Meerlust was the 1975 Cabernet Sauvignon. Nico's flagship red, a Bordeaux blend of Cabernet Sauvignon, Merlot and Cabernet Franc, christened Rubicon, followed in 1980, which was also the first vintage of the Meerlust Pinot Noir. The first Meerlust Merlot apppeared in 1984, and these four wines, together with Meerlust Red (the Rubicon blend in vintages when the quality is not considered quite good enough to bear the 'Grand Vin' label) make up the range of excellent reds produced on this estate. There are now sixteen hectares of Chardonnay, a plantation started five years ago, and 1995 will be the first vintage to go on the market.

The name Meerlust is of German origin, and indicates 'pleasure of the sea'. This is the Stellenbosch estate nearest to the sea, and the cooling breezes from False Bay have a very important effect on the vineyard. They allow for a slower, steadier ripening of the grapes, less loss of aromas in the fruit, and there is lower risk of a crop being spoilt in the event of a sudden excessive rise in temperature, a nightmare occurrence that is not at all uncommon in the hotter vineyards of the Cape.

Giorgio is a warm, open man, and a skilled and dedicated winemaker. He does not believe in irrigation unless it is absolutely necessary, and maintains that quality depends above all on good vineyard management and low yields. Rigorous pruning is essential and, if he ever feels that 'green harvesting' is called for, this is done as soon after the flowering as possible, since taking off bunches a month before harvest leads to loss of aroma.

All Meerlust's red wines are fermented at high temperatures, and all spend time in small casks of French oak. The Pinot Noir is aged for between 15 and 18 months in 2nd-fill casks, the Merlot in

80% new and 20% 2nd-fill for the same period, as are the Cabernet Sauvignon and the Rubicon, though the proportion of new wood can be as high as 100% if the vintage can support it. In 1995 an experimental Pinot Noir is being made, ageing in 100% new casks. Giorgio told me that one of the reasons for the relatively recent improvement in red wine quality in South Africa stems from the high proportion of Afrikaans-speaking winemakers. As they find German a much easier language to learn than French, there has always been a tendency for them to study oenology in Germany, resulting in higher skills in white winemaking, and less understanding of the techniques of red wine vinification, such as high temperature fermentation, etc. This is now changing, and many of the younger winemakers have spent time in Burgundy, Bordeaux, California and Australia, resulting in an ever-increasing production of quality red wines.

Tasting Notes

Pinot Noir 1982: Palish, orangey red; ripe, slightly rustic Burgundian nose; good Pinot Noir fruit, just beginning to dry out.

Pinot Noir 1983: Browner than 1982; a more farmyard nose; still has nice fruit, finishes dry.

Pinot Noir 1985: Shade darker than first two; wild strawberries and truffles on nose; good, ripe Pinot Noir fruit, with good tannins and some structure.

Pinot Noir 1987: Good colour, shading to brown; farmyard and truffly nose; full of fruit and backbone and will last some years – excellent.

Pinot Noir 1989: Deeper red; summer-fruit bouquet; loads of ripe fruit and good, soft tannins; a super Pinot Noir.

Merlot 1984: Deep, intense colour; lovely, rich nose of rich, ripe fruit; lots of ripe, black fruit, and still has amazing structure for an eleven-year-old SA Merlot.

Merlot 1987 (100% new oak): Deeper red than 1984; powerful nose of ripe blackcurrant; mouth-filling wine, with soft tannins and lots of ageing potential.

Merlot 1988: Fine, deep colour; pleasing blackberry nose; more ready than 1987, with less body and fruit.

Merlot 1989 (100% new oak): Dense, blacky red; young Pomerol nose; big mouthful of fruit, with nice, non-aggressive tannins, very long aftertaste – will make a super bottle.

Merlot 1991: Very dark red with blue at edges; good Merlot nose evolving; fine, rich fruit with lots of backbone.

Rubicon 1980: Quite deep red still; toasty, dried fruit nose; plenty of nice fruit there, but tannins almost gone – to drink now.

Rubicon 1981: Shade darker than 1980; nose a bit muted, but some nice fruit there; ripe fruit on palate, with some mileage yet.

Rubicon 1983: Paler colour than 1980 or 1981; slightly cooked nose; still has some fruit, but more evolved than first two.

Rubicon 1986 (first year in small casks): Very deep red; good nose – cassis and some wood; big mouthful of fruit, with fine tannins and lots of backbone – a keeper.

Rubicon 1987: Deeper colour than 1986; nose good, but more closed-up than 1986; fat, round and ripe in mouth, with soft tannins and big structure.

Rubicon 1988: Good red, but less dense than 1986 and 1987; generous, rather earthy nose; less weight, but has nice fruit – to drink in 1–2 years.

Rubicon 1989: Deep colour; nose beginning to open up with ripe berry fruit; good fruit in mouth, with tannins dominating at the moment.

Rubicon 1991: Bluey red; nose still closed; a huge mouthful of fruit with excellent tannins and length – a real winner to drink in 10 years.

Red 1985: Good, bright medium red; good fruit bouquet; nice, ripe fruit with soft tannins – good now.

Red 1990: Deeper colour; open nose of ripe fruit; good fruit and some structure in mouth, but less concentrated than 1985 Red.

Cabernet Sauvignon 1980: Deep red, browning at edges; good, slightly earthy nose; some nice fruit with good tannins, but starting to dry out.

Cabernet Sauvignon 1981: Colour deeper; nose slightly raisiny; same dried fruit on palate, but still has some tannins – good to drink now.

Cabernet Sauvignon 1984 (first year new small casks): Very dark red; nose shy, but truffly; big, concentrated fruit with good structure and length – to keep for some years.

Cabernet Sauvignon 1986: Very deep red; open cassis nose; well structured wine with ripe fruit – will keep.

Cabernet Sauvignon 1991: Fine deep red; big, ripe black-fruit nose; huge, mouth-filling wine with bags of soft tannins and keeping qualities – stunner.

From the cask: The Chardonnay 1995 was tasted from three different new casks, all from different coopers; all had been fermented and aged in the casks, and all tasted completely different. This will be the first release of Meerlust's Chardonnay, and I look forward with interest to the final result.

BLAAUWKLIPPEN

Situated on the left of the Stellenbosch-to-Somerset West road, Blaauwklippen currently has some 100 hectares of vines, planted with a wide variety of cultivars. In a wine country where the consumer is always welcomed, owner Graham Boonzaier, who bought the estate in 1971, offers many attractions to visitors in addition to the excellent range of wines made by cellar-master Jacques Kruger. As well as tasting the wines, you can also buy older vintages from the Vinotheque and bin-ends from the 'bargain barrels'. Good and reasonably priced lunches are also available, and there is a collection of vintage cars and horse-drawn carriages, as well as some fine old furniture. From October to April there are carriage tours of the vineyard, and there is a good range of home-made preserves and cooked meats for sale.

Jacques Kruger is a large, laid-back and very affable man, and his character is reflected in his wines. The highlight of the range of some twenty wines that I tasted was Jacques's Zinfandel. One of only a very small handful of Cape winemakers to favour this esssentially Californian grape, Jacques's Zinfandel consistently wins plaudits and awards in South African competitions: the 1990 was given a Double Gold Veritas rating, but he also gained a further accolade by winning a blind tasting competition in America against the top Californian producers. This is a variety which does well in South Africa, and we may see more South African Zinfandels as the interest in Cape wines of quality expands.

Blaauwklippen, like many other estates and co-operatives, has perhaps too many varieties and too many different wine styles for a winemaker of Kruger's calibre – who could achieve more if he were to concentrate on the wines that he makes best from the cultivars that are best suited to the soil and micro-climate of his vineyards. The explanation for the wide range of wines offered is two-fold.

It is important to remember that, until only very recently, South African wine-producers had to rely almost entirely on the domestic market for sales, and that a large proportion of purchases were made direct from the farms. It was therefore in the interests of every estate and co-operative to have a comprehensive range of wines, so that callers could get all their wines in one stop, rather than buying reds from one farm, whites from another and so on. Second, Graham Boonzaier believes strongly in looking after the domestic market first and, although he recognizes the importance of the export market, he feels that regular customers for all his wines should be assured of continuity of supply.

Tasting Notes

Chardonnay 1993 (40% wood-fermented and aged for 6 months, of which 50% new, 50% 2nd-fill): Bright, pale colour; nice fruit and some wood on nose; well-made Chardonnay with good fruit, some weight and length, wood there, but not too much.

Chardonnay 1995 (4 and a half months oak, 2nd- and 3rd-fill casks only, shaved wood): Medium gold colour; good fruit and some vanilla on nose; nice rounded fruit in mouth, wood just right, some butteriness.

Chardonnay/Sémillon 1995 (no wood): Bright, pale straw; nice nose with good ripe fruit; easy-drinking, with good fruit/acid balance.

Sauvignon Blanc 1995 (Gold Veritas Award, Wine of the Month Club winner): Pale straw; up-front gooseberry fruit bouquet; fresh, crisp fruit, with right acid balance.

Sociable Dry White (named after carriage, Rhine Riesling, Colombard, Sémillon): Bright, pale colour; clean, grapey nose; crisp and clean, with lots of nice fruit, dry but not bone-dry.

White Landau 1995 (Sauvignon Blanc, Rhine Riesling, Muscat Ottonel): Bright, pale straw; strong Muscat nose; clean, grapey fruit, easy, crisp and dry.

Rhine Riesling 1995: Very pale; clean, grapey fruit bouquet; pleasant, easy-drinking wine, off-dry, with good fruit.

Muscat Ottonel 1995: Pale straw; strong Muscat nose; quite dry, with lots of raisiny fruit and length.

Muscat Ottonel 1990: Treacly gold; evolved Muscat nose; rich, spicy, cooked fruit palate, quite long.

Special Late Vintage 1995 (Chenin Blanc, with a touch of Muscat, lower sugar than usual – 32 g/l, as opposed to high 40s): Pale colour; nose quite shy; pleasing fruit taste, medium-sweet.

Special Late Vintage 1989: Quite deep gold; honey and beeswax on nose; rich fruit with some complexity, and right degree of acidity.

Sociable Dry Red (no oak, no vintage; blend of Pinot Noir and Pinotage, with a little Zinfandel): Clear, medium red; open Pinotage fruit nose; ripe, easy fruit on palate – good value.

Red Landau (no vintage, but mostly 1990, blend of Merlot, Cabernet Sauvignon and 3% Zinfandel, all wood-aged): Deep colour; good, open fruit on nose; blackcurrant fruit in mouth, with soft tannins and some structure.

Pinot Noir 1989 (chosen for SAA 1st Class, entered for South Africa/Australia challenge): Quite deep red for Pinot Noir; nose quite Burgundian; ripe fruit in mouth, with some wood, ripe tannin and good structure.

Pinot Noir Reserve 1987 (18 months in small oak): More bricky red; cabbagey, farmyard nose; still has lots of good fruit.

Shiraz 1990 (Veritas Double Gold): Clear, mid-red; very Shiraz nose; a big, mouth-filling wine, with lots of ripe fruit, good tannin and length.

Shiraz 1993: Deep red; powerful Shiraz nose; big, rounded fruit in mouth, with good backbone.

Zinfandel 1989 (Veritas Double Gold – won competition against best of Californian Zins): Bright, mid-red; lots of ripe fruit on nose; nice, chewy mouthful of summer fruit – raspberries, with a lot of body, soft tannin and good length.

Zinfandel 1992: Really deep red; ripe fruit nose; more fruit, but less tannin and structure, perhaps due to less new wood?

Cabernet Sauvignon 1990: Deep red; some cassis on nose; fine fruit, good tannins and some backbone.

Cabernet Sauvignon 1991: Shade darker than 1990; open, black-fruit bouquet; good depth and weight with nice tannins.

Cabernet Sauvignon 1992 (just bottled): Dark, bluey red; nose a bit closed-up, intense berry fruit coming through; good concentration, big, with ripe fruit and soft tannins. Will be good bottle.

Cabernet Sauvignon Reserve 1989 (from best Cabernet plot, 36 months in new Seguin-Moreau casks): Deep, dense red; ripe, toasty fruit bouquet; big mouthful, with lots of fruit and structure – a wine for laying-down.

Cabernet Sauvignon Reserve 1990: Shade lighter than the '89; good cassis fruit nose; more accessible than '89, but good balance – will keep well.

Cabernet Sauvignon Reserve 1992 (same treatment as other two Reserves, but includes some Cabernet Franc): Very deep colour; open, black-fruit nose; good fruit, tannins and structure, but with a touch more fleshiness – from Cabernet Franc?

'*Vintage Port*' *1991* (90% Zinfandel, 10% Pontac, matured for 40 months in 500-litre casks): Good colour, with some tawny hints; rich, plummy nose; figgy and raisiny, quite spirity.

Technical Notes

Area under vines: 100 hectares

Cultivars planted
WHITE: Chardonnay, Sauvignon Blanc, Sémillon, Colombard, Rhine Riesling, Chenin Blanc, Muscat Ottonel
RED: Cabernet Sauvignon, Merlot, Shiraz, Zinfandel, Cabernet Franc, Pinot Noir, Pinotage, Pontac

Useful Information

Owner: Graham Boonzaier
Winemaker: Jacques Kruger
Address: Blaauwklippen Agricultural Estates, Box 54, Stellenbosch 7599
Telephone: 021.8800133 *Fax*: 021.8800136

Tasting/Sales: Weekdays 09.00 to 17.00, Saturdays 09.00 to 13.00; Coachman's lunches from 12.00 to 14.00

NEIL ELLIS WINES

Neil Ellis is a highly intelligent, articulate and skilled winemaker, and his limited range of immaculately presented wines is clear proof of his dedication to quality above all things.

After qualifying in oenology in 1973, Neil began his career in the cellars of KWV. He was cellar-master at Groot Constantia and then at Zevenwacht until 1989. During these years, he became more and more convinced that the way ahead lay in sourcing the best grapes from the best vineyards for each varietal wine, buying them in and vinifying and ageing them at a central point. His first foray into the role of '*négociant*/winemaker', a field in which he now unquestionably leads, was at Zevenwacht, undertaken with the blessing of the then Chairman, Gilbert Colyn.

In 1989 Neil entered into an agreement with Hans Froehling of

Louisvale in the Devon Valley, whereby he made the wine for Louis-vale, in return for which he could use their facilities for making wine from his carefully selected bought-in grapes. It soon became clear that the winery at Louisvale was not big enough for his growing business, and he is now in partnership with Hans-Peter Schröder, owner of the Oude Nektar estate in the beautiful valley of the Jonkershoek mountain on the outskirts of Stellenbosch.

Oude Nektar is now the centre of Neil's operations. There are now some twenty hectares planted to new clones of Cabernet Sauvignon, Merlot, Cabernet Franc, Shiraz, Chardonnay and Sauvignon Blanc, on the cool mountain slopes of the Jonkershoek, of which fourteen hectares are in production and six are newly planted. Plans for future plantings will bring the total area under vines to 35 hectares, but Neil continues to buy in grapes from his regular sources: Pinot Noir, Chardonnay and Sauvignon Blanc from Elgin, the Cape's coolest viticultural region; Sauvignon Blanc from Groenekloof near Darling on the West Coast; and Cabernet Sauvignon, Merlot, Chardonnay, Gewürztraminer and Sauvignon Blanc from carefully selected vineyards in the Stellenbosch area. The relaxation of rules applying to the buying-in of grapes by estates in 1995 has resulted in a huge increase in demand for premium fruit, but Neil's foresight and track-record with his regular sources ensure continuity of supply.

Total production of Neil Ellis Wines is currently around 25,000 cases, which he would like to build up to 35,000 over the next few years. A quarter of sales is accounted for by three very demanding customers – Sainsbury's and Marks and Spencer in the UK, and the Woolworth's chain in South Africa, owned by Marks and Spencer. A total of 35% is sold on the export market.

Tasting Notes

Groenekloof Sauvignon Blanc 1995: Pale, greeny gold; good wafts of gooseberry and elder bark on nose; clean and crisp, with fruit/acid balance right, good length.

Elgin Sauvignon Blanc 1995: Same greeny gold; Sauvignon nose good, but more restrained than Groenekloof; on palate has a touch more weight and fruit, stony acidity and long aftertaste.

Stellenbosch Chardonnay 1995 (fermented and aged in 2nd- and

3rd-fill casks for 6 months): Pale, greenish colour; nose quite closed; initial impression of oak in the mouth, but elegant fruit follows, all in harmony – a Chardonnay of some finesse.

Elgin Chardonnay 1994 (fermented in cask, 30% new, and aged 8–10 months): Same pale colour; pleasing fruit bouquet with some vanilla; wood and fruit together, a shade more fatness than the Stellenbosch wine, possibly due to extra year.

Stellenbosch Pinotage 1994 (aged in cask 14 months, 50% new, 50% 3rd-fill): Bright, medium-deep red; rich, black-cherry nose; lovely ripe fruit attack, but good tannins and structure.

Stellenbosch Cabernet Sauvignon 1992 (aged in cask 24 months, 60% new, 40% 2nd- and 3rd-fill): Deep red with bluey edges; powerful nose of blackcurrant and cigar-box; a big, tannic mouthful of wine, but loads of fruit and the tannins are ripe – will make a great bottle.

Stellenbosch Cabernet Sauvignon/Merlot 1993 (aged in cask 18 months, 25% new, rest 2nd-, 3rd- and 4th-fill): Medium-deep red; rich blackberry nose; loads of good berry fruit, ripe tannins and some backbone – a good Bordeaux blend with ageing potential.

Technical Notes

Area under vines: 20 hectares (14 in production) plus bought-in grapes

Cultivars planted
WHITE: Chardonnay, Sauvignon Blanc
RED: Cabernet Sauvignon, Merlot, Cabernet Franc, Shiraz

Useful Information

Viticultural Consultants: Johann Pienaar, KWV; Eben Archer, USA
Winemaker: Neil Ellis
Address: Neil Ellis Wines (Pty) Ltd., Box 917, Stellenbosch 7600
Telephone: 021.8870649 *Fax*: 021.8870647

Tasting/Sales: Monday to Friday 09.00 to 13.00, 14.00 to 16.30; summer also Saturday 09.00 to 12.30

THELEMA MOUNTAIN VINEYARD

Gyles Webb is one of the golden boys of South African winemaking. Originally an accountant, wine was always a passion for him, and now his passion is his work. Thelema Farm was bought by his wife's family trust in 1983. At that time the beautiful 157-hectare property at the top of the Helshoogte pass had no vines, and was given over entirely to the growing of plums, apples and pears, and the farm, workers' cottages, house and buildings were in a sorry state.

Gyles's love of wine, and particularly his discovery of white Burgundy, led him to quit accountancy and enrol at Stellenbosch University, where he got his B.Sc. Agriculture degree, majoring in Viticulture and Oenology, in 1979. This was followed by a period in the experimental wine department of Stellenbosch Farmers' Winery, a vintage at the Heitz cellars in the Napa Valley, and a couple of years as assistant winemaker at Neethlingshof. By now, the McLean Family Trust had bought Thelema, and Gyles left Neethlingshof in 1985 to throw himself full-time into putting Thelema on the wine map.

Although wine had not been made here since the early part of this century, analyses of the decomposed granite soils, together with the high altitude – between 370 and 640 metres above sea-level – on the principally south-facing slopes of the Simonsberg mountain gave Gyles all the encouragement he needed to plant the noble varieties. Orchards have been grubbed up to make way for vines, and there are currently 38 hectares planted mainly with Cabernet Sauvignon, Merlot, Chardonnay, Sauvignon Blanc and Rhine Riesling.

New farm-workers' cottages have been built and the old ones restored, and the Victorian Cape farmhouse has also been returned to its former glory. In 1987 work began on the new winery, which was completed in time to receive the first Chardonnay grapes in February 1988, and is well equipped to cope with up to 350 tons of grapes.

Of the Thelema white wines, Sauvignon Blanc and Rhine Riesling are made without recourse to oak, but the Chardonnay is all fermented in an equal mixture of new, 2nd- and 3rd-fill 225-litre French oak casks, in which it spends about eight months on the lees. All the reds, Cabernet Sauvignon, Merlot and the Cabernet

Sauvignon/Merlot blend are aged for about eighteen months in a mixture of French oak casks from different forests. The Cabernet Sauvignon/Merlot blend, the Cabernet Sauvignon and Cabernet Sauvignon Reserve all merit a high proportion of new wood each year, but the Merlot is aged in 2nd-fill casks only.

The management team at Thelema is very small, and consists of Gyles, who is in charge of vineyards and winemaking, his wife, Barbara, who attends to the marketing, and her mother who runs the reception and tasting area. The style of Thelema's wines is a cross between New and Old World, and combines many of the best elements of both, and they are a good illustration of the way that South Africa should be going.

Tasting Notes

Thelema Sauvignon Blanc 1995: Pale, greeny gold; elegant, up-front Sauvignon Blanc nose of elder-bark and gooseberry; lovely, long fruit, persistent, clean and crisp. Among the best South African Sauvignon Blancs tasted.

Thelema Chardonnay 1994: Pale straw; oak quite evident on nose; good fruit on palate, with some weight and butteriness, and oak in nice balance with fruit.

Thelema Riesling 1995: Light golden colour; attractive Riesling fruit bouquet; elegant wine with lots of minerally fruitiness, bone dry.

Thelema Merlot 1992: Good, deep red; open, black-fruit nose; approachable mouthful of ripe berry fruit, with some ripe tannins and a bit of structure.

Thelema Cabernet Sauvignon/Merlot 1992: Deep ruby; open, ripe fruit nose; initial sweet fruit attack with a touch of mint, ripe tannins and good length.

Thelema Cabernet Sauvignon 1992: Deep colour, blue at edges; cassis bouquet with a touch of violets; good balance of ripe, minty fruit, with soft tannins and good backbone. (This won Gyles SAA's top Diners Club Winemaker of the Year award in 1994.)

Thelema Cabernet Sauvignon 1991: Fine, deep colour; strong blackcurrant on nose; smooth, ripe mouthful with no mintiness, some good tannins and staying power.

Thelema Cabernet Sauvignon Reserve 1991: Colour still almost black; powerful, ripe bouquet with vanilla hints; huge, fruity, concentrated mouthful of wine, with lots of good tannins and enough backbone to keep it going for several years. (Awarded a rare 5 stars by John Platter.)

Technical Notes

Area under vines: 38 hectares

Cultivars planted
WHITE: Chardonnay, Sauvignon Blanc, Rhine Riesling, Muscat de Frontignan
RED: Cabernet Sauvignon, Merlot

Useful Information

Owner: Thelema Mountain Vineyards (Pty) Ltd.
Winemaker: Gyles Webb
Address: Thelema, Box 2234, Stellenbosch 7601
Telephone: 021.8851924 *Fax*: 021.8851800

Tasting/Sales: Monday to Friday 09.00 to 17.00, Saturday 09.00 to 13.00

MURATIE

There is a timeless magic about this lovely old farm, and it is easy to understand how the former owner, German artist Georg Paul Canitz, was captivated when he came across Muratie by accident on his way to a party nearby in 1925. He came, he saw and he was conquered and, having bought the farm, lived and made wine there until his death in 1959. Canitz was clearly a merry fellow, and his parties were legendary. Although he evidently had a soft spot for the ladies – as is clear from paintings of his favourite models that still adorn the walls, and from the carefully preserved graffiti in his cosy 'party room' – he was lucky to number among his friends an important figure in the history of South African winemaking, Professor Perold of Stellenbosch University.

Perold was a great innovator, and spent a great deal of time helping his friend to establish the vineyards of Muratie, encouraging him to plant mainly red varieties, for which he considered Muratie's soil and situation well-suited. Muratie was almost certainly the first estate to plant Pinot Noir in South Africa, and the birthplace of South Africa's own red variety, the Pinotage, a cross between Pinot Noir and Cinsaut bred by Professor Perold. On the death of Canitz in 1959, his daughter Annemarie took on the responsibility for winemaking at Muratie. This was a bold decision for the time, as female wine farmers were unheard of, or at least viewed with grave suspicion. With the help of winemaker Ben Prins, Annemarie Canitz managed the estate as best she could for nearly 30 years, until it was bought in 1988 by Ronnie Melck, former Managing Director of Stellenbosch Farmers' Winery.

The purchase of Muratie was the realization of a dream for Ronnie Melck, who sadly died in September 1995. A giant of a man with a legendary palate, Melck has left behind a legacy of stories among his innumerable friends throughout the world of wine. He was the seventh generation of a family descended from Martin Melck, a soldier in the service of the Dutch East India Company who came to South Africa in the middle of the eighteenth century. Martin became a free burgher in Stellenbosch, and one of the largest wine farmers in the Cape, owning many fine farms, including Delheim, Uitkyk and Muratie. One can imagine the sense of fulfilment Melck must have felt to have Muratie back in the family during his last years, and the immense satisfaction he must have derived when the 1995 Cabernet from Muratie won the coveted General Smuts trophy for the best of all wines at the SA Young Wine Show.

Muratie was in a dilapidated state when Ronnie Melck bought it, and the first priority was to get the vineyards into shape. The result of this work shows up very clearly in the wines, which are all of very high quality. This can come as a surprise to first-time visitors to Muratie, especially if, before tasting the wine, they glance into the cellars, which are extremely basic and old-fashioned. Open cement fermenting tanks are used, some of them in the open air, and wooden paddles are used to break the cap every two hours during fermentation. The walls are moss-stained, but there are plenty of small oak casks testifying to the serious nature of the winemaking here.

Hennie van der Westhuizen, the estate manager, is fiercely proud of Muratie, and obviously worshipped his late employer. 'He was a big man,' he said several times during my visit, and I felt that tears were not far away. Although there may have to be some extensions to the existing buildings and other minor concessions to twentieth-century winemaking, Hennie explained that it was always Ronnie Melck's wish to keep the appearance and character of Muratie as unchanged as possible, and this they will certainly try to honour.

The range of wines produced at Muratie is simple and limited, as one would expect. All are red, apart from a fortified white wine from the Hanepoot grape called Amber, first made in the year that *Forever Amber* was published, and named by Georg Canitz after the heroine. Shiraz, Pinot Noir, Cabernet Sauvignon, Merlot and a red blend of 50% Cabernet, 30% Shiraz and 20% Merlot are made, as well as an excellent and very popular 'port'. The blended wine is sold as Ansela van de Caab, a name which, like so many things at Muratie, springs from an old story. When the settlement at the Cape was only 47 years old, this property, then known as Die Driesprong, was granted by Governor Wilhem Adriaen van der Stel to one Lourens Campher, who married a freed slave, by name Ansela van de Caab.

Tasting Notes

Muratie Shiraz 1993: Rich, deep colour; strong Shiraz nose, with typical peppery, herby notes; good, powerful fruit, with some porty character, will evolve well with a year or more in bottle.

Muratie Pinot Noir 1994: Very deep colour for Pinot Noir; nose still quite closed, but some nice fruit starting to come through; a lot of wine for a young Pinot Noir, but has ripe tannins, and some raspberry fruit evolving – will be good in a year or two.

Muratie Cabernet Sauvignon 1994: Fine deep red; blackcurrant and chocolate nose; lots of smooth, ripe fruit with soft tannins – already very approachable, but will keep.

Muratie Merlot 1993: Nice garnet colour; ripe fruit on nose; a bit thin in the mouth, with rather harsh tannins – a bit disappointing, possibly due to youth of vines.

Muratie Ansela van de Caab 1993 (blend of 50% Cabernet Sauvignon, 30% Shiraz and 20% Merlot, 9 months in 2nd- and 3rd-fill casks): Very deep red; powerful nose, with Shiraz dominating; big, ripe and mouth-filling, with some backbone.

Muratie 'Port': Deep, blackberry colour; rich Christmas pudding nose; luscious, rich fruit and raisin taste.

Muratie Amber (fortified to 17% alcohol by volume, made from Hanepoot grapes): It has to be said that the colour is amber; rich, hothouse grape bouquet; lovely, grapey fruit with a lot of length.

Technical Notes

Area under vines: 42.5 hectares

Cultivars planted
WHITE: Clairette Blanche, Muscat d'Alexandrie, Chenin Blanc, Riesling
RED: Cabernet Sauvignon, Merlot, Pinot Noir, Shiraz, Cinsaut, Tinta Roriz, Tinta Barocca, Tinta Francisca, Sousao

Useful Information

Owners: Melck Family
Estate Manager: Hennie van der Westhuizen
Address: Muratie Estate, Box 133, Koelenhof 7605
Telephone: 021.8822330 *Fax*: 021.8822790

Tasting/Sales: Monday to Thursday 09.30 to 17.00, Friday 09.30 to 16.00, Saturday 09.00 to 15.00

LOUISVALE

Hans Froehling, former head of the servicing division of Nixdorf computers, decided to opt out of high-pressure city life, and bought the Louisvale farm in the Devon valley at the end of 1988. He and his partner, Leon Stemmet, took possession just before the vintage of 1989, at which time there were just eleven hectares of Chardonnay planted. They could easily have sold their crop at a good price,but decided to take up the challenge of making their own wine.

Providence gave them a hand in the form of winemaker Neil Ellis, who had already embarked on his policy of sourcing the best grapes and making wine at a central point – which at that time was at Zevenwacht, where the 1989 Louisvale Chardonnay was vinified. As Ellis was looking for a winery where he could go it alone, and Hans and Leon were looking for a winemaker, an agreement was soon reached whereby Neil Ellis became the Louisvale winemaker, in return for the use of the Louisvale facilities for making his range of wines from bought-in grapes. This arrangement worked well for both sides, until it became apparent that the Neil Ellis operation had outgrown the Louisvale winery in terms of sheer volume. They parted on amicable terms, Neil going into partnership with Hans-Peter Schröder, owner of the Oude Nektar estate in the Jonkershoek valley, and Hans and Leon taking on Marinus Bredell as their new winemaker.

Although the reputation of Louisvale has been built upon its flagship wine – the Chardonnay, fermented and aged in small oak casks, between 20% and 40% of which are new each vintage – the range of wines made here has been considerably extended in the last two or three years. There are two more Chardonnays, sold under the name of Chavant, one of which is made without the use of oak, and the other only lightly wooded, and they also produce a Sauvignon Blanc/Chardonnay blend. Since 1994 they have been producing three red wines, a Cabernet Sauvignon, a Cabernet Sauvignon/Merlot blend and a straight Merlot, all of which have some cask-ageing (new American and 3rd- and 4th-fill French casks are used). The Chardonnays are made from Louisvale's own vineyards, and all the other grapes are bought in.

The walls of the tasting-room and the office are decorated with many awards, both for the wines of Louisvale, and for the champion Great Danes and miniature Schnauzers that are bred by Hans and Leon.

Tasting Notes

Chavant Chardonnay, Unwooded 1995: Pale straw; nice, ripe Chardonnay fruit nose; full, ripe fruit taste, some weight and good length.

Chavant Chardonnay, Lightly Wooded 1995: Pale gold; good, clean fruit bouquet with touch of vanilla; oak and fruit nicely balanced, good weight.

Sauvignon Blanc/Chardonnay 1995: Pale golden colour; asparagus nose from the Sauvignon; the Sauvignon character also leads on the palate, with some gooseberry flavour, a bit of weight from the Chardonnay, and nice length.

Chardonnay 1994: Bright, golden colour; fruit bouquet good, with some new wood; some good buttery Chardonnay fruit, and quite oaky, needs another year or so in bottle.

Chardonnay 1993: Shade darker than the 1994; lovely, fat Chardonnay fruit now coming into harmony with the oak, both on the nose and in the mouth – a really good Chardonnay with good weight and long aftertaste.

Cabernet Sauvignon/Merlot 1994: Brilliant red; open and slightly gamey nose; ripe fruit with soft tannins and some structure, to drink in 2–3 years.

Merlot 1994: Very deep red; quite closed on nose, but good fruit coming through; a big, mouth-filling wine, with ripe tannins and enough backbone to keep it going for 5–10 years.

Technical Notes

Area under vines: 14.5 hectares, Chardonnay only (other grapes bought in)

Wines produced
WHITE: Chardonnay, Chavant Chardonnay (lightly oaked), Chavant Chardonnay (non-oaked), Sauvignon Blanc/ Chardonnay
RED: Cabernet Sauvignon, Cabernet Sauvignon/Merlot, Merlot

Average production: 10,000 cases Chardonnay (own grapes); 10,000 cases other wines (bought-in grapes)
Sales: two-thirds domestic sales, one-third export – UK, Germany, Holland, Belgium, Japan

Useful Information

Owners: Hans Froehling and Leon Stemmet
Winemaker: Marinus Bredell
Address: Louisvale, Box 542, Stellenbosch 7599
Telephone: 021.8822422 *Fax*: 021.8822633

Tasting/Sales: Weekdays 10.00 to 17.00, Saturday 10.00 to 13.00

CLOS MALVERNE

The previous owner of this farm in the Devon Valley, an Englishman called Colonel Billingham, originally named it Malvern Heights because the surrounding hills reminded him of the countryside around Malvern, his home in England.

Seymour Pritchard, formerly an accountant, bought the farm in 1969, and moved in in 1970. At that time there were seven hectares planted with vines for table grapes. In 1976 he replanted the vineyard with Cabernet Sauvignon, as the soil, exposure and microclimate of Clos Malverne are well-suited to this variety. The grapes were sold to Stellenbosch Farmers' Winery until 1986, at which time Seymour decided to make his own wine. The vinification of his first vintage was fairly rudimentary, and was limited to only 800 bottles, but results were sufficiently encouraging for him to continue. In 1987 he bought new casks, and in 1988 he was joined by winemaker Jeremy Walker, whom he had met on a skiing holiday. There are now nine hectares under vines, a further nine are leased, and he has bought another twenty hectares in the Devon Valley, which will come into production in 1997.

In the nine years since 1986, production has risen from 800 bottles to 27,000 cases. The range, detailed below, notably includes a Pinotage Reserve; an Auret, the estate's flagship blend of Cabernet Sauvignon, Pinotage and Merlot; a Devonet, a 50/50 blend of Cabernet Sauvignon and Merlot and currently unwooded; and a Blanc de Noir made from Cabernet Sauvignon and an unwooded Sauvignon Blanc. The quality of Clos Malverne's wines is consistently high, and future plans will increase production of Pinotage.

Tasting Notes

Sauvignon Blanc 1995: Very pale straw colour; lots of up-front fruit on the nose; clean and fine, with all the right gooseberry, grassy Sauvignon flavours, good length.

Blanc de Noir 1995: Pale onion-skin colour; attractive summer fruit bouquet; light, bone dry and easy-drinking.

Devonet 1995: Deep red; big black-fruit nose; loads of ripe fruit in the mouth, with some good soft tannins.

Pinotage 1994: Brilliant, deep red; powerful Pinotage fruit nose; quite tough and tannic, but lots of good fruit, and will repay keeping.

Pinotage Reserve 1994 (12 months in small oak, pressed juice added, 3 days skin-contact): Very deep colour; rich, ripe fruit bouquet; a huge mouthful of chewy fruit, with great structure and the right kind of tannins – a smasher!

Cabernet Sauvignon 1993 (12 months in small oak, pressed juice added, 3 days skin-contact): Very deep, almost black colour; powerful blackcurrant nose; loads of blackcurrant fruit in the mouth, ripe tannins and good backbone, a super Cabernet that will reward patience.

Technical Notes

Area under vines: 9 hectares at Clos Malverne; 9 hectares leased nearby; 20 hectares purchased, in production 1997; plus grapes bought in

Cultivars planted
WHITE: Sauvignon Blanc
RED: Cabernet Sauvignon, Pinotage, Merlot, Shiraz

Wines produced
WHITE: Blanc de Noir (made from Cabernet Sauvignon and Sauvignon Blanc)
RED: Auret (blend of Cabernet Sauvignon, Pinotage and Merlot), Cabernet Sauvignon, Pinotage, Pinotage Reserve, Devonet (unwooded 50/50 blend of Cabernet Sauvignon and Merlot)

Average production: 27,000 cases

Sales: 60% domestic, 40% export

Useful Information

Owner: Seymour Pritchard
Winemaker: Michael Bucholz
Address: Clos Malverne, Box 187, Stellenbosch 7600
Telephone: 021.8822022 *Fax*: 021.8822518

Tasting/Sales: Weekdays 08.30 to 17.30, Saturday 09.00 to 13.00

LIEVLAND

Not many people know this, but Lievland was, before the Second World War, a small state in eastern Europe which has now disappeared – quite literally according to *Encyclopaedia Britannica* – without trace. In the early 1930s a Lievland aristocrat by the name of Baron von Stiernhielm purchased the farm that was then known as Beyers Kloof. The Baron died in 1936, leaving a widow with four children to bring up. The Baroness, who was a Dutch lady, must have been a tough egg, for she decided to run the farm, which she promptly renamed Lievland, and to make the wine there. She studied winemaking under the redoubtable Professor Perold, and in only four years was making her first vintage. Initially she was aided by a winemaker, but soon dispensed with his services and assumed total responsibility for running the farm and winemaking.

When Lievland was purchased by the Benadé family in 1973, it was planted mainly with Chenin Blanc, Cape Riesling and Cinsaut, all high tonnage yielders and favoured by many wine farmers at that time. The Benadés' first step was to launch into a massive replanting programme, replacing many of the old vines with Cabernet Sauvignon, Cabernet Franc, Merlot, Ruby Cabernet and Shiraz for red wine production; and Bukettraube, Weisser Riesling, and more recently a little Sauvignon Blanc and Chardonnay for white. A new underground cellar for maturation and storage was completed in 1987.

Paul Benadé is a tough and able businessman, and suffers neither fools nor bureaucrats gladly. He and his gifted winemaker, Abé

Beukes, make a formidable team, and the countless medals and prizes won by Lievland's wines bear witness to the drive of the former and the ability of the latter. Abé studied at Stellenbosch University, where he gained a B.Sc. in Viticulture, Oenology and Microbiology. As a student he worked with Jan Boland Coetzee at Kanonkop, did two years' viticultural research at Nietvoorbij, and worked as winemaker at both Eikendal and Simonsig. His special passion is the making of Noble Late Harvest wines, and the 1993 which I tasted was a superb example. Both Paul and Abé are devoted to wine, winemaking and to the continuing improvement of the already fine quality of Lievland's wines. They travel the world promoting the image of Lievland, and are constantly studying and tasting the wines of the world.

D. V. B., Lievland's top-of-the-range red, is a blend of roughly equal parts Cabernet Sauvignon, Merlot and Cabernet Franc, and is aged in between 50% and 100% new Nevers casks; the Cabernet Sauvignon ages in between 30% and 40% new Nevers oak; the Shiraz in 30% to 40% new Alliers; and Lievlander, the estate's easy-drinking red blend of Cinsaut, Ruby Cabernet, Cabernet Franc and Merlot, spends between two and six months in a mixture of shaved and unshaved used barrels. This varying use of oak comes as a result of long study and much experimentation, and is typical of the attention to detail exercised at Lievland.

Tasting Notes

Shiraz 1992 (some American oak used, now abandoned): Brilliant, deep colour; slightly farmyard nose; lots of fresh, ripe fruit with spices, finishes quite dry.

Shiraz 1992 (100% Nevers oak): Colour a touch deeper than the first wine; good fruit nose, less of the farmyard; good, concentrated fruit, ripe tannins, with the same dry finish.

D. V. B. 1992 (33% each Cabernet Sauvignon, Franc and Merlot): Very deep, dense red; excellent ripe fruit nose; a mouthful of ripe berry fruit, good tannins and structure with long aftertaste. A winner.

Cabernet Sauvignon 1989 (includes about 10% Merlot): Still has very deep colour; good cassis on nose, with some farmyard hints; very concentrated fruit with dry tannins, will keep well and make a fine bottle.

Noble Late Harvest Reserve 1991 (fermented in stainless steel and then transferred into oak, 30% new): Rich golden colour; honey and apricot nose; very rich apricot and raisin fruit, high alcohol (14.5%) and glycerol, low acidity.

Noble Late Harvest Reserve 1993 (fermented and aged 12 months in 100% new oak): Lovely treacle colour; tremendous concentration of rich fruit on nose; wonderful symphony of honeyed fruit, and has the essential 'green spine' of all great sweet whites. Smashing.

Noble Late Harvest 1989 (no wood): Deep, browny gold; rich, dried-fruit bouquet; raisins, sultanas, prunes and dried apricots on palate, finishes quite dry.

Also tasted from the cask: 1995 Chardonnay; 1995 Lievlander; two different casks of 1995 Shiraz (one from new virus-free clones, one from twenty-year-old vines); 1995 blend of 50% Merlot, 25% Cabernet Sauvignon and 25% Franc, all fermented together, and will, subject to last minute adjustments, form the 1995 D. V. B.; and finally the 1995 Cabernet Sauvignon, to which up to 10% Merlot may be added later. All were excellent.

Technical Notes

Area under vines: 65 hectares

Cultivars planted
WHITE: Chenin Blanc, Sauvignon Blanc, Weisser Riesling, Bukettraube, Chardonnay, Cape Riesling, Clairette Blanche, Kerner
RED: Cabernet Sauvignon, Cabernet Franc, Merlot, Shiraz, Cinsaut, Ruby Cabernet

Wines produced
WHITE: Chardonnay, Sauvignon Blanc, Weisser Riesling, Cheandrie (semi-sweet, Chenin Blanc, Weisser Riesling, Bukettraube blend), Natural Sweet Wine (Chenin Blanc, Weisser Riesling blend), Noble Late Harvest, Noble Late Harvest Reserve
RED: Lievlander (Cinsaut, Ruby Cabernet, Merlot, Cabernet

Franc blend), Shiraz, Cabernet Sauvignon, D. V. B. (Bordeaux blend)

Sales: 50% domestic, 50% export

Useful Information

Owner: Paul Benadé
Winemaker: Abraham Beukes
Address: Lievland Estate, Box 66, Klapmuts 7625
Telephone: 02211.5226 *Fax*: 02211.5213

Tasting/Sales: Weekdays 09.00 to 17.00, Saturday 09.00 to 13.00

DELHEIM

The core of the present Delheim estate is a 25-hectare farm, known as De Drie Sprong, granted in 1699 to a German settler, Lorenz Kamfer, by Wilhem Adriaen van der Stel. This land is all on the lower slopes of the Simonsberg mountain. The freehold of De Drie Sprong passed through the hands of nine different owners until it was bought in 1857 by Jan Andries Beyers, who had been busy acquiring land above and around De Drie Sprong since 1813.

The upper part of the estate, although it did not comprise any of the land originally granted to Kamfer, had been divided away from the property assembled by Jan Andries Beyers in 1903 by the then owners, and had kept the De Drie Sprong name. This land was purchased in 1938 by a successful builder, Hans Otto Hoheisen as a retirement home for himself and his wife Deli, for whom he renamed the estate Delheim – Deli's home. Hoheisen was a close friend of Paul Canitz, owner of the neighbouring Muratie estate, and it was on his advice that he bought the property, and with his encouragement and that of Professor Perold that he began to plant Delheim with vines for winemaking, initially using Cape Riesling, Cabernet, Hanepoot and Pinot Noir.

These were pioneering days in the production of red and dry white table wines in the Cape. The taste of South African consumers was focused almost entirely on brandy, fortified sweet wines, 'ports' and 'sherries', and there was virtually nowhere to turn for help or advice on matters of viticulture or vinification.

These difficulties were further compounded by shortages of plant material, chemicals, bottles, corks and machinery caused by the war years. In spite of all these problems, Hoheisen forged ahead, and his wines, sold as Drie Sprong HOH Muscat Dessert, HOH Cabernet, etc., met with a degree of success, in spite of some of his earlier efforts being offered for sale in second-hand beer bottles.

Hans and Deli Hoheisen worked all the hours that God sent, and then some more, both on the farm and in the cellar, as well as in the marketing of their wines. They had no children to help them, and this had, after all, been intended as the dream home of their retirement. On a visit to Germany, Deli met up with her nephew, Spatz Sperling, who had farming experience and was looking for new horizons. It was agreed that Spatz would travel to South Africa to help his aunt and uncle on their farm. In 1951 Spatz set sail from Southampton aboard the *Winchester Castle* for South Africa, equipped with £10 spending money for the two-week voyage. This was a salutary lesson in the value of money for young Spatz, and he arrived in Cape Town having spent only just over £1, mainly on lemonade at two-pence a glass.

With Spatz's help, the Hoheisens kept Delheim going as a wine farm through the difficult years of the early 1950s, extending the activities of the estate into the planting of pine trees on the higher ground. Spatz's knowledge of forestry and love of trees not only provided additional revenue, but also a valuable source of shade and protection for the vines from the devastating winds that howled down the slopes of the Simonsberg. The market for table wines was still very difficult, and in 1957 Hans Hoheisen decided to call it a day, preferring to go and help his father on the 14,000-hectare farm he had bought in the Eastern Transvaal. The running of Delheim was turned over to Spatz on a profit-sharing basis, and for a while there were not many of these.

Spatz's first vintage at Delheim yielded 22 tons of grapes for winemaking. This gave hardly enough to live on, but Deli Hoheisen, who believed passionately in the future of Delheim as a wine estate, had turned her hand to growing vegetables. In a good week, the vegetables could realize as much as £16 in the Mowbray market, which paid the weekly wage-bill, and left enough for lunch for her and Spatz.

Although Spatz was not a winemaker by training, he was not, and still is not afraid of a challenge. He was lucky in that a number of young winemakers in the Cape had also fled from the depression of post-war Europe, many of them from Germany. All were keen to further the name and quality of South Africa's wines by pooling their knowledge and helping each other. An example of such a challenge met and overcome has now become a classic of South African wine-lore.

It must first be explained that Sperling in German means sparrow, and that Spatz is in the diminutive form. The scene is set in the Delheim cellars at the end of the 1950s, when Spatz was entertaining a group of friends to a Sunday afternoon of eating, drinking and swimming. An integral part of all such days in the winelands includes a visit to the cellar to taste the latest efforts of the winemaker. One particular tank of rather dark brown, sweet liquid was tasted, and one lady guest gave her verdict: 'But Spatz, this is really *dreck*'. Not to put too fine a point on it, *dreck* is the German for shit. The gauntlet had been thrown down, and Spatz picked it up. By the 1961 vintage, Spatzendreck became a well-made late-harvest sweet wine. The name was born, and the cheeky label showing a fat sparrow, rear-view, producing its quota of *dreck*, became part of the Delheim legend. They say that all publicity is good, and Spatzendreck proved this by winning *Decanter*'s Worst Wine Label of the Year Award in 1970.

The 50 hectares of the Drie Sprong farm are really best suited to varieties for the production of delicate white wines, and are planted to Sauvignon Blanc, Chenin Blanc, Weisser Riesling, Gewürztraminer and Chardonnay. The only red variety planted on the Simonsberg slopes is the Pinot Noir for the making of Sparkling Rosé. Spatz, never one to miss out on market trends, was on the lookout for some land for growing red cultivars right at the start of the 1970s. He found and bought 80 hectares on Klapmutskop, only three kilometres north-west of Drie Sprong, in 1975. The soil, exposure and micro-climate here are the same as those of the great red wine estate of Kanoncop, and were quickly planted with Cabernet Sauvignon, as well as Merlot, Cabernet Franc, Shiraz and, later, Pinotage.

In addition to their suitability for growing the red 'noble' varieties, the conditions on Klapmutskop are also favourable for the development of the spores of the 'noble rot', and Chenin Blanc and Sémillon were added to the range of cultivars. This resulted in the production of Edelspatz, Delheim's Noble Late Harvest wine.

In 1988 a further 35 hectares were bought, adjoining the Klapmuts vineyard, already planted, and Delheim's range now includes Dry Red, a lighter blend of several varieties, a Pinot Noir, a Shiraz, a Cabernet Sauvignon, and Grand Reserve, the estate's flagship red, which is predominantly, and sometimes exclusively, Cabernet Sauvignon, and of very high quality.

Spatz followed Hans Hoheisen's precedent by naming the Klapmuts vineyard Vera Cruz, in honour of his very hard-working and supportive wife, Vera. Tongue in cheek, as always, Spatz says that the name is partly derived from his wife's extensive travels in Spanish-speaking South America and partly in recognition of the cross that she took up when she married him. All joking aside, this is very much a family business. In theory Spatz is supposed to have retired, but he is very active in all aspects of the farm, as indeed is his mother, his son Victor and his daughter Nora, and the two younger children, Maria and Nicky.

Tasting Notes

Sauvignon Blanc 1995: Pale gold colour; lots of up-front Sauvignon fruit on the nose; a clean, correct wine with nice gooseberry and asparagus flavours, good balance and length.

Chardonnay 1995: Mid-golden colour; oak quite strong on nose, but good fruit as well; excellent rich fruit, some breadth, with oak a bit dominant, but will balance out in time.

Gewürztraminer 1995: Very pale colour; lovely spicy Gewürz bouquet; same spiciness on palate, with a touch more sweetness than Alsatian counterparts.

Edelspatz 1994 Noble Late Harvest: Deep, golden colour; a concentrated bouquet of clover honey; rich, figgy-pudding taste, more roasted than botrytized.

Cabernet Sauvignon 1992 (12 months in 2nd-, 3rd- and 4th-fill casks, mostly new clones): Bright, mid-red; good cassis nose with minty tones; well-balanced wine with some structure – good now, but will keep and improve for a year or two.

Grand Reserve 1992 (up to 18 months in 50% new, 50% 2nd-fill casks, this wine 70% Cabernet Sauvignon, 30% Merlot, but

1990 100% Cabernet Sauvignon, as will be 1994): Deep, dense red; nose of ripe black fruit; a big mouthful of ripe fruit, with fine ripe tannins, and good structure.

Pinotage 1995 (4 months in 8,000-litre wooden vat, with oak chips added): Nice deep colour; typical Pinotage nose of summer fruit; big, mouth-filling, a fresh, fruity Pinotage with some good tannins.

Technical Notes

Area under vines: 150 hectares

Area under forest: 170 hectares

Cultivars planted
WHITE: Chenin Blanc, Colombard, Sauvignon Blanc, Cape Riesling, Rhine Riesling, Gewürztraminer, Chardonnay, Sémillon
RED: Pinotage, Shiraz, Cabernet Sauvignon, Merlot, Cabernet Franc, Pinot Noir

Average production: 1,000 tons, approx. 1,000,000 bottles

Useful Information

Owner: Spatz Sperling
Winemaker: Philip Constandius
Address: Delheim Wines (Pty) Ltd., PO Box 10, Koelenhof 7605
Telephone: 021.882.2033 *Fax*: 021.882.2036

Tasting/Sales: Weekdays 08.30 to 17.00, Saturday 08.30 to 15.00, Sunday (1 November–28 February) 11.30 to 15.00; Vintners Platters (1 October–30 April); Country Soup (1 May–30 September)

EERSTERIVIER CO-OPERATIVE

The Eersterivier Co-operative, founded in 1954, is the youngest co-operative movement in the Stellenbosch area. There are currently seventeen members, each farming between 20 and 120 hectares, and producing between 100 and 1,500 tons of grapes apiece. This gives the cellar an average annual volume of around 10,000 tons, which equates to approximately 8 million litres of wine. Roughly 10% of this is bottled under the Eersterivier label for sale on the local market, and the balance is sold in bulk to merchants and to VINFRUCO, for blending and for export and bottling overseas. The co-operative's wines are available in the UK under the name of First River Winery through Walter S. Siegel Ltd.

In the early days of the co-operative, most of the wine was sold to the KWV for brandy, and for making their own wines. The current general manager, Manie Rossouw, has run the affairs of Eersterivier very capably for over a quarter of a century, since his appointment in 1970. He reports to a board of five directors elected from among the members. He is assisted by winemaker Marius Lategan, and marketing manager Marius Burger, a post created in 1991.

The accent at Eersterivier is very much on quality. There is a very user-friendly tasting facility, and ex-cellar sales account for a high proportion of the sales of bottled wines on the domestic market. There is a range of sixteen wines currently on offer, all very reasonably priced and attractively labelled.

Tasting Notes

Hanseret Edelblanc (blend of Sauvignon Blanc, Cape Riesling and Chenin Blanc): Very pale colour; quincy Chenin nose; fruit rich, ripe and clean with nice length.

Sauvignon Blanc 1995: Pale straw; nose quite muted, but definite Sauvignon character; crisp, clean and fruity with right level of acidity.

Chardonnay/Sauvignon Blanc 1995 (60/40 mix, with Sauvignon wood fermented and aged): Pale golden; rich fruit and some oak on nose; a better-than-usual marriage of these two grapes, but presently oak-dominated.

Chenin Blanc 1995: Very pale colour; typical Chenin quincy nose; loads of ripe, off-dry fruit, with good length.

Riesling 1995: Pale lemon yellow; nice Riesling bouquet; good fruit in mouth, acid balance right for a bit of ageing.

Cabernet Sauvignon 1992: Very deep colour; big blackcurrant bouquet; a fat mouthful of ripe black fruit, drinkable now, but enough tannins and structure to keep for a year or two.

Pinotage 1995: Deep colour for young, unwooded Pinotage; apricots and banana on nose; lots of cheerful, quaffable fruit, and good length.

Pinotage 1978 (for academic interest): Colour starting to brown; still has nice fruit, though slightly cooked, on the nose and in the mouth, with some soft tannins.

Technical Notes

Co-operative: 17 members

Average production: 10,000 tons

Bottled wines: 90,000 cases approx.

Wines bottled
WHITE: Hanseret Edelblanc, Sauvignon Blanc, Riesling, Muscat d'Alexandrie, Chardonnay/Sauvignon Blanc, Chenin Blanc, Weisser Riesling, Hanseret Bouquet Blanc, Special Late Harvest Gewürztraminer
RED: Hanseret Claret, Pinotage, Cabernet Sauvignon, Grand Reserve
SPARKLING: Demi-Sec
FORTIFIED WINE: Hanepoot Jerepiko

Useful Information

General Manager: Manie Rossouw
Winemaker: Marius Lategan
Finance/Marketing: Marius Burger
Address: Eersterivier Kelder, Box 2, Vlottenburg 7604
Telephone: 021.8813870 *Fax*: 021.8813102

Tasting/Sales: Weekdays 08.30 to 17.00, Saturday 09.00 to 13.00; Light meals served December school holidays

GRANGEHURST WINERY

To say that Jeremy Walker's fermenting cellar is a little cramped would be a masterpiece of understatement. However, in spite of there being not enough room to swing the proverbial cat, Jeremy is making red wine in this converted squash court that can hold its head up with South Africa's finest.

Jeremy started his winemaking career with Seymour Pritchard at Clos Malverne, later establishing his own winery on the slopes of the Helderberg in 1992. Although he has plans to plant half a hectare of his own vines, Jeremy currrently makes his wines from very carefully selected grapes from the neighbouring farm, Firgrove and, not surprisingly, from the Devon Valley. He is at present producing about 2,500 cases annually, but plans to increase this to 8,000 within the next five years. In order to achieve this he is building a new fermentation cellar, which will contain additional fibre-glass open fermentation tanks, and six stainless-steel tanks which will be used for blending. His existing cask cellar, which is a conversion from his former bachelor quarters, is adequate for current volumes. Plans to increase space for barrels were not mentioned, but I have absolutely no doubt that the Walker gift for squeezing quarts into pint pots will solve that problem when it arises.

The Grangehurst record to date is impressive. For the winery's maiden 1992 vintage, three wines were entered in the South African Young Wine Show, and all received medals – two golds and one silver, and the Cabernet Sauvignon/Merlot blend carried off four trophies, including the General Smuts Trophy for the Champion South African wine. A further mark of Grangehurst's quality may be seen in the rapid take-up of the 100 debentures offered to wine investors.

Tasting Notes

Cabernet Sauvignon 1992 (20% Merlot, marked 90 by *Wine Spectator*): Clear, deep red; good cassis nose; ripe fruit and firm structure harmonizing well, with good length.

Cabernet Sauvignon 1993 (14% Merlot): Very deep colour; nice open nose of ripe black fruits; fine fruit, ripe tannins, good structure and length – excellent.

Reserve 1993 (73% Cabernet Sauvignon, 27% Merlot – all new wood, 85% French, 15% American oak): Very deep red with bluey edges; good ripe fruit on nose, with oak evident; a fine, balanced blend, with loads of good ripe fruit, soft tannins and considerable structure.

Pinotage 1994: Good deep colour; nice berry fruit nose; fine well-made wine, balanced, with good tannins and some nice structure.

Technical Notes

Wines produced
RED: Cabernet Sauvignon, Cabernet Sauvignon/Merlot, Pinotage, Reserve

Useful Information

Owner/Winemaker: Jeremy Walker
Address: Grangehurst Winery, Box 206, Stellenbosch 7599
Telephone: 024.553625 *Fax*: 024.552143

Tasting/Sales: Weekdays 10.00 to 17.00, Saturdays 09.00 to 13.00

JOHN PLATTER WINES, CLOS DU CIEL

John Platter's sixteenth annual South African Wine Guide appeared during my months of research at the end of 1995. The publication of this slim volume of some 315 pages is an eagerly awaited event each year. It is packed with information on every estate, winery and co-operative in South Africa: maps of each wine region, showing clearly the position of each entry, details of restaurants, hotels, bed-and-breakfast establishments, addresses and telephone/fax numbers of wine routes/trusts/associations for each region and the numbers of the Publicity Associations for each area. More importantly, every wine that is currently available from every winery is tasted and rated by either John himself, or by a member of his able team. Platter's marking for wines is by a system of stars, from one (ordinary) to five (Cape Classic), and it is the star-ratings in his guide that every South African winemaker holds his breath for with the appearance of each new edition. The most coveted five-star award is not handed out often; in fact I could only find nine such wines in the entire 1996 guide.

John is a quiet, unassuming fellow with an enormous depth of knowledge which, as with many wine writers I have met, he is more than willing to share, and I am extremely grateful to him for all the invaluable help, advice and information that he gave me. Erica, his wife, edits his guides and is a humorous and talented columnist in her own right.

The Platters live in an attractive house on the slopes of the Helderberg mountain. He has two hectares of vines at the Clos du Ciel vineyard, which are exclusively Chardonnay, from which he produces between 300 and 400 cases a year. It is the dream of most wine writers to make their own wine, and John has not only achieved this goal, he has also achieved it with some distinction.

In view of the relatively short history of Clos du Ciel as a vineyard, and the very small quantity produced, we did not do a formal tasting during my visit, but John kindly gave me a bottle of his 1994 vintage to take away. I tasted the wine, and then drank it with one of my solitary suppers at Stellenzicht. It had a nice golden colour, and a good Chardonnay nose with only hints of oak; in the mouth it has good weight and fruit, and a long finish. If I ever get the chance to make wine and produce something as good as that, I shall be well pleased.

Technical Notes

Area under vines: 2 hectares

Cultivars planted: 100% Chardonnay, 10 different clones

Viticulture: Minimum sulphur used, minimum pesticides

Vinification: Whole cluster pressing, fermentation started in tank and transferred to casks – 2nd-, 3rd- and 4th-fill, 9 months on lees with regular batonnage, one racking, one light filtration.

Useful Information

Owner and Winemaker: John Platter
Address: Clos du Ciel Vineyards, Box 3162, Stellenbosch 7602

Not open to public

MORGENHOF

The early history of Morgenhof is confused and confusing. When the land was first granted in 1680, the farm was called Harmony, and the name was later changed to Onrus. By the time the property was acquired by 'Stil Jan' Momberg, the partially retired present-day owner of Middlevlei, the name was Morgenhof. Momberg did much to restore the farm and the wines, which had been sadly neglected. The next owner was a Johannesburg-based company, Rhine Ruhr Holdings (Pty) Ltd., whose managing director, Gert Grobe, bought Morgenhof in 1982. The company continued the programme of improvement, and also did much towards the restoration of the fine Cape Dutch buildings.

In 1993 the property changed hands once more, when it was bought by a French couple, Alain and Anne Huchon. Anne, in addition to being a member of the Cointreau liqueur family, also has a strong vinous background. Her grandfather was responsible for the development of the great Cognac house of Remy-Martin, and her family still owns businesses and estates in the Cognac area. Anne herself is involved with her brother and sisters in the ancient Champagne house of Gosset. Both Alain and Anne are highly qualified in marketing and business management, and they have already created an air of Gallic professionalism at this 300-year-old estate.

Possibly the most exciting innovation under the Huchon ownership is the creation of the huge underground maturation cellar. Inspired by the cask cellar at Château Lafite-Rothschild, the 1,250 square metre octagon can hold up to 2,000 casks, or 450,000 litres of wine. Designed by Michael Dall and associates, the cellar complex, which also includes a tasting room and vinotheque, combines a classical French style with a taste of the Cape. The whole is surmounted by a tower, which will be used initially for conferences and special functions, but will be converted eventually for use as a restaurant.

In addition to all the investment and financial know-how brought to Morgenhof by the Huchons, the actual winemaking is in the very capable hands of Jean Daneel. Jean is one of the best winemakers in South Africa, a fact which was recognized when he won the coveted Diners Club 'Winemaker of the Year' award in 1992 whilst working for the Buitenverwachting Estate.

Tasting Notes

Sauvignon Blanc 1995: Pale, greeny gold colour; lovely asparagus and elderflower nose; beautiful clean, crisp fruit with good length.

Chardonnay 1994: Pale gold colour; good fruit and notes of vanilla; in the mouth the wine is quite fat and buttery, and the oak is well integrated with the fruit.

Merlot 1993: Deep, dense red; lots of rich, ripe fruit on the nose; loads of ripe black fruit on the palate, with nice ripe tannins and good structure – a wine that will repay keeping.

Cabernet Sauvignon 1993 (old clones, but virus-free): Very deep, blacky red; powerful cassis nose; a big mouthful of wine with a lot of backbone and powerful but non-aggressive tannins.

Technical Notes

Area under vines: 80 hectares

Cultivars planted
WHITE: Sauvignon Blanc, Chardonnay, Chenin Blanc, Cape Riesling, Rhine Riesling
RED: Cabernet Sauvignon, Merlot, Cabernet Franc, Malbec, Pinotage, Tinta Barocca

Wines produced
WHITE: Sauvignon Blanc, Chardonnay, Chenin Blanc, Blanc de M (75% Chenin Blanc, with Rhine Riesling)
RED: Merlot, Merlot/Cabernet Sauvignon, Cabernet Sauvignon, Pinotage. (Bordeaux Blend planned.)

'PORT': 'Ruby Port' (Tinta Barocca, Pinotage)
SPARKLING: Cap Classique, Brut (45/55 Chardonnay/Pinotage)

Useful Information

Owners: Alain and Anne Huchon
Winemaker: Jean Daneel
Oenologist: Rianie Geldenhuys
Address: Morgenhof Wines, Box 365, Stellenbosch 7599
Telephone: 021.889.5510 *Fax*: 021.889.5266

Facilities: Lunch 12.00 to 14.00 Monday–Saturday year round, Sunday November–April; picnics in summer, soups in winter. Function/conference facilities
Visits/Tasting: Monday–Friday 09.00 to 16.30, Saturday 10.00 to 15.00, Sunday (November–April) 10.00 to 15.00

MULDERBOSCH

Larry Jacobs bought this 48-hectare farm in 1989 with the express purpose of creating a quality wine estate. A huge amount of work has been done in terms of earth-moving, vineyard preparation and building. The vineyards are well situated to the east of the Koelenhof road, facing north-east and south-east and rising from 130 metres above sea-level up to 300 metres.

Quite apart from the geological and climatic suitability of this part of Stellenbosch, Mulderbosch is doubly blessed in having Mike Dobrovic as winemaker. He is keen, dedicated and so highly qualified that I can only understand about half of his oenological patter. This is not to infer that Dobrovic bores one with technospeak; he is more inclined to let his excellent wines speak for themselves, whilst he regales the taster with some of the funniest (and dirtiest) jokes I have heard since I worked in the City of London.

The first wine that Mulderbosch produced was a barrel-fermented Blanc Fumé 1991 from bought-in Sauvignon Blanc grapes, for which Mike won a Veritas Double Gold award. Since then he has continued to make a Blanc Fumé, but it is perhaps his unwooded Sauvignon Blanc that has really put Mulderbosch on the wine map. This is one of South Africa's most sought-after white wines, and most of it is sold on a kind of black market even before the vintage is released. There is also a fine Chardonnay which is 60% barrel-fermented, half in new oak and half second fill. Unfortunately the reputation of the Sauvignon Blanc is so high that the Chardonnay is somewhat undeservedly overlooked.

Two red wines are also produced from grapes grown on the lower slopes. There is a Bordeaux blend which is sold under the name Faithful Hound. This relates to a dog which belonged to the previous owner of the property who died; the dog stayed near the shack where they had lived, faithfully waiting for his master to return. The grapes for the Bordeaux blend are Cabernet Sauvignon, Cabernet Franc, Merlot and Malbec, and are grown on a plot of land near to the shack. There is also a pure Merlot and I tasted a 1993, which was an experimental blend from four different new oak barrels, one of which was American and the rest Nevers oak from three different French coopers.

The winemaking buildings are on two levels, and have been carefully sited so as to cause minimum disruption to the lie of the land, as well as to allow as much movement of the wine as possible to take place by gravity rather than by pumping. The barrel-maturation cellar is partly underground, which makes it much easier to keep cool.

Tasting Notes

Chardonnay 1994 (mixture of Davis and French clones; 60% barrel-fermented, 50% of which new): Palish, greeny gold; nice, open Chardonnay nose, with vanilla and cumin; lots of fat fruit, a bit tropical, and nicely in tune with the wood.

Blanc Fumé 1993 (about 60% cask-fermented): Nice, pale gold; good, clean Sauvignon nose, restrained, but good fruit showing; fruit and acidity in harmony, good length and some finesse.

Sauvignon Blanc 1993 (no wood): Very pale greeny gold; nose of gooseberry, mango and slight curry; nice mouthful of fruit, but fades fast.

Sauvignon Blanc 1994: Same very pale colour; asparagussy, elder-bark nose; lovely fruit, acidity still high, but just coming into balance, good length.

Sauvignon Blanc 1995: Very pale, greenish gold; fine grassy nose with gooseberry fruit, but still quite closed; big in the mouth, very long, with loads of fruit and tremendous aftertaste.

Faithful Hound 1993 (60% Merlot, 36% Cabernet Sauvignon, 4% Malbec): Fine, dark colour; excellent nose of cassis and vanilla; fruit, tannins and aromas all coming together, but has enough structure to keep it going for many years.

Faithful Hound 1995 (38% Cabernet Sauvignon, 38% Merlot, 12% Cabernet Franc, 12% Malbec, 25% new casks, rest 2nd- and 3rd-fill): Good, deep, dense red; very strong oak on nose – sample taken from a new Taransaud cask; a very big mouthful of fruit with huge structure and fine tannins, a real keeper.

Merlot 1993: Very dark red; big nose of ripe, black fruit with hints of oak; lots of good, ripe fruit, nice tannins and good structure – a winner.

Technical Notes

Area under vines: 17 hectares, with possibility of another 6–7

Cultivars planted
WHITE: Sauvignon Blanc, Chardonnay
RED: Cabernet Sauvignon, Merlot, Cabernet Franc, Malbec

Useful Information

Owner: Larry Jacobs
Winemaker: Mike Dobrovic
Address: Mulderbosch Vineyards, Box 548, Stellenbosch 7599
Telephone: 021.882.2488 *Fax*: 021.882.2351

Not open to the public

J. P. BREDELL

Until very recently, the 'ports' of J. P. Bredell were only known by a very lucky few. This is surprising, not only because of the extraordinary quality of the wine, but also because this is the largest 'port' producing property in South Africa. The explanation is simple: for many years this huge wine property has produced 'port', as well as other wines and grapes, for the KWV, and it is only in the last few years that they have decided to produce some premium wines under their own label.

'Port' production on Helderzicht, the main part of the J. P. Bredell property, began as early as 1933, and the famous Professor Perold, head of Stellenbosch University's Agricultural Sciences Department, chose this farm in 1942 for his experiments in the cultivation of 'port' varieties, as it had the soil and micro-climate nearest to that of Pinhao in the Douro. The farm was bought by the Bredell family in 1965, the neighbouring Onder Rustenberg was acquired soon after, and the two farms became known as J. P. Bredell Farms. They are on three slopes on the foothills of the Helderberg, very close to False Bay, and the vines benefit greatly from the cooling sea-breezes. Anton Bredell farms Helderzicht, and his brother Albert farms Onder Rustenberg, but it is the gentle giant Anton who makes the wine.

Although the J. P. Bredell winery still produces very large amounts of 'port' for the KWV as well as grapes and table wine, Anton's main passion is in the making of 'vintage port' to sell under his own label. He says that this is true 'vintage port', but in South-African style rather than a copy of the Portuguese original. This may very well be so, but I have managed to infiltrate a bottle of J. P. Bredell's 1991 vintage into a tasting of the same year of one or two well-known Portuguese shippers' wines, with the wine-makers present. Only one Portuguese taster recognized the wine as not being from Portugal, and he said this was because it had a whiff of cherries, a scent never found in Portuguese 'port'.

The 'port' varieties planted are Tinta Barocca, Souzao, Touriga Francesa and, more recently, Touriga Nacional, and a little Cinsaut is also included. These are all planted on the westernmost of the three slopes on the Bredell farm, which is well-drained with some clay. Fermentation is in open lagars, and although treading is not done by foot as in the Douro, Anton is considering this for future vintages. Currently the cap is broken constantly by the use of long wooden paddles, which is truly back-breaking work.

Anton started keeping back stocks of vintage wines in 1988, but it was really the 1991 that became the first J. P. Bredell 'vintage port' in the style he was looking for. The wine, labelled as J. P. Bredell Vintage Reserve 1991, spent two years in 500-litre barrels and is made of 50% Tinta Barocca and 50% Souzao. Only 200 cases were made. The wine is widely acclaimed by all who have tasted it, and has won several awards. Perhaps the mark of recognition that has given Anton Bredell the greatest pleasure was winning the 'vintage port' category during the 1994 Calitzdorp 'Port' Festival.

Tasting Notes

J. P. Bredell Vintage Reserve 1991: Very deep, blackish colour; rich and succulent Christmas pudding nose; a huge, complex and concentrated mouthful of plummy fruit and tannins with enough structure to age for many years.

Technical Notes

Area under vines: 232 hectares

Average production: 2,000 tons (1,000 cases own-label)

Cultivars planted
'PORT': Tinta Barocca, Souzao, Touriga Nacional, Touriga Francesa, Cinsaut
RED: Pinotage, Cabernet Sauvignon , Merlot, Cinsaut
WHITE: Chenin Blanc, Sauvignon Blanc, Chardonnay, Riesling

Useful Information

Winemaker: Anton Bredell
Address: J. P. Bredell Wines, Box 5266, Helderberg 7135
Telephone/Fax: 024.422478

Tasting/Sales: Monday–Friday 08.30 to 17.00

WARWICK FARM

Norma Ratcliffe is Canadian by birth and, from the winemaking point of view, she is decidedly French by inclination. During the 1980s she spent a lot of time in France, and at one time was the winemaker for Charles de Guigné at Château Sénéjac in Bordeaux. This was a time of evolution and excitement in Bordeaux, and I am certain that Norma caught much of her enthusiasm from the likes of Peter Vinding Diers, Martin Bamford and John Salvi.

Named by an earlier owner – Colonel Alexander Gordon, a Boer War veteran of the Warwickshire regiment who stayed on in South Africa after the war ended – Warwick Farm was originally part of a vast estate called Good Success. When Stan Ratcliffe bought Warwick Farm in 1964, there was not a single vine planted on the property. At that time winemaking did not form part of Stan's plans for Warwick, but he nevertheless decided to start planting Cabernet Sauvignon vines, which soon began to produce grapes of such high quality that they became highly sought after by wholesalers and other wineries.

It was not until Norma's arrival at Warwick in 1971 that the serious business of making wine began. To Stan's original plantings were added Cabernet Franc and Merlot. Not surprisingly, Norma's whole attitude and approach to winemaking has always had more than a touch of the Médoc. Although the winery, and in particular the fermentation equipment, has all the latest in technological aids, tradition is the keynote. Regular pumping-over during fermentation and a three-week maceration are the order of the day. Each grape variety is vinified separately, and racked into 225-litre French oak casks, and it is only after nine months to one year that the final 'assemblage' is made. Once again following the Médocain 'modus vinificandum', only fresh egg-whites are used for fining – 3–5 egg-whites per 100 litres, depending on the vintage – and no filtration is practised.

The first vintage at Warwick was in 1985, and the wine was a 100% Cabernet Sauvignon. This was followed in 1986 by the first Bordeaux blend, the now famous Warwick Trilogy, a classic Médoc mixture – 60% Cabernet Sauvignon, 32% Merlot and 8% Cabernet Franc in the case of the 1993 vintage. This wine, like all the Warwick babies, is a consistent winner of gold Veritas awards, and is a regular feature on the SAA First and Business Class wine lists.

The Ratcliffe portfolio of wines now includes the Trilogy, which spends sixteen months in a mixture of new and 2nd-fill casks, as does the Cabernet Sauvignon. There is also a Cabernet Franc and a Merlot, which both spend a little less time in wood. Watch out for her first release of Pinotage, the 1995 vintage. I tasted the wine from two different casks – see notes below – and I think that Beyers Truter across the road may have a rival in the years to come. Norma is also making a Chardonnay; 1994 was her first essay, and she was not sure whether to continue. I find the 1994 to be drinking beautifully now, and the 1995 certainly justifies her decision to try again.

Tasting Notes

Chardonnay 1995: Very deep golden colour; rich fruit on nose with strong vanilla; soft, ripe fruit, with lemony citrus notes. Excellent.

Chardonnay 1994: Lighter colour than the 1995; soft and easy bouquet, not much wood evident; oakiness there in the mouth, but not excessively, lovely soft and buttery, with full fruit.

Merlot 1993 (5% Cabernet Sauvignon – 20% new oak, rest 2nd-fill): Deep red, almost black; ripe blackberries on nose; a big mouthful of ripe fruit and chocolate, with good tannins and structure.

Cabernet Franc 1993 (a little Cabernet Sauvignon): Very dense blacky red; ripe bouquet with spicy hints; a nice mouthful of accessible fruit, slightly minerally.

Cabernet Franc 1991: Colour beginning to show brown at edges; nice ripe fruit nose; good, smooth fruit in the mouth, with some nice, soft tannins, and that same mineral taste.

Cabernet Sauvignon 1993: fine bluey-black colour; restrained but definite cassis nose; lovely fruit, ripe tannins and lots of backbone for a long life.

Warwick Trilogy 1993: Lovely deep red; strong cassis nose; a nicely balanced blend, with rich berry fruit in the mouth, plus fine tannins and a good skeleton for keeping.

Pinotage 1995 (from a new high-toast Burgundy cask): Very deep colour; rich, plummy, biscuity nose; soft and mouth-filling, with great complexity and length.

Pinotage 1995 (from a 2nd-fill Vicard cask): Colour and nose quite similar, but less sweetness in the mouth, though fruit and structure are all there.

Technical Notes

Area under vines: 55 hectares – and still planting

Cultivars planted
WHITE: Chardonnay
RED: Cabernet Sauvignon, Merlot, Cabernet Franc, Pinotage

Wines produced
WHITE: Chardonnay
RED: Trilogy, Cabernet Sauvignon, Merlot, Cabernet Franc, Pinotage

Useful Information

Owners: Stan and Norma Ratcliffe
Winemaker: Norma Ratcliffe
Assistant: Marcus Milner
Address: Warwick Estate, Box 2, Muldersvlei 7606
Telephone: 021.884.4410 *Fax*: 021.884.4025

Tasting/Sales: Weekdays 09.00 to 12.00, 13.30 to 16.00 and preferably by appointment. Saturdays by appointment only

KANONKOP

The present Kanonkop estate was originally part of neighbouring Uitkyk, property of the late Senator J. H. Sauer. In 1930 the larger part of the Uitkyk estate was sold to Baron Hans von Carlowitz, and the Sauer family named the remaining portion Kanonkop. The name derives from a *kopje*, or small hill, from which a cannon used to be fired when sailing ships, plying the trade routes between Europe and the Far East, entered Table Bay for a victualling stop-

THE WINES OF SOUTH AFRICA

over. There were a series of these signal guns scattered around the farm lands of the Cape, so that the farmers could load their wagons, inspan their oxen and journey to Cape Town to sell or barter fresh fruit and vegetables to the ships, which had been many months at sea.

The Honourable P. O. Sauer, son of J. H. Sauer, began wine farming at Kanonkop with Danie Rossouw in the early 1930s. Sauer, who was Minister of Transport for some years and was respectfully known as Oom Paul, died in 1975. The farm is now run by Oom Paul's grandsons Johann and Paul Krige. Winemaking before the arrival of Beyers Truter in 1980 was in the hands of the redoubtable Jan 'Boland' Coetzee, who did much to establish the reputation of Kanonkop for the production of high-quality wines.

Beyers Truter is something of a pop star among winemakers of the Cape. His special ability lies in the making of Cabernet Sauvignon, a Bordeaux blend called Paul Sauer, and most importantly the famed Kanonkop Pinotage. There are a handful of South African winemakers who are putting enormous effort into revitalizing this neglected and only exclusively South African variety. There is certainly a great deal of interest in and demand for Pinotage, and the style of wine does not really seem to matter as long as the quality is good. It is a variety which lends itself to classic winemaking procedures, and cask ageing, which produces a wine of considerable structure and longevity. But it can also be vinified to give a light and fruity wine without the use of wood that may be drunk young with great pleasure. Beyers Truter was the driving force behind the formation, in November 1995, of the Pinotage Producers' Association. The founders' meeting was attended by 120 producers, and they came from every wine region of South Africa. Their objective is the promotion of Pinotage on a worldwide basis as a quality red wine grape, and at the same time to improve the quality of both grape and wine. There are two similar associations in South Africa, one for the promotion of sparkling wine and one for 'port', and both have proved of great value to producers.

There are 100 hectares currently under vines at Kanonkop, now almost entirely red varieties, grown in the ideal micro-climate and soil of the Simonsberg slopes. Fermentation is in open fermenters, which are like port lagars. For the Pinotage Beyers allows the must to ferment on the skins for two to three days at about 28 degrees

Celsius, during which time the cap is constantly broken by the use of wooden paddles and adequate dosings of SO_2 are added. The juice is then run off the skins and pulp, and is allowed to continue fermenting in stainless steel tanks at between 18 and 20 degrees until completely dry.

The Cabernet Sauvignon ferments and remains on the skins at between 26 and 28 degrees for four or five days until almost dry. Barrel maturation is taken very seriously at Kanonkop and, after much experimentation, they have narrowed their suppliers to a shortlist of three French coopers – Seguin-Moreau, Nadalee and Vicard. The Paul Sauer Bordeaux blend of 80% Cabernet Sauvignon, 10% Cabernet Franc and 10% Merlot spends 18 months in a mixture of 70% new and 30% 2nd-fill casks; the Cabernet Sauvignon between 16 and 18 months in one-third new, one-third 2nd-fill and one-third 3rd-fill casks; and the Pinotage stays between 14 and 16 months in 15–20% new oak, the rest being a mixture of 2nd- and 3rd-fill casks.

All this care and attention to detail produce wines that win prizes with clockwork regularity. The Kanonkop Cabernet Sauvignon has won gold medals at the Stellenbosch Bottled Wine Show since 1981, and both the Paul Sauer and the Pinotage 1990 won Double Gold awards. Beyers won the Robert Mondavi Winemaker of the Year trophy at the International Wine and Spirit Competition in London in 1991, and the 1991 Paul Sauer blend won the Pichon-Longueville, Comtesse de Lalande Trophy in 1994. The Kanonkop Pinotage Auction Reserve, a wine made specially for the Cape Independent Winemakers' Guild annual auction, not only regularly fetches the highest price at the auction, but it is also one of only nine wines to be awarded the coveted five stars in John Platter's 1996 Guide.

Tasting Notes

Pinotage 1989 (20% new oak, rest 2nd- and 3rd-fill): Deep colour; ripe fruit nose; very big mouthful of ripe fruit, huge structure, lots of length and fine tannins.

Pinotage 1990 (50% new oak, rest 2nd-, 3rd-, 4th- and 5th-fill): Same brilliant, deep red; typical plum and banana nose of Pinotage (Beyers says archetypal Kanoncop); again a big wine with loads of ripe, plummy fruit, soft tannins and the right backbone to keep it going for a long time.

Pinotage 1991 (50% new oak, 50% 2nd-fill): Lovely deep colour; fine Pinotage nose; tremendous fruit, but good tannins and big skeleton make this a wine to wait a few years for.

Pinotage 1992 (20% new oak, rest 2nd- and 3rd-fill): Very deep, clear red; some farmyard and leather on nose; fine fruit, very long with lots of body.

Pinotage 1993 (50% new oak, 50% 2nd-fill): Colour very deep and bright; nice fruit coming through, with a trace of leather, but still quite closed; a monster of a wine, with loads of luscious fruit, terrific structure and very fine tannins – will make a very fine bottle.

Beyerskloof Pinotage 1995 (from a separate Krige/Truter operation – this wine is made from bought-in Pinotage grapes from 20–40-year-old, non-irrigated bush vines): Bright, medium red; open, ripe-fruit nose; excellent mouthful of fruit with some non-aggressive tannins.

Cabernet Sauvignon 1989: Deep, bluey red; nose of cassis and leather; plenty of good, ripe fruit, fine backbone and good length.

Cabernet Sauvignon 1990: Same lovely deep colour; good cassis bouquet; leaner than '89, with considerable charm and class, fine fruit and plenty of backbone.

Cabernet Sauvignon 1991: Brilliant mid-red; strong blackcurrant nose; good fruit, with more structure and ageing potential than '89 or '90. (Beyers will continue with this style.)

Paul Sauer 1989: Deep, dense colour; nice fruit on nose, with some spiciness; a well-made, nicely balanced blend with good fruit and structure.

Paul Sauer 1990: Fine, deep colour; strong, up-front fruit nose; loads of ripe, rounded fruit, with good tannins and structure.

Paul Sauer 1991: Same fine, deep colour; nose quite closed; fine, broad palate, a well-made wine with super fruit and a lot of backbone.

Paul Sauer 1992: Deep ruby; very open bouquet; more up-front fruit than the preceding three vintages, nice soft tannins.

Technical Notes

Area under vines: 100 hectares

Cultivars planted
RED: Cabernet Sauvignon 45%, Pinotage 35%, Merlot 14%, Cabernet Franc 3%, Ruby Cabernet 3%

Wines produced
RED: Paul Sauer – Bordeaux blend, Cabernet Sauvignon, Pinotage, Kadette Dry Red (10 months oak, easy drinker, blend of Merlot with Cabernet Sauvignon and a little Cabernet Franc – prior to 1994 the blend used to contain Pinotage as well)

Useful Information

Owners: Johann and Paul Krige
Winemaker: Beyers Truter
Address: Kanonkop Estate, Box 19, Elsenburg 7607
Telephone: 021.884.4656 *Fax*: 021.884.4719

Tasting/Sales: Weekdays 08.30 to 17.00, Saturday 08.30 to 12.30; closed New Year's Day, Christmas Day, Good Friday
Facilities: Traditional snoek barbecue, with sweet potatoes, home-baked bread, etc., by appointment for groups of minimum 15 people

VRIESENHOF AND TALANA HILL

It has long been my theory that one can tell the kind of wine a man makes within ten minutes of meeting him. This was definitely not the case with the legendary Jan 'Boland' Coetzee. To describe Jan as the strong, silent type would be akin to describing Château Petrus as a nice little claret. The former Western Province and Springbok rugby player is built like the proverbial brick vathouse, speaks very little until he has got your measure, and has the reputation of not suffering fools, bureaucrats or journalists at all. The wines produced by Jan at Kanonkop during the 1970s are just the style I would expect from such a man: big, tough and very slow to give of themselves. There is, however, much more to Jan than first meets the eye, as the ensuing fifteen years has shown.

Feeling the need to follow his own star, Jan set about looking for a farm to suit his winemaking needs. He finally left Kanonkop in October 1980, and went in search of south-facing slopes to the south of Stellenbosch. He found what he was looking for in Vriesenhof, an 85-hectare farm nestling between the Stellenbosch and Helderberg mountains. The micro-climate here is quite different from Kanonkop; firstly it is much cooler, due to the sea-breezes from the Indian Ocean, and secondly there are relatively fewer hours of sunshine at the foot of the Helderberg. These factors give Jan the possibility of making wines that are lighter, finer and more elegant than the blockbusters of higher, hotter Kanonkop.

The purchase was made in December 1980. There were vines on the farm, but they were old Chenin Blanc, grown for quantity sales at the guaranteed minimum price set by the KWV for brandy production, and not for the making of fine wine. Jan's first priority, therefore, was the planting of the vineyard. He has deliberately been very slow and cautious about this – the secret of making good wine, he says, lies in the marriage of the right clones, rootstocks and sites and then the care of the winemaker, and if you do not get the first three right, you have wasted fifteen years of your life. Initially Jan set aside the Pinotage with which he had suceeded so brilliantly at Kanonkop, and concentrated his efforts on Cabernet Sauvignon, Cabernet Franc, and Merlot for his red wine, and Chardonnay for white, believing that these were the varieties best suited to the soil, exposure and micro-climate of Vriesenhof. He also planted some Pinot Noir to 'play with'. First love dies hard, however, and there are now Pinotage vines at Vriesenhof. The wine, which he will not release until he is 100% happy with it, will bear the name Kallisto, which he translates from the Greek as 'the best of the best' – definitely a wine to watch out for. Jan also believes that a blend of Merlot and Pinotage may be a marriage of the future.

Next in order of priority was the construction of a winery and underground cellar, which extends beneath the homestead. This work was completed in 1981. It was not until 1982 that Jan and his wife, Annette, moved into the property which, over the past fourteen years, they have slowly and painstakingly restored to its present state. In true Cape Dutch style, the rooms are tall and cool, and there are huge fireplaces for cold winter nights. The staircase that leads directly down into the cellar is a reminder that Jan is living 'above the shop'.

Large investment and steady progress are all very well, but it cannot have been easy from the financial point of view for Jan and his family over the fifteen years since he bought Vriesenhof. Jan's reputation and skill as a winemaker has been a help here, as he works as consultant to a number of wineries, including Buitenver-wachting, Eikendal, Lanzerac, Graham Beck, Morgenster, Yonder Hill and Helderenberg. Until recently he also used to make the wine at the neighbouring property Talana Hill, but this has now been incorporated into the Vriesenhof operation.

The range of wines currently made in the Vriesenhof cellar include Vriesenhof Kallista (a Bordeaux blend of Cabernet Sau-vignon, Merlot and Cabernet Franc), Vriesenhof Cabernet Sauvignon and Vriesenhof Chardonnay. This is also the birthplace of Talana Hill Royale, a more St Emilion style of Bordeaux blend with Merlot predominating and some Cabernet Franc, as well as Talana Hill Chardonnay. There is also a range of three wines sold under the name Paradyskloof Red (a blend of Merlot, Cabernet Sauvignon and some Shiraz), White (which is made from Char-donnay, Pinot Blanc and Sauvignon Blanc), and an easy-drinking Pinotage. The grapes that go into the Paradyskloof wines may have come from either property, and the wines are good value for money. Another wine made at Vriesenhof which reveals yet one more facet of Jan's character is a Limited Edition blend of mainly Merlot, with varying amounts of Cabernet. Five hundred specially designed and beautifully presented magnums of this wine are made each year, and all the profits go towards the protection of the Lesser Kestrel, a small, endangered species of raptor, migrating between Africa, Europe and Asia. This typifies Jan's care for the country and its creatures: it is his dream to make his vineyards a model for the future generations, and he plans to leave a minutely docu-mented record of everything he has ever done here.

Jan has spent a lot of time visiting other wine-producing coun-tries, especially France – he spent an entire vintage season in Burgundy in 1981, transferring Annette, two daughters and a baby son from the beginning of August until mid-December. He worked in the cellars of Drouhin, *négociant* and vineyard owner in Beaune, and there learned a great deal about the French approach to the Pinot Noir and the Chardonnay, as well as the importance of the correct use of oak. In 1995 he went to France, this time taking hundreds of samples of his own wines – the purpose? – to meet with coopers, taste his wines with them, and then ask them to supply the casks best suited to his wine. He has taken delivery of the first barrels, and awaits the results with interest.

During a pre-tasting talk on the Vriesenhof terrace, overlooking Talana Hill, Jan asked me if I liked Pinot Noir. Having replied that that depended entirely on the Pinot Noir, Jan disappeared and returned with bottle, corkscrew and glasses. It was certainly the most extraordinary Pinot Noir I have ever tasted: deep, blackish red in colour, with great wafts of Pinot Noir on the nose, big and fat in the mouth, with huge structure and very fine tannins. This is a Coetzee special – made from a clone that he likes; this was the 1991 vintage, and it has been in 2nd-fill casks for 40 months, bottled in December of 1994. He thinks he will now plant this particular clone in more serious quantity, and I think he is right.

With lunch – smoked fish, eggs, salad and cheese – we drank the 1992 Chardonnay, a mature 1982 Cabernet Sauvignon, and finished with a luscious 1983 Noble Late Harvest from 100% Chenin Blanc; a fitting end to a marvellous visit.

Tasting Notes

Paradyskloof White 1995 (Chardonnay/Sauvignon Blanc): Pale straw colour; nice fruit on nose with Chardonnay dominant; fruit/ acidity balance just right, with full Chardonnay flavours and some nice Sauvignon coming through.

Vriesenhof Chardonnay 1995: Nice pale, golden colour; good, ripe Chardonnay fruit on nose, with some oakiness; nice fruit, some fatness and ageing potential, good length.

Talana Hill Chardonnay 1994: Mid-gold colour; curious, faintly coconut nose; a heavier, fatter style than the Vriesenhof, with rich fruit – just a touch of oxidation?

Paradyskloof Red N. V. (blend, see text above): Good, deep red; lively fruit bouquet, some Shiraz; ripe Cabernet Sauvignon and

Merlot fruit with soft, pleasing tannins – ready and pleasing to drink now.

Vriesenhof Cabernet Sauvignon 1991: Deep, ruby colour; slight toastiness on nose; nice, raisiny fruit, with good structure and length – a stayer.

Vriesenhof Kallista 1992 (blend, see text above): Brilliant mid-red; blackcurrant and ripe summer berries on nose; a wine of some finesse, with ripe fruit, good backbone and soft tannins, and finishes long.

Talana Hill Royale 1992 (blend, see text above): Fine, deep red; luscious nose of black fruit, blackberries and cassis; same full, ripe fruit in the mouth, with *goût de terroir* and big structure – one to lay down.

Vriesenhof Auction Blend 1991 (special barrel selection for annual Cape Independent Winemakers' Guild auction, blend of Merlot and Cabernets): Deep, dense red; rich, rounded fruit bouquet with some oakiness; this is a big wine, with lots of tannins, but all the other elements there to make a memorable bottle in 2 or 3 years that will then keep and improve.

Vriesenhof Auction Blend 1992: Same dense, bluey red as 1991; powerful fruit, with touch more oak than 1991 on nose; lovely, rounded fruit, tannins softer, but lots of good backbone for keeping – I marginally preferred it to the '91.

Technical Notes

Area under vines: Vriesenhof – 16 hectares; Talana Hill – 7 hectares

Cultivars planted
Vriesenhof: Cabernet Sauvignon, Cabernet Franc, Pinotage, Pinot Noir
Talana Hill: Chardonnay, Merlot, Cabernet Franc

Wines produced
WHITE: Paradyskloof Chardonnay/Sauvignon Blanc, Vriesenhof Chardonnay, Talana Hill Chardonnay
RED: Paradyskloof Red Blend, Paradyskloof Pinotage, Vriesenhof

Cabernet Sauvignon, Vriesenhof Kallista, Talana Royale, Vriesenhof Auction Blend

Useful Information

Owner/Winemaker: Jan Coetzee
Sales Enquiries: Liza Kriek, André Haasbroek
Address: Vriesenhof, Box 155, Stellenbosch 7599
Telephone: 021.880.0284 *Fax*: 021.880.1503

Tasting/Sales: by appointment only

RUSTENBERG

Situated on the edge of the rather unattractive Stellenbosch suburb of Cloetesville, Rustenberg is, in fact, everybody's idea of what a Cape farm should look like and be like. There is a timeless and peaceful beauty about the thatched and gabled Cape Dutch buildings, constructed around a square of lawn and shaded by ancient oaks. There are two homesteads, which house offices and the tasting-room, the cattle-shed which houses Rustenberg's beautiful dairy herd, and the winery, built in 1792 and still in use today. Rustenberg is an amalgam of three farms – Schoongezicht, meaning beautiful view in Afrikaans, Glenbawn, which is a fruit farm, and Rustenberg itself.

This is a 1,000-hectare estate, and is polycultural. There is a large fruit farm, a dairy herd, sheep and vineyards – pastures, orchards and vines climb up and away from the farm on the west, south-west and east-facing slopes of the Simonsberg. The present owner Simon Barlow's father, Peter Barlow, bought Rustenberg in 1940, and Schoongezicht five years later. Glenbawn, the fruit farm, was added later still. Wine has been bottled here continuously since 1892, a record thought to be unmatched by any other estate. Another curious fact, which may be due to the air, the quality of the wine, or just the quality of life in general at Rustenberg, is that there have only been three winemakers in the last one hundred years. An English immigrant named Alfred Nicholson came here to help the owner, John X. Merriman to re-establish the fruit farms and the vineyards following the devastation of phylloxera in the late 1890s. He was followed by his son, Reg Nicholson, in 1945. Reg was joined by Etienne le Riche, a graduate in Oenology and Agricultural Economics from Stellenbosch University in 1974, and was succeeded by him on his retirement the following year. Etienne le Riche is still responsible for winemaking today.

Simon Barlow took over management of the estate in 1987, but lives at his own farm, Nooitgedacht, near Somerset West, where he also has vineyards on the slopes of the Helderberg. The vines are mainly Merlot and Cabernet, with Chardonnay and Sauvignon Blanc for white wine. The first wines, also made by Etienne le Riche, were produced for Lay & Wheeler of Colchester, England in 1994, and are sold under the name Westpeak.

The approach to winemaking at Rustenberg has always been very traditional, and even now open fermenters are still in use for the red wine, whilst the white wines are allowed to settle in stainless steel tanks, inoculated and then transferred to oak casks for fermentation, followed by a period on the lees. Like Reg Nicholson before him, Etienne insists on the use of the vineyard's own natural yeasts in the red wines. The first disciple of this tenet that I came across was Peter Vinding Diers, who was making the wine at Château Rahoul in the Graves in the early '80s. All this talk of yeast strains was quite new and revolutionary to the Bordeaux winemakers at that time, although their importance is now universally recognized. Imagine my surprise when Etienne le Riche showed me a copy of my Bordeaux book, telling me that it was a present to him from Peter Vinding: 'He worked here as a trainee, you know.' It would seem that the Old World can still learn a few things from the New-World wine producer.

The wind of change is blowing gently in the vineyards at Rustenberg: a programme of introduction of new clones has been launched by viticulturist Kevin Watt, with the assistance of consultant John Pienaar. It is early days, however, and it will be a year or two before we see the effects of introducing new-clone Cabernets into Rustenberg's blends. One change brought about by this programme does not seem to have done Rustenberg any harm – Etienne le Riche found that new-clone Cinsaut does not produce the fruit intensity that the old vines used to add to Rustenberg's old favourite, Dry Red. He has replaced most of the Cinsaut in the blend with Merlot, and nobody has so far complained.

The four mainstay wines of Rustenberg are Cabernet Sauvignon,

Rustenberg Gold (a Bordeaux blend), Dry Red (a blend of Cabernet, Merlot and Cinsaut) and Pinot Noir. For the export market they are also producing a Merlot/Cabernet blend, Chardonnay, Sauvignon Blanc and a 'Vintage Port'.

Tasting Notes

Sauvignon Blanc 1995: Pale straw; big, up-front, gooseberry fruit; classic asparagus/grassy Sauvignon with nice length and correct fruit/acid balance.

Chardonnay 1995 (one-third fermented in new oak, 3 months on lees, two-thirds no wood): Pale straw; nice citrussy nose; good lemony/grapey fruit, some weight and nice balance.

Dry Red 1993: Good deep colour; ripe nose of black fruits; medium body, good fruit, well-structured, fine value.

1993 Merlot/Cabernet (export only): Medium red; nice fruit with some oak on nose; good open fruit aromas on palate, with soft, smooth finish.

Cabernet Sauvignon 1992: Nice medium red; nose of cassis; a well-balanced wine, with good fruit, some structure and a long aftertaste, will keep.

Cabernet Sauvignon 1986: Colour holding well; rounded, ripe-fruit nose; same rounded fruit in mouth, hint of strawberry, still has good structure, excellent.

Rustenberg Gold 1992: Brilliant mid-red; black fruit and vanilla on nose; fruit good with backbone and soft tannins.

Pinot Noir 1992: Bright, medium red; nice fruit with some farmyard; good mixture of Burgundian vegetation and fruit, with some good tannins and structure.

'Vintage Port' 1990 (80% Souzao with Cabernet, bottled in 3rd year after wooding in large vats): Deep, dense red; very powerful ripe fruit nose; plummy, figgy fruit, great length and concentration.

Technical Notes

Area under vines: 65 hectares, 85% red, 15% white

Cultivars planted
WHITE: Chardonnay, Sauvignon Blanc
RED: Cabernet Sauvignon, Merlot, Cabernet Franc, Pinot Noir, Cinsaut
'PORT': Souzao, Touriga Nacional

Wines produced
RED: Cabernet Sauvignon, Gold (Bordeaux blend), Dry Red (Cabernet, Merlot, Cinsaut), Pinot Noir

Export only
WHITE: Chardonnay, Sauvignon Blanc
RED: Merlot/Cabernet, Vintage Port

Useful Information

Owner: Simon Barlow
Winemaker: Etienne le Riche
Marketing: Charles Withington
Address: Rustenberg Estate, Box 33, Stellenbosch 7600
Telephone: 021.887.3153 *Fax*: 021.887.8466

Tasting/Sales: Weekdays 08.30 to 17.00, Saturday 09.00 to 14.00
Facilities: Picnics (bring your own) encouraged under the oaks

NEETHLINGSHOF

One of the most imposing of the South African wine estates, Neethlingshof is hard to miss. Five miles west of Stellenbosch on the Kuils River road, the gateway is flanked by flags of fourteen nations. To the right is a small lake from the centre of which a fountain rises about fifteen metres into the blue South African sky. A magnificent avenue of pines leads you up the one-kilometre drive to the beautifully restored estate buildings.

The first recorded owner of the land was a German immigrant called Willem Barend Lubbe, to whom it was granted by Simon van der Stel in 1692. The wheel has now come full circle, for the present owner, Hans-Joachim Schreiber, is also German-born. A banker and financier by profession, Schreiber retired from his post as a Managing Director of the Dresdner Bank of Frankfurt in 1981. He had spent 40 years with the bank, finishing up in charge of the Treasury, Money Market, Precious Metals and Foreign Exchange activities. Schreiber had extensive dealings with South Africa as a bank executive, and became convinced that, in spite of the uncertain and sensitive political climate at the time, there was great investment potential in South African wine. His first purchase was Klein Welmoed, which is not a wine farm, followed by the old Alphen property, now renamed Stellenzicht, which was bought from the Bairnsfather-Cloete family in 1981. Neethlingshof, the jewel in the Schreiber crown, was acquired in 1985.

Originally, the land that is now Neethlingshof was christened 'De Wolwedans' by Willem Barend Lubbe. This translates as 'Dance of the Wolves', and probably refers to packs of jackals. After a number of other owners, the land was acquired by the Neethling family in 1816, and it is from them that the estate took its present name. Johannes Henoch Neethling was evidently a bit of a lad, and became known as 'Lord' Neethling for his flamboyant dress and lifestyle. It was he who completed the elegant homestead, started by Charles Marais, the previous owner. Neethling sold the estate to his son-in-law, Jacobus Louw, in 1871. It may be that his profligate life had forced this decision upon him, for he also had three sons, and would surely have left it to them had he been in a position to do so.

The property remained in the Louw family until 1963, when Nico Louw sold it to Jannie Momberg of Middlevlei, and his cousin 'Stil Jan'. At this time, Neethlingshof was known as being one of the best wine farms in the area, but Jan was far from happy with the winemaking facilities, and made no wine there until he had modernized the winery to his exacting standards. In fact, from 1963 until the early 1970s, all the grapes from the estate were sold to Stellenbosch Farmers' Winery. By the time that Hans-Joachim Schreiber bought Neethlingshof in 1985, Jannie Momberg had become the sole owner, having sold his share in Middlevlei to Stil Jan, and bought Stil Jan's share in Neethlingshof.

A programme of investment, building and replanting of the vineyard on an enormous scale followed Schreiber's purchase of Neethlingshof, and it is only now, ten years later, that the results are there to be seen as well as tasted. The most radical part of Neethlingshof's redevelopment took place in the vineyard, where detailed viticultural research and soil analyses were undertaken. These investigations were followed by large-scale up-rooting of redundant and unsuitable vines, and replanting with new, virus-free clonal selections on sites especially chosen to suit each varietal. There are currently some 160 hectares of vines planted on the slopes of the Bottelary hills, mainly facing east towards the Helderberg and south towards False Bay and varying in altitude between 70 and 282 metres above sea-level.

In the early years of Schreiber's wine venture, winemaking was in the hands of ex-Nederburg guru Gunter Brozel, who designed the superb facilities at Stellenzicht, and then at Neethlingshof. Both Schalk van der Westhuizen at Neethlingshof and André van Rensburg at Stellenzicht agree on one thing, that the quality they are now achieving in both places is certainly in some measure due to the technical excellence and versatility of Brozel's designs. Schalk van der Westhuizen was born in 1953 on the estate, where his father was Estate Manager for 30 years. Having studied viniculture, he became Neethlingshof's winemaker in 1973; in 1985 Schreiber made him Farm Manager, and it was under his supervision that the vast and all-important reconstruction of the vineyard was carried out. Now that this vital task is complete, Schalk is back in the cellar doing what he loves best and does exceedingly well – making the wines of Neethlingshof.

The refurbishment and restoration of Neethlingshof's historic buildings is now finished. The old manor-house is now the Lord Neethling Restaurant, where excellent food is served to complement Neethlingshof, Stellenzicht and other top South African wines, and next door the Palm Terrace Restaurant offers more informal sustenance. The original homestead now holds the reception and a suite of very comfortable and modern offices. Across the square from these three buildings are the winery and cellar – completely restructured to house the latest in high-tech vinification equipment with an astonishing 1.8 million litre capacity – and a state-of-the-art maturation area. Living and working conditions for vineyard, cellar and estate workers were matters of importance in Schreiber's plans, and he has developed a model village of 26 self-contained houses, a crèche, community-hall and playground.

For all the wines made at Neethlingshof, the emphasis is on

quality above everything else. This has been achieved firstly by the vineyard improvement programme described above – when Schreiber took over here, production was 80% Chenin Blanc, and not all of very high quality. Low yields also mean high quality and good concentration – the average at Neethlingshof is between 6 and 10 tons per hectare, or 39 to 45 hectolitres per hectare. These sort of yields are achieved by pruning, green harvest when necessary and minimal irrigation – in fact it is only possible to irrigate about one-third of the total vineyard area at all.

In the past, Neethlingshof's main claim to fame was for the quality of its Noble Late Harvest wines. These, mainly from Weisser Riesling, are still consistent prize-winners – indeed a Neethlingshof N. L. H. was one of the very few SA wines to win its category in the recent, rather ill-conceived Australia v. South Africa wine Test Match. But the whole range of Neethlingshof's wines, reds and dry whites as well, are now figuring regularly among the Veritas Gold Awards, on SAA's wine lists, and in many international wine competitions.

Like so many of South Africa's estates, wineries and co-operatives, Neethlingshof is totally geared to the receiving of visitors. For a modest charge, you can taste the whole range of wines produced on the estate, as well as those of Stellenzicht, seven days a week, all the year round, except on Christmas Day, New Year's Day and Good Friday. Tours of the cellar are arranged on request, and the latest facility is the Vineyard Tour – this includes a tour of the cellars, a trip round the vineyards in a comfortable tractor-drawn trailer, ending high up at 'Ilanga', a specially constructed, open-sided shelter with unbelievable views of the surrounding vineyards, mountains and the ocean. Here you taste the range of wines, and then partake of a sumptuous *braavleis*, washed down with the wine of your choice. The all-inclusive price of this tour is R75.00 per person, with children at half-price (the charge is increased between 1 December and 15 January to R95.00).

Hans-Joachim has achieved a great deal in the fifteen years since he first bought land in the Cape, and the beauty of his properties as much as the success of his wines must be a source of tremendous personal satisfaction. He is also giving a great deal back to South Africa in the process, since the two things that this country needs most are foreign investment and export. Schreiber is very conscious of the environment, and this is reflected in the way that his vineyards are run. He is also extremely aware of the social problems that beset the new South Africa, and he has shown generous financial support to the Nelson Mandela Children's Fund. I would also like to add a personal word of thanks to Hans-Joachim for his unstinting help during my stay in South Africa, and in particular for his generous hospitality in allowing me the use of the beautiful apartment at the Stellenzicht Mountain Winery.

Tasting Notes

Sauvignon Blanc 1995 (Veritas Gold): Pale golden; good, up-front Sauvignon fruit on nose; crisp, clean fruit with right balance of acidity.

Chardonnay 1995 (50% fermented in mixture of new American and 2nd- and 3rd-fill French oak, then kept 3 months on lees): Pale straw; good fruit on nose with oaky hints; ripe and full in the mouth, with just the right amount of wood.

Cape Riesling 1995: Good bright colour; fresh bouquet; easy-drinking, grapey fruit with slight 'spritzig'. Good for summer drinking and picnics.

Blanc de Noir 1995 (blend of Cabernet Franc and Cabernet Sauvignon): Palest onion-skin pink; surprising – for a white wine – Cabernet nose; off-dry, nice fruit and good length.

Weisser Riesling 1995: Pale straw colour; delicate table-grape nose; elegant, light and fruity with a touch of sweetness.

Neethlingshoffer 1995 (blend of Weisser and Cape Riesling, Gewürztraminer, Sauvignon Blanc, Bukettraube and Chenin Blanc, 12.2 g/l sugar): Clear, pale straw; nose quite shy, but good fruit coming through; lots of quite sweet ripeness, and good length.

Gewürztraminer 1995: Greeny gold; spicy Traminer nose; lots of ripe and spicy fruit in the mouth, but lacks acidity.

Neethlingsrood 1992 (blend of 45% Cabernet Sauvignon, 45% Shiraz, 10% Merlot): Good, deep colour; powerful Shiraz nose; a big, mouth-filling wine, with soft tannins and some spine.

Merlot 1993: Nice medium red; black fruit bouquet; easy middle-weight, very slurpable, but has some keeping character.

Shiraz 1993: Deep red; 'hot-stone' nose of Rhône from Shiraz; good, fat ripe fruit, some nice tannins and a bit of structure, but ready now.

Pinotage 1993: Dark red; soft nose with hint of banana; a pleasing, easy wine, with some character.

Cabernet Sauvignon 1992: Bright, medium red; clarety cassis on nose; an easy-drinking Cabernet, with ripe fruit and some soft tannins.

Lord Neethling Reserve 1992 (blend of 67% Cabernet Sauvignon, 18% Merlot, 15% Shiraz): Dark ruby colour; blackcurrant nose; loads of good, ripe fruit and a lot of backbone. Will keep 5 years and more.

Weisser Riesling Noble Late Harvest 1995: Medium-deep gold; lovely nose of beeswax and honey; lovely, rich and complex, with lots of botrytized fruit, tremendous concentration.

Technical Notes

Area under vines: 155 hectares

Average yield: 6 tons per hectare

Average production: 80,000 to 100,000 cases

Cultivars planted
WHITE: Chenin Blanc, Chardonnay, Sauvignon Blanc, Cape Riesling, Weisser Riesling, Bukettraube, Muscat de Frontignan, Gewürztraminer
RED: Cabernet Sauvignon, Cabernet Franc, Merlot, Shiraz, Pinotage, Tinta Barocca, Pinot Noir

Wines produced
WHITE: Sauvignon Blanc, Chardonnay, Weisser Riesling, Cape Riesling, Gewürztraminer, Neethlingshoffer
RED: Cabernet Sauvignon, Merlot, Shiraz, Pinotage, Neethlingsrood

Useful Information

Owner: Hans-Joachim Schreiber
Winemaker: Schalk van der Westhuizen
Farm Manager: Jaco van den Berg
General Manager Marketing: Guy Kedian
Address: Neethlingshof Estate, Box 104, Stellenbosch 7599
Telephone: 021.883.8988 *Fax*: 021.883.8941

Tasting/Sales: Weekdays 09.00 to 17.00, Saturday/Sunday 10.00
to 16.00; closed Christmas Day, New Year's Day and Good
Friday; cellar tours on request
Facilities: Vineyard Tours, including tasting; *Braavleis* with wine
of your choice, at R75.00, booking essential. Tours depart
Neethlingshof at 11.00, 12.00 and 13.00; Lord Neethling and
Palm Terrace Restaurants – Telephone 021.883.8966

STELLENZICHT MOUNTAIN WINERY

The vineyards of Stellenzicht were bought by German financier
Hans-Joachim Schreiber in 1981. The previous owners were the
Bairnsfather-Cloetes, and the wines that they made there were sold
under the Gilbey's Alphen label. This family are direct descendants
of the original Hendrik Cloete, who was responsible for making
the dessert wine of Constantia into one of the world's most sought-
after wines among the courts of Europe in the late eighteenth
century. This perhaps gives a clue to the potential of this 228-
hectare estate, for no member of this illustrious wine family would
waste time or effort on land that was anything less than prime.

Site, soil and micro-climate are all favourable for the vine – 150
hectares are currently planted on the slopes of the Helderberg
mountain between 100 and 400 metres above sea-level, which
benefit from the cooling breezes off the Atlantic only six kilometres
to the south. The potential for making fine wine here is confirmed
by the neighbouring estates – Jan 'Boland' Coetzee's Vriesenhof
and Talana Hill lie to the immediate north, and Rust-en-Vrede and
Alto to the south. If you add to the natural advantages of Stellenzicht the far-sighted attitude and investment policies of Hans-
Joachim Schreiber, the lively interest on the part of consumers
worldwide in quality wine from South Africa, and a highly talented

and ambitious winemaker, you have an unexploded wine-bomb of momentous scale.

After purchasing the estate, exactly as he was to do five years later at Neethlingshof, Schreiber set about an extensive replanting programme in the Stellenzicht vineyard, in conjunction with the building of a massive high-tech winery. The latter was also designed by the vinification master Gunter Brozel, formerly *éminence grise* of Nederburg. The winery is superbly equipped with all that is best in vinification equipment: temperature-control, mash-cooling and a spacious, air-conditioned and humidified wood-maturation cellar, housing a huge range of large capacity wooden vats and small American and French oak casks.

André van Rensburg is, as I write these words, in the middle of his fourth vintage at Stellenzicht. After a brilliant academic career at Stellenbosch University, André cut his winemaking teeth at Saxenberg and then Warwick. He is one of several very special people that I have been lucky enough to meet during the time I have spent writing about wine, and I count myself privileged to call him friend. His knowledge of every aspect of viticulture and vinification, not only in South Africa but worldwide, is encyclopaedic, and he is more than willing to share his secrets and his tremendous enthusiasm. During my six-week stay in the apartment at Stellenzicht, André gave me a generous amount of his very valuable time, patiently explaining what he does and how he does it and, just as importantly for me, how everybody else does it.

Although he is, in my opinion, one of the best winemakers in the Cape today, André is not part of what is loosely termed 'the establishment'. One of his most endearing characteristics is his total lack of guile – what he wants to say, he says, and hard luck on anyone who does not like it. He charges through life with all the finesse of an enraged buffalo, but underneath all the shouting and swearing beats a heart of pure gold, and a degree of sensitivity and artistry without which it would be impossible for him to produce the quality of wines for which Stellenzicht is becoming renowned.

He has two varieties to which he is particularly dedicated, the Sémillon and the Shiraz – his winemaking talent with both cultivars is clearly demonstrated in the Stellenzicht Sémillon 1995, and the Shiraz 1994 and 1995. André's dream is to spend a vintage with Guigal in the northern Rhône, and I hope very much that this can

be arranged. There is a small plot of Viognier planted at Stellenzicht: could André's plan be to emulate the master by incorporating
some of this idiosyncratic white grape into the Stellenzicht Shiraz?

Towards the end of 1995 the wine Test Match took place
between Australia and South Africa, organized and sponsored by
SAA. I am not sure that the timing was right, as South Africa, in
spite of the incredible strides made in the last three years, has only
been exposed to international market forces for a very short time.
The result was fairly predictable, and out of 100 categories, Australia won 88, and South Africa only 12. I relate this tale again
because Stellenzicht had two wines placed respectively 2nd and
3rd in their categories – Shiraz 1994 and Sauvignon Blanc 1995.
To André's great delight, his Shiraz beat the redoubtable Grange
by several places and, as he is not slow to point out, the Stellenzicht
wine sells at approximately one tenth of the price commanded
by its Antipodean counterpart. Subsequent accolades include a
staggering success at the Canadian Mondial international wine
competition in 1996. Out of 1,715 entries from all over the world,
only 25 wines were given gold medals. Three of these were from
South Africa, and only one from Australia. Of the South African
golds, two were awarded to Stellenzicht wines – the 1994 Shiraz,
which was also classified best South African wine, and the 1995
Chardonnay.

Between December 1995 and March 1996, Hans-Joachim
Schreiber has bought three more farms (two of which are neighbouring Thelema on the slopes of the Simonsberg) which will
eventually add a further 90 hectares of prime vineyard to his
holdings. The new vineyards will all come under the umbrella
of Stellenzicht, which promises an interesting challenge for Gyles
Webb.

Tasting Notes

Heerenblanc 1995 (50% Sauvignon Blanc, 25% Sémillon, 25%
Chenin Blanc – no wood): Pale, greeny gold; penetrating green
fruit nose; clean and crisp, nice fruit, good balance – Veritas Gold
and SAA Business Class.

Sauvignon Blanc 1995: Pale, greeny gold again; lovely elder-bark
nose; beautiful fresh gooseberry fruit, aromatic, long and

beautifully balanced – Veritas Double Gold, Stellenbosch Champion White Wine, Champion Sauvignon Blanc.

Sauvignon Blanc/Sémillon 1995 (65% Sauvignon Blanc, 35% wood-fermented Sémillon): Pale straw colour; Sémillon and oak dominate the bouquet; excellent fruit flavours, with oak a bit powerful at the moment; will be better balanced in a year, but all sold out – and probably drunk! Veritas Gold.

Grand Vin Blanc 1995 (51% Sauvignon Blanc, 23% Chardonnay, 16% Sémillon, 10% Auxerrois – all wooded): Pale greeny gold; nice, heavy fruit nose with vanilla; excellent ripe fruit on palate, a structured wine, oak and fruit in harmony.

Chardonnay 1995 (whole bunch pressed, fermentation 1 week in stainless-steel then transferred to a mixture of Nevers and Alliers casks for 6 months on lees): Very pale colour; fruit good on nose with quite strong oak; oak to the fore in the mouth, but will balance out with 6 months in bottle – good for 3 to 5 years.

Sémillon 1995 (100% wood-fermented and aged, 30% new American, rest 2nd- and 3rd-fill French): Pale straw; nose a bit shy at first, but good fruit and some oak beginning to show; a big mouthful of ripe fruit with oak quite strong – leave for a year, and will go on for some time – a star.

Merlot 1994 (25% spends 14 months in small oak, 75% 12 months in large oak vats, fined with fresh egg-whites): Deep, bluey red; open, black-fruit nose; rounded, ripe fruit in the mouth, with surprisingly good tannins and structure for a wine that is only 25% aged in small casks.

Cabernet Sauvignon 1993 (90% Cabernet Sauvignon, which spends 15 months in small wood, then 6 months in large oak vats, 10% Cabernet Franc 1994, all of which was aged in small oak): Good, deep colour; ripe, cassis Cabernet Sauvignon nose; Cabernet Franc detectable in the mouth by its added softness, but loads of Cabernet Sauvignon structure with ripe tannins – already drinkable, but will train on.

Stellenzicht 1994 (blend of 69% Cabernet Sauvignon, 22% Merlot, 9% Cabernet Franc, all aged separately for 12 months in small wood, then blended and aged for a further 6 months in small wood with egg-white fining): Dense, blackish red; very concentrated blackfruit nose; a really big, mouth-filling wine, with excellent ripe fruit, soft tannins and backbone – needs 5 years, and will then keep for many more.

Shiraz 1994 (92% Shiraz, 8% Merlot, 12 months in 25% new American oak 75% 3rd- and 4th-fill French): Very deep, dense red; big, northern Rhône nose; huge, fat mouthful of ripe fruit, with big but non-aggressive tannins – will be a great bottle in time.

Shiraz 1993 (85% old clones, 15% new): Paler colour than 1994; soft, open fruit nose; easier drinking old-style Shiraz – won Veritas Gold, while 1994 only took silver!

Sauvignon Blanc/Sémillon, Noble Late Harvest 1995 (60% Sauvignon Blanc – barrel-fermented and aged, 40% Sémillon – no wood): Medium-pale gold; honey and beeswax nose; luscious, sweet taste of honey and flowers, but has the essential green backbone of all fine botrytized wines.

Technical Notes

Area under vines: 150 hectares

Cultivars planted
WHITE: Sauvignon Blanc, Chardonnay, Sémillon, Chenin Blanc, Auxerrois, Viognier
RED: Cabernet Sauvignon, Cabernet Franc, Merlot, Shiraz, Pinotage

Wines produced
WHITE: Heerenblanc, Sauvignon Blanc, Chardonnay, Grand Vin Blanc, Sémillon, Sauvignon Blanc/Sémillon, Noble Late Harvest
RED: Stellenzicht Bordeaux Blend, Merlot, Cabernet Sauvignon, Shiraz

Useful Information

Owner: Hans-Joachim Schreiber
Winemaker: André van Rensburg

Address: Stellenzicht Mountain Winery, Box 104, Stellenbosch 7600

Telephone: 021.880.1104 *Fax*: 021.880.1107

Tasting/Sales: at Neethlingshof, q. v.

ZEVENWACHT

Zevenwacht is an impressive 353-hectare estate on the Bottelary Hills between Stellenbosch and Kuils River, with wonderful views over False and Table Bays. The name is an elision of the names of two estates put together in 1979 by the Cape Town architect Gilbert Colyn, who bought first Zevenfontein, and then the next-door property of Langverwacht. At that time Colyn already had a farm, Avonduur, on the Helshoogte Pass, which is now known as Delaire. It could have been the ownership of this fine but small vineyard that fired Colyn to make wine on a far bigger scale, or it could have been an atavistic inclination from his ancestral connections with the Colijns of Groot Constantia. Whatever the motivation, it may be that he bit off more than he could chew. Zevenfontein at the time of purchase was very run down, and the entire vineyard had to be replanted, extensive building and restoration work was necessary on both properties, and a new cellar had to be built. In 1992 the entire property was sold to Harold Johnson, a construction engineer and property developer, who coincidentally also has a farm near the Helshoogte Pass, Zeven Rivieren, from where the grapes come for the Private Collection range.

Harold and his wife Denise are an energetic couple with a lot of vision, and have already invested much in the way of both resources and effort at Zevenwacht. The results are there to be seen. Apart from being a serious wine estate, Zevenwacht is very much geared to the conference business. As well as the Look Out Conference Centre, high up among the vines, there is a large party and conference suite called the Al Fresco within the winery complex; an excellent restaurant overlooking the dam in the old manor-house; and an amazing network of picnic and *braai* sites, some complete with bar, around the banks of the dam. In addition, a fourteen-suite inn with further conference facilities is under construction for completion in 1996.

At the moment there are about 170 hectares under vines at Zevenwacht, with another 32 hectares under preparation, and 10 more planned for the future. Production is at present split roughly equally between red and white wine, and the winemaking, having been for some years in the hands of Eric Saayman, has passed into the able care of Hilko Hegewisch, late of Boschendal.

Tasting Notes

Sauvignon Blanc 1995: Pale straw; grassy, asparagus nose; clean, crisp fruit with nice acidity and good length – a fine Sauvignon Blanc.

Gewürztraminer 1995: Pale greeny straw; nose has some spiciness, but quite closed; bone dry, clean and crisp with good length.

Rhine Riesling 1995: Pale greenish gold; good fruit and some pepper on nose; slightly spritzig, fresh, dry, grapey fruit with good length.

Chardonnay Zevenrivieren, Private Collection 1995: Pale gold colour; fruit and oak in harmony on nose; some nice Chardonnay fatness in the mouth, fruit and oak together.

Pinot Noir 1994: Brilliant mid-red colour; lovely raspberry nose; excellent Pinot Noir fruit, with some nice tannins and a bit of structure – really good.

Technical Notes

Area under vines: 170 hectares

Cultivars planted
WHITE: Sauvignon Blanc, Gewürztraminer, Chardonnay, Rhine Riesling
RED: Cabernet Sauvignon, Merlot, Shiraz, Pinot Noir

Wines produced
WHITE: Sauvignon Blanc, Rhine Riesling, Gewürztraminer, Bouquet Blanc, Stein

RED: Cabernet Sauvignon, Pinotage, Merlot, Zevenrood, Pinot Noir
Plus: From Harold Johnson's Banhoek vines – Zevenrivieren Chardonnay, Private Collection and Zevenrivieren Shiraz, Private Collection

Useful Information

Owners: Harold and Denise Johnson
Winemaker: Hilko Hegewisch
Address: Zevenwacht, Box 387, Kuils River 7580
Telephone: 021.903.5123 *Fax*: 021.903.3373

Tasting/Sales: 7 days a week 09.00 to 17.00
Facilities: Formal restaurant, coffee terrace, picnic baskets, Malaysian barbecues, Sunday buffet lunch

OVERGAAUW

The Overgaauw farm has been in the van Velden family since 1783, but has been a wine estate only since 1905, when vines were first planted by Abraham van Velden. Abraham's son David took over from his father in 1945, and Braam, the present generation, has been in charge of Overgaauw's 130 hectares since 1978. A total of 70 hectares are planted with vines on south-facing slopes aspected towards False Bay. The soil is mostly Hutton and Clovelly decomposed granite, and the micro-climate, benefiting from the cooling Atlantic breezes, is perfect for the culture of the vine.

Overgaauw has always been a bit of a pioneering estate, and can boast many 'firsts'. David van Velden went to France with Frans Malan of Simonsig to buy casks from Demtos, and Overgaauw became the first estate to age Cabernet Sauvignon in new French barrels. Braam also lays claim to being the estate first to plant a number of different varieties in South Africa, including Cinsaut/Hermitage in 1970, Merlot in 1982, Sauvignon Blanc in 1983 and Chardonnay in 1986. Overgaauw were also the first to plant Sylvaner, and are the only wine estate still making wine from this varietal today. They were also, along with Welgemeend and

Meerlust, the first to make a Bordeaux Blend, which is still made under the name Tria Corda.

In 1949 David van Velden planted a number of Portuguese varieties for the making of 'port', including Tinta Barocca, Tinta Francisca, Sousao, Tinta Roriz, Cornifesto and Malvasia Rey (since grubbed-up). A later addition was the Touriga Nacional, which they made in 1992 as a single-varietal 'Vintage Port'. Apart from the Touriga Nacional, all the 'port' varieties are picked and fermented together in open stainless-steel fermenters, and then aged in large vats of 1,300- and 1,700-litre capacity, plus a little in smaller 2nd- and 3rd-fill casks.

Tasting Notes

Sylvaner 1995: Nice pale gold; aromatic, asparagus nose; lovely crisp, grapey fruit, good balance and length.

Sauvignon Blanc 1995: Pale straw colour; nose fine, but not overpowering; clean, crisp fruit, slight grassiness with nice length – Sancerre style.

Chardonnay 1995 (40% new oak, 30% 2nd-fill, 30% 3rd-fill, fermented and then 6–8 months on lees): Pale straw; nose good, but quite shy; nice fruit there, but wood needs time to soften.

Chardonnay 1991: Quite deep colour; good fruit, white Burgundy nose; fat, buttery, broad palate with oak and fruit in balance and good length.

Pinotage/Cabernet Franc 1994 (60% Pinotage, 40% Cabernet Franc, aged 18 months in 2nd- and 3rd-fill casks): Deep colour; plummy fruit with some leather on nose, Cabernet Franc to the fore; Pinotage comes through in the mouth with slight banana flavours, some structure.

Merlot 1993 (14 days maceration, 24 months in 30% new, 70% 2nd-fill casks): Deep, dense red; open nose of blackberry and blackcurrant; big, soft and ripe, soft tannins and fine structure.

Cabernet Sauvignon 1992: Deep red; cassis and oak nose; fine, balanced wine with fruit and soft tannins, good structure and excellent length.

Cabernet Sauvignon 1988: Very deep colour for an eight-year-old; open cassis nose; very fine, well-balanced, just starting to sing, but loads of fruit, soft tannins and backbone to keep it going for years.

Tria Corda 1988 (65% Cabernet Sauvignon, 25% Merlot, 10% Cabernet Franc): Brilliant medium-dark red; fine, soft, ripe fruit on nose; all elements in harmony, a beautiful Bordeaux blend, just approaching readiness, but with a long future.

'Vintage Port' 1985: Slight tawny tinge; rich, slightly chocolatey nose; nice Christmas Pudding flavours, quite sweet and spirity.

Vintage Touriga Nacional 1992 (single varietal 'vintage port' made for Cape Independent Winemakers' Guild Auction, priced at R1,000 per case): Very deep, almost black colour; rich, ripe dried fruit nose; a huge mouthful of figgy pudding fruit, with big structure and length – very Portuguese in style, to keep for years.

Technical Notes

Area under vines: 70 hectares

Cultivars planted
WHITE: Chenin Blanc, Chardonnay, Sémillon, Sauvignon Blanc, Sylvaner
RED: Cabernet Sauvignon, Cabernet Franc, Malbec, Merlot, Pinotage, Shiraz
'PORT': Tinta Barocca, Tinta Francisca, Sousao, Cornifesto, Touriga Nacional

Wines produced
WHITE: Sylvaner, Sauvignon Blanc, Chardonnay
RED: Cabernet Sauvignon, Tria Corda, Merlot, Pinotage/Cabernet Franc
'PORT': 'Vintage Port', Vintage Touriga Nacional

Useful Information

Owner: Braam van Velden
Winemaker: Braam van Velden with Chris Joubert
Address: Overgaauw Wine Estate, Box 3, Vlottenburg 7604

Telephone: 021.881.3815 *Fax*: 021.881.3436

Tasting/Sales: Weekdays 09.00 to 12.30 and 14.00 to 17.00,
Saturdays 10.00 to 12.30
Facilities: Cellar tours – Wednesday 14.30 and 16.00

MIDDLEVLEI

The 160-hectare farm of Middlevlei was bought by two Momberg
brothers in 1930, and passed into the hands of their two sons,
both called Jan, and known as 'Stil' Jan and Jan 'Bek', or Jan the
Silent and Jan the Mouth. Jan Bek, or Jannie as he is called, is a
public figure of some note, and is currently an ANC member of
parliament. In 1963 he sold his share in Middlevlei to Stil Jan and
bought Neethlingshof. Stil Jan, now the sole owner, shares the
work with his two sons: Tinnie makes the wine, Ben is in charge
of the vineyard and, as Tinnie put it, 'Dad carries the cheque-
book.'

Middlevlei is on the lower slopes of the Papegaaiberg, about a
kilometre up the road from Stellenbosch Farmers' Winery's Oude
Libertas complex. There are 130 hectares under vines, which grow
at between 120 and 240 metres above sea-level. The soil here seems
to suit the Pinotage very well, and Jan has always been successful
with this variety, even during the years when it was out of favour.
The prolific bush-vines are pruned heavily, reducing yield but
improving concentration. The press wine is added to the free-run
juice, and the wine is matured for 16 months in a mixture of 2nd-
and 3rd-fill small oak. Jan's success with this traditionally made
red wine encouraged him to plant Cabernet Sauvignon – the first
vintage was 1981, which was not released until 1985. The practice
with Cabernet Sauvignon is to age the wine for 22 months in 70%
new oak, and 30% 2nd-fill casks, and an excellent, structured wine
is the result – both the 1986 and 1987 vintages won Veritas Double
Golds. There is also a good Shiraz made under the Middlevlei label
and, since 1995, a Chardonnay. Merlot, Cinsaut and Tinta Barocca
are also grown, but the wine is sold in bulk to the Bergkelder, of
which Middlevlei is a member. In addition to the Chardonnay,
Chenin Blanc and Sauvignon Blanc are grown, but are sold as
grapes to the Bergkelder.

The cellar, built in 1941, is simple but functional: fermentation is in cement tanks for the red wines, and all wine movement is by gravity. The system was not designed out of respect for the wine, but simply because there was no electricity at Middlevlei in 1941 on which to run the pumps. Stil Jan, he who carries the cheque-book, has promised Tinnie that if he can guarantee to make better wine five years in a row with new equipment, he will gladly pay for it. It is only the initial stages of vinification that take place in the Middlevlei cellar; all barrel-ageing and bottling are carried out in the Bergkelder's cellars in Stellenbosch. Like the other participating wineries, all Middlevlei's marketing is handled by the Bergkelder, but Middlevlei is one of the few that sell their wine direct to the public from the estate. Visitors cannot fail to be impressed by the immaculately tended gardens and beautifully maintained buildings. Everything about the place is sparkling clean – even the donkey that was rather surprisingly in the tasting-room appeared to have been freshly shampooed.

Tasting Notes

Shiraz 1990: Brilliant, mid-red; open, powerful Shiraz fruit on nose; a medium-bodied wine with very pleasing raspberry fruit and a bit of backbone.

Pinotage 1991: Deep, dense red; ripe blackberry nose; a big mouthful of ripe fruit, nice soft tannins and some structure.

Cabernet Sauvignon 1987: Nice deep colour, just beginning to lighten at the edge; strong cassis and some vanilla on the nose; a ripe and ready wine, but with enough good tannins and skeleton to keep it going for some time.

Technical Notes

Area under vines: 130 hectares

Cultivars planted
WHITE: Chardonnay, Sauvignon Blanc, Chenin Blanc
RED: Cabernet Sauvignon, Pinotage, Shiraz, Merlot, Cinsaut, Tinta Barocca

Wines produced
WHITE: Chardonnay
RED: Pinotage, Shiraz, Cabernet Sauvignon (plus Merlot, Cinsaut
and Tinta Barocca sold in bulk to Bergkelder)

Useful Information

Owner: Jan Momberg
Winemaker: Tinnie Momberg
Vineyard Manager: Ben Momberg
Address: Middlevlei, Box 66, Stellenbosch 7600
Telephone: 021.883.3308

Tasting/Sales: Weekdays 09.00 to 16.00, Saturday 09.00 to 12.00.
Wines also marketed by the Bergkelder

ALTO

Alto is part of a larger estate that used to be called Groenrivier.
Hennie Malan, who owned Groenrivier in 1919, split the land,
and sold half to his brother-in-law. The part that he kept he farmed
with his son Manie, and they christened the new estate Alto, partly
because of the high altitude of the upper slopes, and partly for the
high quality at which they were aiming. At that time there were
few if any vines planted on this steep and narrow strip of land,
and the Malans had a hard task turning Alto into a quality wine-
producing estate.

It is important to remember that only comparatively recently
have most wine farmers enjoyed the benefits of soil analyses, viticultural expertise, and knowledge of and access to the plant
material – rootstocks, virus-free clones, etc. In 1919 the only way
to plan your planting was by instinct, and an all-important feel for
the soil. Fortunately Hennie Malan must have been blessed with
all the right farmer's gut feel, as he decided that the Alto land was
well-suited to the planting of red noble varieties, choosing mainly
Cabernet Sauvignon, plus Cinsaut and Shiraz. The latter two varieties were chosen for purely economic reasons: Cabernet Sauvignon
takes too long to mature for a struggling farmer on a new enterprise, so Hennie decided on a blend incorporating the quicker

maturing, softer wine from these two. This was no bad thing, for it brought about the birth of Alto Rouge, one of the oldest-established and continuously successful South African red wines made and sold on the domestic and export markets. In 1923 Hennie sent samples of his new blend to Burgoyne's, a highly reputable wine merchant of the day in London, who proceeded to place a substantial order for five years' supply – thus forging the first link in a chain that was to last for three decades, and doubtless giving great satisfaction and financial security to Hennie and his son.

Manie Malan continued the tradition at Alto until 1956 when he sold the farm to Advocate Broeksma, Attorney General of the Cape. Piet du Toit, who learned his winemaking from Manie Malan, became winemaker in 1959, and later bought a share in the property. In 1983 he retired and handed over the reins to his genial giant of a son, Hempies, a well-known rugby Springbok. It is perhaps fortunate that the three wine estates currently owned by rugby heroes, Alto, Rust-en-Vrede and Vriesenhof, all make superb wine. Even if their wines were not as good, I am sure that South Africans, who treat the game as a religion, would still flock by the car-load to buy their wine from people who are their equivalent of the twelve disciples.

1968 was an important year for Alto, and for the South African wine industry in general, for it was then that Alto entered into partnership with the giant Distillers Corporation, thus becoming, along with Theuniskraal, the first of the Bergkelder wine estates. Although some of Alto's wine is aged here, the majority goes to the Bergkelder cellars for wood maturation and bottling. Marketing is handled by the Bergkelder and, like a few of the other participating estates, it is only very recently that tastings and sales have been offered at the property.

Although the focus remains on Alto Rouge, a pure Cabernet Sauvignon has been made here for some years. This is made from low-yielding, non-irrigated vines high up on the mountainside, aged in almost entirely new oak, and is always kept in bottle until it is six years old before it is released. The result is an excellent, well-structured wine with firm tannins that keeps extraordinarily well. His 1987 Cabernet won a Gold Medal at Vinexpo 1995, 1986 was nominated Best South African Red at the International Wine and Spirit Competition in London in 1994, and the 1984 won a Grand Prix d'Honneur at Vinexpo in 1993.

The modern blend of Alto Rouge has changed a little since the prototype of the 1920s: up to, and including, the 1989 vintage, this was dominated by Shiraz, which gave a full, gutsy wine of 13.5% alcohol by volume; but this was changed in 1990 to a 78% Merlot majority; and has settled down in 1991, the current release, to a more even mix of 28% Cabernet Sauvignon, 27% Cabernet Franc, 20% Merlot and 25% Shiraz. Apart from these varieties, Hempies also grows some Pinot Noir, which is for inclusion in the Bergkelder's Cap Classique sparkler, Pongracz, named after the colourful Hungarian soldier, who spent some time as viticulturist to the Bergkelder.

Tasting Notes

Alto Rouge 1991: Attractive garnet red; open fruit bouquet, with Shiraz uppermost; good, mouth-filling fruit, with nice soft tannins and a bit of backbone.

Cabernet Sauvignon 1987: Deep red, just starting to shade at edges; nose of ripe, up-front blackcurrant; really nice ripe fruit flavours in the mouth, with soft tannins and some way to go.

Cabernet Sauvignon 1982: Blackish, dense colour (wine unfiltered); terrific nose, lots of ripe, black fruit; this is a stunning, big Cabernet, with a mass of luscious, cassis fruit, beautiful tannins and tremendous structure – a try, and a conversion.

SIMONSIG

Simonsig is very much a family business. Frans Malan is the 'pater-familias', and although supposed to be a semi-retired figure, still has a finger in every pie on this large estate. Pieter is in charge of sales and marketing, Johan is the winemaker and François runs the vineyards. There are currently 270 hectares under vines, and these are on three separate farms, which are all entitled to use the Simonsig estate label.

Frans Malan took over the first farm, de Hoop – which is where the homestead and wine buildings stand today – from his father-in-law in 1953, having obtained an M.Sc. in Oenology at Stellenbosch

University. The farm was at that time a mixed one, but Frans lost no time in improving and enlarging the vineyard and in modernizing the winemaking facilities. Obviously he was well pleased with his early winemaking experience, for in 1964 he bought the nearby Simonsig farm, so named for its wonderful views of the Simonsberg. He put the two farms together, and registered them as a wine estate under the name of Simonsig, since the de Hoop name was not available. In 1980 the third farm, Morgenster, was acquired, situated on the cool slopes near Neethlingshof. As if all this were not enough, a further parcel of vineyard was added, when in 1989 the Malans took a lease on the famous Kriekbult vineyard, which adjoins de Hoop, and is famed for its Pinotage.

Frans Malan has always been at the sharp end of the wine industry, and has served on many committees and boards, legislative, viticultural, tourism – you name it, and he has undoubtedly done it, if not invented it. He it was, for example, with Spatz Sperling, who started the Stellenbosch Wine Route, leading the way for all the other regions to follow. He says that this was in imitation of what he had seen on visits to Europe – but I can vouch that, from both tourist's and wine lover's points of view, South Africa has all the European wine regions knocked into a cocked hat when it comes to visiting, tasting, finding your way around and, most important of all, being made to feel welcome.

Other innovations provided by Frans include the first 'Méthode Champenoise' – now called Cap Classique – sparkling wine to be made in the Cape. The now famous Kaapse Vonkel was first made in 1971, and at that time was made entirely from Chenin Blanc, as was almost everything else. It is now a sparkler of considerable elegance and finesse, made from a classic mixture of 60% Pinot Noir and 40% Chardonnay. He also bottled the first Chardonnay in South Africa in 1978, and was one of the pioneers of 'bag-in-the-box' wines, which he dreamed up in 1975, after losing an important part of his regular sales to Distillers and the Stellenbosch Farmers' Winery.

My first reaction on glancing at the Simonsig price list was one of concern at the number of different wines offered. All too often in the Cape one finds winemakers trying to produce fifteen or more wines from a relatively small vineyard. This is a hangover from the days of a purely domestic market and 'one-stop-shopping': if you did not have a whole range of wines your client simply drove up the road to some farm that did. This often meant poor-quality wines: few winemakers are good at everything and each farm will be suited only to certain varieties. This, however, is certainly not the case at Simonsig. First, Johan Malan does seem to make every wine equally well, and second, with three farms to play with, there are endless combinations of soil, exposure and climate to suit virtually every grape.

Tasting Notes

Chenin Blanc 1995: Pale straw; pleasing, quincy nose; nice, clean fruit, good length.

Cape Riesling 1995: Very pale colour; good fruit on nose; lots of nice grapey fruit, a well-rounded wine.

Chardonnay Reserve 1991 (30% fermented in new oak casks, 4 months on lees, one racking and back in cask for another 4 months): Pale golden colour; lovely ripe Chardonnay fruit nose, oak not too strong; a fine, well-balanced Chardonnay, with nice buttery weight.

Dry Weisser Riesling 1991: Beautiful greeny gold; ripe fruit bouquet; long and rich, with lots of nice fruit.

Adelblanc 1994 (Sauvignon Blanc/Chardonnay): Pale straw; good but subdued fruit on nose; clean, crisp and pleasing. (Frans tells me the 1995 has a higher proportion of Sauvignon, and fruit is therefore more accentuated.)

Vin Fumé 1994 (100% Sauvignon Blanc, barrel-fermented, 4 months on lees): Very pale colour; traces of wood on the nose, but too much to hide the Sauvignon fruit; a really good, well-balanced Sauvignon Blanc.

Chardonnay 1995: Palish straw; more wood on the nose than the 1991 Reserve; harmonious on the palate, some nice Chardonnay fatness, very good.

Sauvignon Blanc 1995: Pale golden colour; classic, up-front Sauvignon nose of elder-bark and gooseberry; loads of crisp, asparagussy fruit, slight green peppers, long aftertaste.

Adelberg 1993 (Cabernet Sauvignon, Pinotage, Merlot): Deep red; good fruit nose, with Pinotage to the fore, slight acetone; good fruit, easy-drinker and good value.

Pinotage 1994 (made without wood): Deep colour; ripe berry nose and palate, with some nice tannins.

Shiraz 1992 (18 months wood in 2nd-fill casks): Deep, lively red; strong Rhôney nose of Shiraz; wood very evident in mouth but loads of good fruit – needs time, and will be good.

Cabernet Sauvignon 1992 (18 months in 20% new oak): Very deep colour; rich cassis and vanilla nose; big mouthful of ripe fruit, soft tannins and lots of backbone – a keeper.

Tiara 1991 (100% new oak for 24 months): Fine, deep red; open nose of cassis; well-balanced, ripe fruit and soft tannins, will stay for years.

Mustique 1994 (blend of different Muscats): Pale golden; loads of spicy, grapey fruit on nose; delicious table grape taste, medium dry.

Sonstein 1994 (Bukettraube and Chenin Blanc): Pale gold; clean, grapey nose; luscious, sweet fruit flavours, very long.

Pinotage Rosé 1995: Pale pink; good raspberry fruit nose; fresh, sweetish fruit – a pleasing and refreshing rosé.

Franciskaner 1995 Special Late Harvest (Chenin Blanc and Gewürztraminer): Nice golden colour; grapey nose; ripe and luscious in the mouth, but not at all cloying.

Gewürztraminer 1994 Special Late Harvest: Mid-gold; lychees and roses on the nose; very complex, luscious fruit, but finishes quite dry.

Bukettraube 1990 Noble Late Harvest: Deep, treacle gold; lovely figs and raisins nose; a little like drinking a liquid Christmas pudding – delicious and complex.

To finish the tasting and freshen the palate, I took a glass of the Simonsig Cap Classique, Kaapse Vonkel 1992: this is a high-class sparkler, very much in the Champagne style, which may be partly due to the presence of a Champenoise winemaker at Simonsig during that vintage.

Technical Notes

Area under vines: 240 hectares

Cultivars planted
WHITE: Chenin Blanc, Weisser Riesling, Chardonnay, Clairette Blanche, Sauvignon Blanc, Palomino, Bukettraube, Gewürztraminer, Colombard, Muscat Ottonel, Morio Muscat, Cape Riesling
RED: Cinsaut, Pinotage, Merlot, Cabernet Sauvignon, Pinot Noir, Shiraz

Wines produced
WHITE: Chenin Blanc, Sauvignon Blanc, Weisser Riesling, Riesling, Adelblanc, Chardonnay Reserve, Vin Fumé, Mustique, Gewürztraminer, Franciskaner, Sonstein, Bukettraube Noble Late Harvest
RED: Tiara, Cabernet Sauvignon, Shiraz, Pinotage, Adelberg
ROSÉ: Pinotage Rosé
SPARKLING: Kaapse Vonkel (Cap Classique), Jean le Riche Sec, Jean le Riche Doux

Useful Information

Owners: Malan Family
Winemaker: Johan Malan
Marketing Manager: Pieter Malan
Vineyard Manager: François Malan
Address: Simonsig, Box 6, Koelenhof 7605
Telephone: 021.882.2004 *Fax*: 021.882.2545

Tasting/Sales: Weekdays 08.30 to 17.00, Saturday 08.30 to 12.30 (in low season closed weekdays 13.00 to 14.00)
Facilities: Cellar tours, 10.00 and 15.00

SAXENBERG

The name of this 80-hectare vineyard high above the Kuils river derives from the original grantee, a free burgher named Joachim Sax. The property has passed through many hands, and was bought by the present owner, Swiss real-estate magnate Adrian Bührer in

1989. He and his wife, Birgit, have made the manor-house their home, and are heavily involved with the running of the estate on a day-to-day basis. Thanks to their enthusiasm and investment, winemaker Nico van der Merwe is producing some exceptional wines at Saxenberg. They decided at the outset that they would not register Saxenberg as an estate, as they prefer to have the flexibility to buy in grapes as and when they need them.

Although Saxenberg is historically a white wine estate, and there are more white varieties planted than red, there is currently more red wine being made, aged and bottled here than white – a great deal of the white wine is being sold in bulk on both the domestic and export markets. Nico certainly seems to be more interested in, indeed passionate about, the making of red wine and is fascinated by the role of wood in the maturation process. We tasted many cask samples, including an excellent, black, concentrated Pinotage 1995 from a new American oak cask, a deeply coloured Merlot from new French oak, two different clones of Cabernet Sauvignon and a superb Shiraz.

Tasting Notes

Sauvignon Blanc 1995: Pale golden; elegant gooseberry and elderflower bouquet; same grassy, gooseberry fruit on palate, clean, crisp and bone dry.

Chardonnay 1994 (two-thirds in 4 different new oaks): Pale, greeny gold; vanilla and fruit bouquet; all elements together, oak, fruit and acidity, with some nice fatness – good.

Shiraz 1993: Powerful Rhôney nose; a very big mouthful of ripe, black fruit – a super fat wine, one of John Platter's rarely awarded five-star wines, and deservedly.

Technical Notes

Area under vines: 80 hectares, to be increased to 100

Cultivars planted
WHITE: Sauvignon Blanc, Chardonnay
RED: Cabernet Sauvignon, Merlot, Shiraz, Pinotage

Wines produced
WHITE: Sauvignon Blanc, Chardonnay, Les Deux Mers
Chardonnay/Sauvignon Blanc, Les Deux Mers Bouquet Blanc,
Noble Late Harvest Le Rêve de Saxenbourg
RED: Cabernet Sauvignon, Pinotage, Shiraz, Merlot (plus all these
in 'Private Collection' range)
SPARKLING: Le Phanton Brut, Cap Classique

Useful Information

Owners: Adrian & Birgit Bührer
Winemaker: Nico van der Merwe
Address: Saxenberg, Box 171, Kuils River 7580
Telephone: 021.903.6113 *Fax*: 021.903.3129

Tasting/Sales: Weekdays 09.00 to 17.00, Saturday 09.00 to 16.00
Facilities: Restaurant, Ralph's at The Guinea Fowl

UITKYK

The early history of Uitkyk is of only passing interest, since from
1712, when it was granted to one Jan Oberholzer, the estate was
mainly used for sheep and cattle. In the late eighteenth century, it
was bought by the legendary Martin Melck, ancestor of the late
Ronnie Melck of Stellenbosch Farmers' Winery, and latterly of
Muratie. Martin Melck was a wine farming pioneer, and possessed
many vineyards, all of them of high quality, including the present-
day Kanonkop, Uitkyk, Elsenberg and Muratie. Uitkyk passed
from Melck to his son-in-law, Johan David Beyers, who was an
ancestor of Beyers Truter, winemaker at Kanonkop today, and
'King of Pinotage'. This came as a complete surprise to Beyers,
who did not know of the connection when he arrived at Kanonkop
for the first time, and was amazed to see a number of tombstones
in the local churchyard bearing the name Beyers. Kanonkop was
part of the Uitkyk estate until 1930, when Baron Hans von Carlowitz bought the major part of the property.

Carlowitz, a Prussian nobleman, was really the first to recognize
the potential of the high slopes of Uitkyk for the growing of vines.
The farming activities were divided into three parts – wheat on the

lower land, vines on the middle slopes, and timber on the highest and steepest land. The Baron's two sons were given charge of the farm: the elder, Hans, ran the arable and forestry side of things, while Georg, the younger son, was responsible for the vineyards. He planted Chenin Blanc and Cape Riesling for white wine, and Cinsaut and Cabernet Sauvignon for red, and it was from these varieties that two of South Africa's early and enduringly popular branded blends were produced. Carlonet was made from Cinsaut and Cabernet Sauvignon, while the white blend of Uitkyk was Carlsheim. The Carlonet label still exists, but it is now made from 100% Cabernet Sauvignon, and aged for about 18 months in small oak by the Bergkelder.

Von Carlowitz, in spite of all his careful attention to the vineyards and the winemaking, was forced to sell in 1963. The buyer was one Gerry Bouwer, a highly successful entrepreneur, who had the agency for both Chrysler and Singer in South Africa. Bouwer's son-in-law, a dentist named Dr Harvey Illing, gave up his practice and joined his father-in-law as winemaker at Uitkyk, a job at which he excelled.

The Bergkelder are now sole owners of Uitkyk, having recently purchased it from the Illing family, and it is now possible to visit and taste at this historic estate for the first time in decades, as it was always kept as a private house for the Illings. The homestead itself is one of the grander wine farmhouses in the area. It was built by Johan David Beyers in 1788, and the architect was a French immigrant named Louis Michel Thibault, and it has more the appearance of an elegant townhouse of the period than a farm. During the renovations undertaken by the Bergkelder, some fairly spicy murals were uncovered in the hallway, dominated by a buxom female nude above the door.

Tasting Notes

Cape Riesling 1995: Greeny gold colour; nice, grapey fruit bouquet; pleasing, crisp fruitiness.

Sauvignon Blanc 1995: Pale straw; up-front Sauvignon nose; good fruit, but acidity a touch low.

Chardonnay 1993 (50% fermented and aged 3 months in new and 2nd-fill casks, 50% tank-fermented): Pale colour; open

Chardonnay nose with vanilla; plenty of oak, but enough fruit and fatness, a French-style Chardonnay – good.

Chardonnay 1994 (30% barrel-fermented and aged 4 months in new and 2nd-fill casks, 70% tank-fermented, only cask wine had malolactic): Pale gold; oak and fruit on nose; wine developing well, enough oak, good fruit.

Cabernet/Shiraz 1991 (50/50 combination, 15 months new and 2nd-fill casks): Deep colour; Shiraz dominates nose, with smoky hints; fine blend, coming together well, with good fruit, nice tannins and a bit of structure.

Shiraz 1986: Still has good deep colour; gamey, leathery nose, with good fruit; beautiful, old-fashioned Cape Shiraz.

Carlonet 1991 (100% Cabernet Sauvignon, 15 months wood): A fine, deep red; cassis on nose; ripe fruit, soft tannins and good backbone.

Carlonet 1984: Still has good colour; blackcurrant and gaminess on nose; a fine, mature Cabernet with some way to travel yet.

Technical Notes

Area under vines: 180 hectares, plans for 250 in 5 years; 60% white, 40% red

Cultivars planted
WHITE: Cape Riesling, Chardonnay, Sauvignon Blanc
RED: Cabernet Sauvignon, Shiraz, Merlot

Wines produced
WHITE: Cape Riesling, Chardonnay, Sauvignon Blanc
RED: Carlonet, Cabernet Sauvignon/Shiraz, Shiraz

Useful Information

Owners: The Bergkelder
Winemaker/Manager: Theo Brink
Address: Uitkyk Estate, Box 3, Elsenburg Cape 7607
Telephone: 021.884.4710

Tasting/Sales: Weekdays 08.30 to 17.00, Saturday 08.30 to 12.30

UNVISITED

Estates and Wineries: Bertrams Wines, Beyerskloof, Bodega, Delaire, De Trafford Wines, Eikendal, Goede Hoop, Hartenberg, Hazendal (new), Helderenberg (new), Jacobsdal, Jordan, Kaapzicht, Klawervlei, Lanzerac (new), Le Bonheur, Longridge Winery, Meinert Winery, Rozendal, Somerbosch, Spier, Uiterwyk, Veelverjaaght (formerly Petite Provence), Vergenoegd, Vredenheim, West Peak (see Rustenberg), Yonder Hill, Zevenrivieren (see Zevenwacht)

Co-operatives: Bottelary, Helderberg, Koelenhof, Vlottenberg, Welmoed

6

Somerset West and Walker Bay

══════

Although Somerset West officially lies within the Stellenbosch district, it seems sensible to follow John Platter and group it with the wines of the Overberg district. The vineyards are geographically and climatically more akin to those of Villiersdorp, the Bot river and Hermanus than to those in the Stellenbosch area. Vergelegen, for example, lies on the western foothills of the Hottentots Holland mountains, and benefits as much from the cooling sea breezes from Walker Bay as from those from False Bay.

This is a large and mountainous area to the east and south-east of Stellenbosch, extending eastwards to Villiersdorp and south to the attractive seaside resort of Hermanus. The soil is mainly sandy, and farming activities tend more towards the production of wheat and fruit, although there are a few pockets where the classic wine grapes do well. The best of these are in the north-east sector near Somerset West, and the south-eastern corner inland from Hermanus. There is also an increase in the plantation of fine white varieties, particularly Sauvignon Blanc, many of which are bought in by the new breed of *négociant* winemakers like Neil Ellis of Stellenbosch.

VERGELEGEN

Wilhem Adriaen van der Stel, son of Governor Simon, was granted the land at Vergelegen in 1700. Both he and his father were progressive and efficient administrators, though it must be said that if they had a fault, it was a tendency to line their pockets at the expense of the Dutch East India Company, whose servants they were. If the ruling Lords XVII could turn a blind eye on Simon's

Somerset West and Walker Bay

peccadilloes, who engineered himself a land grant of over 800 hectares when the norm was a fraction of that size, they could hardly ignore the scale of his son's gerrymanderings. Quite apart from seizing for himself the vast estate of Vergelegen, his over-weening pride, his arrogance and greed so enraged the free burghers of the Cape that they sent representations to the Lords XVII in Holland, complaining to them about their unjust steward. What-ever they wrote, it was evidently sufficiently damning, for van der Stel, together with the plaintiffs, was summoned to Amsterdam for a court of enquiry. The result was Wilhem Adriaen's permanent exile from the Cape, and the seizure and division of all his lands and properties.

Whatever else he may have been, the Governor was a man of vision and enquiring mind. He was both fascinated and well-versed in matters horticultural and agricultural, and in the short span of his occupation of Vergelegen, turned it into a model estate. By 1706 he had a million and a half vines planted, farmed 1,000 cattle and 1,800 sheep, raised orchards and orange groves, as well as a mass of oaks and camphors; and he engineered an efficient irri-gation system by diverting the Lourens river, and digging channels across his arable lands. In addition he built a magnificent home-stead and farm buildings, surrounding all with a double octagonal wall for fortification. For all his faults, he made a significant contri-bution to the future of farming and winemaking in the Cape.

A succession of owners followed van der Stel's expulsion from Vergelegen. In 1798 it was acquired by the Theunissens, who held it for just over a hundred years. They did much for the vineyards, and built the cellar that was later turned into a library by Sir Lionel Phillips. Following the difficult early years of the century, it was Sir Lionel and Lady Florence Phillips who became the owners of Vergelegen in 1917. Phillips was a 'Randlord', who had made a fortune out of diamonds and gold. They had lived at the splendid Villa Arcadia in Johannesburg, and had Tynley Hall in Hampshire as their English home. They found the homestead and the estate in a sorry state on their arrival, and set out with a will, and a lot of money, to restore the estate to its former glory.

Lady Florence remodelled the house, laid out the lovely gardens much as they are today, built a new bridge to carry motor traffic and had a wall constructed on the foundations of van der Stel's octagonal original. Roads and dams were built, and all the vines were rooted out and the land put to use for mixed farming. On Lady Florence's death in 1941, the estate was bought by Charles 'Punch' Barlow. He did restart the vineyards, but his efforts were not a success, and they were abandoned in 1962. He took great pride in his herd of Jersey cows, but these were sadly wiped out by a batch of poisoned cattle feed. Thereafter the main activity was fruit farming, until his son Tom took over in 1966, who replaced the Jersey herd with Friesians.

Anglo-American Farms Limited, who already owned Boschendal across the mountains in Franschhoek, bought the estate in 1987. The price paid was R2,000,000, for which they got 3,000 hectares of land (about half of which is arable) lying between 75 and 700 metres above sea level, and situated near Somerset West in the foothills of the Hottentots Holland and Helderberg mountains. The company's objective was, and is, to run Vergelegen as a modern polycultural farming enterprise, including the growing of pears, plums, nectarines and soft citrus fruits, running a 1,000-head dairy herd of Holstein/Friesian cattle and the re-establishment of Vergelegen's vineyards.

A two-year period of careful planning followed, during which detailed analyses were made of the varied soils on the estate, and weather statistics were minutely recorded at three automatic and six manually-read monitoring stations. All this information was then studied in order to select the best sites and best plant materials for all the crops planned.

For the vineyards, the plan from the outset has been to produce only a limited range of wines of the very highest quality. To this end, as a result of all the meticulous research and with the help of Boschendal's viticulturist, Gerrie Wagener, the varietals decided upon were Chardonnay, Sauvignon Blanc and Sémillon for white wines, Cabernet Sauvignon, Cabernet Franc, Merlot and Pinot Noir for the reds.

The next step was the construction of a winery, but this had to be something very special, practical, state of the art, and above all it had to blend in with the beauty of this stunning estate. Architectes Associés of Paris were chosen – they had designed the superb new winery, cask cellar, bottling line and visitor centre at Château Pichon Longueville Baron in Bordeaux for Axa Millésimes. Their work at Pichon was done in full consultancy with Axa Millésimes' chief winemaker, Daniel Llose. Consequently all the requirements of fine winemaking were well understood, and the site was chosen on the top of a hill called Rondekop. The top was taken off the hill, rather like decapitating a boiled egg, and a hole excavated to a depth of ten metres to accommodate the structure. The hole is lined with reinforced concrete, and an 800-mm gap left between the excavation wall and the internal, non-structural wall. The sunken cylinder construction allows for gravity-flow, beneficial for the wines, and the insulation provided by the wall cavity makes for much easier temperature control.

Vinification equipment is the best available. Upright, stainless-steel fermentation and storage vats, all equipped with computer-controlled cooling and heating systems and of varying sizes for flexibility, are ranged around the octagonal underground fermentation and blending cellar. Grapes arrive on the upper level, which also acts as a viewing platform for tourists, and are sorted on conveyor belts to remove any leaves, unripe or rotten fruit. The same conveyor belts are used for moving grapes wherever possible, as the traditional augurs are abrasive, and damage the skins unnecessarily. There are two barrel cellars on the lower level, where there is room for 2,000 casks of red and 500 of white wine.

Winemaker Martin Meinert has been with the project from the beginning. He is an intelligent and dedicated winemaker, and has travelled widely in pursuit of further knowledge. He worked frequently with Gilbert Rokwam, late of Château Lafite-Rothschild, even travelling to the Rothschild Los Vascos winery in Chile, and is still just as keen and excited about Vergelegen as he was at the beginning. He is very busy, and I thank him for the time he spent with me, and for the excellent lunch he gave me in Vergelegen's restaurant – from which you can see five of the camphor trees planted by Wilhem Adriaen van der Stel, and which are now classified as a National Monument.

Tasting Notes

Les Enfants Sauvignon Blanc 1992 (first vintage, no wood, lots of bought-in grapes): Quite deep gold; restrained bouquet; clean, crisp Sauvignon, but a touch of greenness.

Sauvignon Blanc 1993 (no wood): Greenish gold; more elder-bark Sauvignon nose; lovely, grapey fruit, elegant and long.

Sauvignon Blanc 1994 (barrel-fermented): Pale greeny gold; nose slightly musty (Martin said this was not a good bottle); fruit OK, but same rather musty flavour as on nose.

Sauvignon Blanc 1995: Very pale straw; nose restrained and not giving much, but fruit emerging; some nice, rather tropical fruit, balance good, and some length.

Les Enfants Chardonnay 1992 (first vintage, 60% barrel-fermented with 6 months on lees, 40% tank, also on lees): Quite deep golden; butterscotch aromas; good fruit, some weight, velvety finish.

Chardonnay 1993: Bright gold; slightly cheesecloth nose; nice fruit, some weight and good length.

Chardonnay 1994: Greeny gold; nose a bit closed, but nice fruit coming out; a touch green and harsh, but fruit there.

Chardonnay 1995 (90% wooded): Pale straw; oaky nose, but good fruit also; nice, lemony fruit on palate, oak evident on taste too, but in balance, good length.

Pinot Noir 1995 (Sainsbury's label): Palish Pinot colour; farmyard and leather on nose; some nice young fruit, but no great pretensions.

Mill Race Red 1993 (76% Cabernet Sauvignon, 24% Merlot): Good, deep red; some nice, chocolatey fruit on nose; a bit green, tannins and fruit lack ripeness.

Mill Race Red 1994 (a bit more Merlot in blend, picked riper): Shade lighter colour than '93; ripe, open bouquet; more smooth, riper fruit and softer tannin.

Merlot 1994: Very deep colour; powerful blackberry nose; a big mouthful of ripe fruit, good tannins and structure.

Merlot 1995: Deep red; nose spicy and peppery; huge and mouth-filling, loads of ripe fruit, with some ripe tannins and a lot of backbone that will keep this one going for years.

Technical Notes

Area under vines: 102 hectares

Cultivars planted
WHITE: Sauvignon Blanc, Chardonnay
RED: Cabernet Franc, Cabernet Sauvignon, Merlot, Pinot Noir

Wines produced
WHITE: Sauvignon Blanc, Chardonnay, Vin de Florence
RED: Mill Race Red, Merlot

Useful Information

Owners: Anglo-American Farms Limited
General Manager: Don Tooth
Winemaker: Martin Meinert
Address: Vergelegen, Box 17, Somerset West 7129
Telephone: 024.517060 *Fax*: 024.515608

Tasting/Sales: Monday–Saturday 09.30 to 16.00
Facilities: Entrance to Heritage Core area – R6 (weekdays, children & pensioners R4); Lady Phillips Tea Garden/Rose Garden – light lunches/teas; winery tours – Monday–Saturday, book by telephone on 024.517061

BOUCHARD FINLAYSON

The motivation that drives people to make wine out of Pinot Noir is difficult to fathom. It is notoriously difficult to grow, and even more difficult to make good wine from. The Burgundians, who are the acknowledged leaders for this variety, get it wrong more often than they succeed. The goal must be triumph over adversity, for when it does come right, a good Pinot Noir with a bit of age ranks with the world's greatest reds. In a totally different way, the same could be said about the Chardonnay, another Burgundian native. The last couple of decades have proved that you can make white wine from this grape virtually anywhere in the world, but to make a great Chardonnay, that is another kettle of fish.

After a long and meticulous search, Tim Hamilton Russell first bought land in the Hemel-en-Aarde valley for the planting of Pinot

THE WINES OF SOUTH AFRICA

Noir and Chardonnay back in 1975. His story is told in the next section, but it is relevant here, for he was joined by Peter Finlayson as winemaker in 1979. Peter, a graduate oenologist of Stellenbosch University, studied further at Geisenheim, and has travelled a great deal, especially to Burgundy, in his quest for knowledge. He also spent three valuable years at Boschendal before joining Hamilton Russell in time to oversee the building of the cellar there.

Peter gained much valuable experience in handling these two tricky grapes at Hamilton Russell, and the wines enjoyed commercial success and acclaim both at home and abroad. In the heart of every winemaker, the ultimate goal is to make wine from your own grapes rather than those of another, and Peter Finlayson was no exception. His ambition was shared by Michael Clark, who worked in the marketing and administration side at Hamilton Russell. In 1989 Paul Bouchard, then head of Bouchard Aîné in Burgundy, came over to act as a judge on the Diners Club Winemaker of the Year Award panel – the winner was Peter Finlayson with the 1986 Hamilton Russell Pinot Noir. The travel bursary that goes with this honour took Peter to Burgundy, where he visited Bouchard, and thus the link was forged that led to the first French investment in Cape vineyards since the Huguenots arrived three hundred years ago. Within a year Peter, together with Michael Clark, left Hamilton Russell and, backed by a syndicate of local businessmen and the all-important Paul Bouchard, bought the next farm up the valley from Hamilton Russell, and set about his plans.

They decided not to register as an estate, since they needed to generate cashflow from the start and had to be free to buy in grapes and make wine immediately. This was all valuable experience, for they managed to source grapes from two particularly good locations, one in Elgin, and the other in Villiersdorp, which they still use to supplement the produce of their own vines. This may have to continue for some while, as demand is strong, and to date there are only 6 hectares of Pinot Noir, 1 hectare each of Chardonnay and Pinot Blanc, plus 2.5 of Sauvignon Blanc.

The Bouchard-Finlayson project was a runaway success from the start, which one cannot help feeling must be a slight thorn in the flesh for Tim and Anthony Hamilton Russell next door. The range now includes a wine blended from Kerner, Rhine Riesling and Gewürztraminer (all bought-in grapes) at the lower end of the price spectrum, as well as Sauvignon Blanc, Chardonnay and the Pinot Noir. Prices are unashamedly high: 'Quality = rigorous selection at all stages = small quantity = high cost,' says Finlayson.

Tasting Notes

Pinot Noir 1995 (from vat): Good, quite deep red for Pinot Noir; good, ripe fruit nose; lots of good, crushed strawberry fruit, with some nice soft tannins.

Pinot Noir 1994 (aged in new oak casks, from Burgundy cooper, where else?): Very good, deep red; a year in bottle has silenced the exuberant bouquet; good fruit, more depth and structure than 1995.

Chardonnay 1995: Pale gold; good fruit with some woodiness; quite lean, with citrussy lemon fruit, some oakiness, and good length.

Blanc de Mer 1995: Nice, pale greeny colour; ripe and spicy nose; lean and racy, nice grapey, spicy fruit and good length.

Sauvignon Blanc 1995: Bright, greeny gold; elderflower nose; loads of gooseberry fruit with Sauvignon grassiness, long.

Sauvignon Blanc 1993 (part barrel-fermented, 9 months on lees): Medium to deep gold; ripe Sauvignon with oak on nose; fruit in harmony with oak, nice length.

Technical Notes

Area under vines: 11 hectares, plus bought-in grapes

Cultivars planted
WHITE: Chardonnay, Sauvignon Blanc, Pinot Blanc
RED: Pinot Noir

Wines produced
WHITE: Blanc de Mer, Chardonnay, Sauvignon Blanc
RED: Pinot Noir

Useful Information

Owners: Bouchard Finlayson
Winemaker: Peter Finlayson
Administration: Michael Clark
Address: Bouchard Finlayson, Box 303, Hermanus 7200
Telephone: 0283.23515 *Fax*: 0283.22317

Tasting/Sales: Open weekdays, Saturday by appointment only

HAMILTON RUSSELL VINEYARDS

From the advertising jungle of J. Walter Thompson to winemaking may seem a curious move, but this is exactly what JWT Chairman Tim Hamilton Russell did in 1975. From his childhood in the Constantia district to his university days in Oxford, Tim had always been exposed to wine. During his student period in England, he formed a particular attachment to the wines of Burgundy, and became determined to prove that it was possible to make Pinot Noir and Chardonnay wines of equal quality in his native Cape.

Having achieved considerable success and financial independence from his business career, he set about realizing his dream. A long and detailed study of soils and climatic conditions led to his choice of the cool Hemel-en-Aarde Valley near Hermanus – the spot benefits from the cool breezes off the bay, whilst being protected from the worst effects of the south-easters by a range of low hills between the vineyards and the ocean.

Planting began in 1976, the cellar was constructed in 1980, and the first vintage was in 1981. The rest is history: the Hamilton Russell Pinot Noirs became internationally famous, and demand was soon outstripping supply, as is the case with all the HRV wines. Production is limited to 22,000 cases, and the problem is not how to sell the wine, but how to allocate it. The quality is still among South Africa's best, and the prices, though relatively inexpensive by European standards for wines of this class, are among the highest for Cape wines.

Tim Hamilton Russell has given me a great deal of help and encouragement, from my first efforts to launch a European-written book on the wines of South Africa in 1987, right up to the period of my researches for this book, and I thank him profoundly for all his help and support over the years. He is now in semi-retirement, living in the most beautiful house at the western extremity of Hermanus. The reins have passed to his son Anthony, a business-school graduate, an ex-merchant banker in London, and now a passionate and voluble wine producer. He is very much an evangelist for the individuality of wines, and the importance of sticking to a style that is not a carbon-copy of something else. Like his father, he is dedicated to quality, which will ensure the continuity of the Hamilton Russell policy of keeping it small, but keeping it good.

Since Anthony's arrival in 1991, there has been a definite wind of change at HRV, though one might describe it more accurately as a breeze. I think it would be fair to say that father Tim's original idea was to make Burgundy, or as near to it as he could manage, whereas Anthony feels that wine should reflect the character of its birthplace. New clones have been introduced and new vinification and viticultural techniques are employed – no matter if they are of New-World or Old-World origin, so long as they are beneficial to the style of HRV's wines.

All the Pinot Noir is aged for at least 18 months in French oak, and the same wood is used for barrel-fermentation of the Chardonnay. Winemaker Kevin Grant, a new arrival for the 1995 vintage, with which he seems to have done wonders, is similarly keen and innovative (though less talkative than Anthony, whom Platter describes as 'the rap artist of the winelands'). The two of them have launched Southern Right Cellars, making Sauvignon Blanc and Pinotage, and a proportion of their profits will go towards research and protection for the Southern Right Whale. Pinotage given the luxury treatment and wood-ageing of the HRV cellars will be an interesting one to watch out for – the '95 vintage is already out, but I have not had the opportunity to taste it.

Tasting Notes

Chardonnay 1994: Good pale golden colour; open citrus and tropical fruit, with some toastiness; rich, smooth lemony fruit with some weight and good length.

Chardonnay 1991: Slightly deeper gold; lemon fruit and wood on nose: more together than 1994, a nice fat Burgundian Chardonnay.

Pinot Noir 1992: Bright, medium-deep red; nice nose of summer fruit with slight mushroom notes; plummy fruit on the palate, with some meatiness and good tannins.

Pinot Noir 1985: Colour quite pale, starting to brown; nose open and ripe with nice fruit; excellent and quite complex Pinot Noir, now approaching peak maturity.

Technical Notes

Area under vines: 56 hectares

Cultivars planted
WHITE: Chardonnay, Sauvignon Blanc
RED: Pinot Noir

Wines produced
WHITE: Chardonnay, Sauvignon Blanc, Chardonnay/Sauvignon Blanc
RED: Pinot Noir

Useful Information

Owners: Hamilton Russell family
Winemaker: Kevin Grant
Address: Hamilton Russell Vineyards, Hemel-en-Aarde Valley, Box 158, Hermanus 7200
Telephone: 0283.23595 *Fax*: 0283.21797

Tasting/Sales: Weekdays 09.00 to 17.00, Saturday 09.00 to 13.00

UNVISITED

Estates and Wineries: Beaumont Wines, Cloete Wines, Goedvertrouw, Hermanus Rivier, Whalehaven, Wildekrans Cellars

7
Paarl

The Paarl wine district lies to the north of Stellenbosch, and is bordered by the town of Wellington to the north-east, and the mountains of the Groot and Klein Drakenstein and Franschhoek ranges to the south-east. The western half, from the foothills of the Paarl mountain to the Perdeberg co-operative in the north and Villiera Estate in the south, is flatter and more given over to fruit and wheat than vines. This low-lying land has an important role, however, in that it allows passage for the cooling Atlantic breezes to the eastern sector.

There are three main types of soil in the Paarl wine district: along the Berg river, which runs through the town of Paarl from the south to the north of the eastern sector, the vines are grown on the sandy soil of Table Mountain sandstone; on the mountain slopes around Paarl and in the south-east the soil is decomposed granite; and in the north-east it is Malmesbury shale. The pH content in the soils of the Paarl district is low, as it is in Stellenbosch, and deep ploughing with liberal application of agricultural lime is necessary during soil preparation. The valley land requires supplementary irrigation in the hot growing season before the harvest, but the vineyards on eastern slopes, having better water retention, frequently need none at all.

Historically Paarl was a region known for the production of fortified wines and sherries; demand for these wines has diminished, and growers, both members of the co-operatives and estate owners, are turning more towards the making of good table wines. The town of Paarl is dominated by the headquarters of the KWV at the southern end of the town, and those of Nederburg to the north.

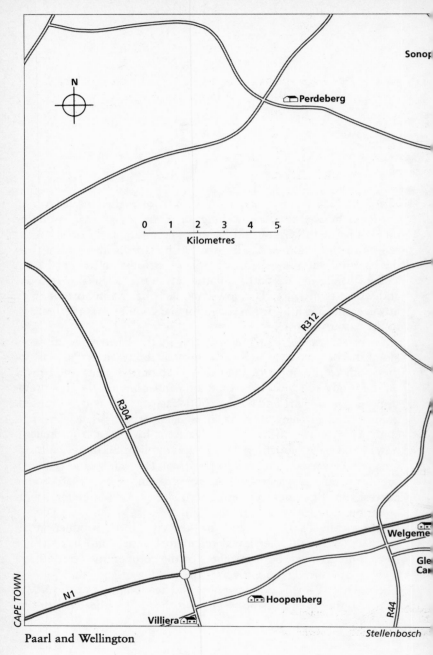

Paarl and Wellington

Stellenbosch

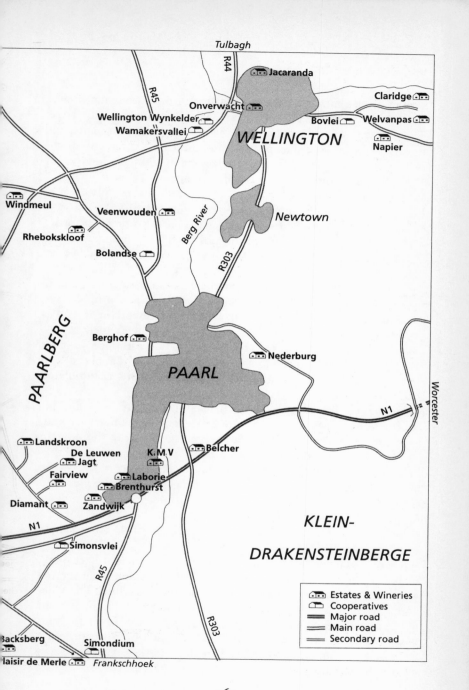

Tulbagh

R44

Jacaranda

Claridge

Onverwacht

Wellington Wynkelder
Wamakersvallei

Bovlei

Welvanpas

WELLINGTON

Napier

R45

Windmeul

Veenwouden

Berg River

Newtown

Rhebokskloof

R303

Bolandse

PAARLBERG

Berghof

Nederburg

PAARL

N1

Worcester

Landskroon
De Leuwen
Jagt

K.M.V

Belcher

Fairview

Laborie
Brenthurst

Diamant

Zandwijk

KLEIN-

N1

Simonsvlei

DRAKENSTEINBERGE

R45

Estates & Wineries
Cooperatives
Major road
Main road
Secondary road

Backsberg

Simondium

R303

Plaisir de Merle

Frankschhoek

BACKSBERG

Sydney Back's father, a Jewish immigrant from Lithuania, bought the farm that was then known as Klein Babylonstoren in 1916. The first wines that he made there were sold under that name, and mostly went either for export to the United Kingdom or to the KWV, always in barrel. Charles Back was joined by his son Sydney in 1938, who proudly made his 58th vintage on the estate in 1996. Father and son laboured mightily to make Backsberg into one of the Cape's leading producers of quality wine.

Not only can they boast an impressive array of prizes to prove their success, but everywhere you go, both in South Africa and overseas, you only have to mention South African wine and Sydney Back's name crops up persistently. Sydney Back is a brilliant wine-maker – Champion Winemaker of the Year in 1978 and again in 1982 at the Cape Championship Wine Show – and a kind, considerate and thoughtful man. Early on in my research trip, I was talking to somebody about the difficulty of choosing which estates, wineries and co-operatives to visit for my book – without a second's pause, the answer came: 'Go and see Sydney Back.' This I did, and he gave me a lot of his time, and the benefit of his accumulated knowledge, which is encyclopaedic.

Sydney was joined by his son Michael in 1975, at the end of his studies in oenology and viticulture at Stellenbosch University and, with the help of winemaker Hardy Laubser, he now shoulders a good portion of the work at Backsberg. This is not to infer that Sydney is taking it easy – the Back seat in this family is always the driving seat. His new, high-quality brandy has just been launched to great acclaim – it won the Domecq Trophy for best brandy at the 1995 International Wine and Spirits show – and he has just planted a new twenty-hectare experimental vineyard, with the help of Australian guru Dr Richard Smart.

There are currently 180 hectares planted with vines at Backsberg, mainly Cabernet Sauvignon, Shiraz, Merlot and Pinotage for red wine and Chardonnay and Sauvignon Blanc for white. The vineyards are mostly on the well-aspected decomposed granite soil of the Simonsberg. Thirty hectares of the estate are down to fruit: twenty of clementines and ten of plums, which both ripen before Christmas, in time for the United Kingdom market. The Backs can also use the picking force before the grape harvest begins.

Sydney has always believed in looking after the home market, and limits his exports to 20% of total production. He has built up an enormous mail-order business, and has offered a three-day service to Johannesburg clients since 1971. He is also proud, and rightly so, of the loyalty of his workforce, who seem to feel very much part of this family-driven estate.

Tasting Notes

Sauvignon Blanc 1995: Nice golden colour; typical, grassy Sauvignon bouquet; asparagus, elder-bark and gooseberries, very long and fine.

Chardonnay 1994 (75% barrel-fermented, batonage for 3 months, total time on lees 8 months): Pale straw; fruit and oak nicely in balance on nose; big, fat, buttery Chardonnay – excellent.

Merlot 1993 (15-year-old vines, 12 months in used casks): Deep red; powerful nose of ripe black fruit; a big mouthful of ripe fruit and soft tannins that is good now and will keep and improve.

Cabernet Sauvignon 1993 (2 weeks maceration, 15 months oak, with not much new wood): Good, deep colour; nose of cassis with minty undertones; clean, ripe fruit with some nice tannins, already drinking well, but will keep a few years.

Klein Babylonstoren 1993 (50% Cabernet Sauvignon, 50% Merlot, 15 months in wood): Very deep colour; open fruit nose, with hint of chocolate; a mass of fruit, non-aggressive tannin and backbone in the mouth – a classy wine to wait a year or two for.

Pinotage 1992 (no small wood used, only 5,000-litre vats): Lovely garnet red; wafts of good fruit – raspberries and plums; a load of good summery fruit, with a bit of structure.

Technical Notes

Area under vines: 180 hectares

Cultivars planted
WHITE: Chardonnay, Sauvignon Blanc, Chenin Blanc, Rhine Riesling, Gewürztraminer, Bukettraube, Hanepoot
RED: Cabernet Sauvignon, Merlot, Shiraz, Pinotage, Pinot Noir

Wines produced
WHITE: Sauvignon Blanc, Chardonnay, Rhine Riesling, Bukettraube, Chenin Blanc, Blanc de Blancs, Hanepoot, Special Late Harvest (Chenin Blanc/Hanepoot), John Martin (barrel-matured Sauvignon Blanc)
RED: Cabernet Sauvignon, Shiraz, Pinotage, Pinot Noir, Merlot, Klein Babylonstoren (blend of Cabernet Sauvignon and Merlot), Backsberg Dry Red
SPARKLING: Backsberg Cap Classique Brut, Backsberg Rosé Sec Cap Classique

Useful Information

Owner: Sydney Back
Winemaker: Hardy Laubser
Vineyard Manager: Michael Back
General Manager: Gerrit Lots
Address: Backsberg Estate, Box 1, Klapmuts 7625
Telephone: 021.875.5141 *Fax*: 021.875.5144

Tasting/Sales: Weekdays 08.00 to 17.30, Saturdays and non-religious public holidays 08.00 to 13.00
Facilities: Closed-circuit TV guide to winemaking process

BOLANDSE CO-OPERATIVE

The Boland Wine Cellar, as it is now called, is one of the largest co-operatives in the coastal area. There are 130 members and the two wineries process around 25,000 tons of grapes every year. As with most of the co-operatives, only a very small percentage is bottled for the domestic market, and even wines destined for sale in bottle on the export market, which represent 10% of total production, are exported to Macon in France in bulk, because bottling costs are much lower there. A further 10% is sold in bulk to the KWV, SFW and Distillers, and a further 20% of the cheaper wines are sold in bag-in-the-box containers, etc.

Both the cellar in Paarl and the one on the Malmesbury road to the north of the town are well equipped with modern vinification plant, including fermentation tanks of varying sizes. This enables winemakers Anthony De Jager and Jacques du Toit to vinify small amounts of grapes from individual vineyards separately. There is a cultivar-planting programme managed in co-operation with the KWV to identify special blocks for the cultivation of popular varieties. The area of the member-farms is very widespread and the varying climates and soil types provide ideal growing conditions for the noble varieties, allowing the co-operative to produce a wide range of wines, many of them of top quality.

The initial interview and tasting were conducted in the cellar in the town, and afterwards General Manager Altus le Roux took me to see the huge cellar and visitor complex on the Malmesbury road. Here they are already well set up for tasting and sales, with a large outdoor area, a children's playground and a panoramic view of the Paarl Valley. A vaulted underground tasting room for special events and press receptions is currently under construction.

Tasting Notes

Colombard 1995 (tank sample on lees): Good greeny gold; nice fruit bouquet; clean fruit with good balance of acidity and length.

Sauvignon Blanc 1995: Pale straw with pinkish tinge; quite restrained fruit on nose; clean, crisp fruit in the mouth.

Chenin Blanc 1995 (Veritas Double Gold): Pale greeny gold; nice guava fruit bouquet; dry with depth and length.

Chardonnay 1995 (mature vines barrel-fermented, 50% in new wood 50% old, rest in tank): Pale straw; good fruit nose with some vanilla; some nice fat Chardonnay fruit, with oak nicely balanced.

Pinotage 1993 (30% wood-aged, 6 months in 2nd- and 3rd-fill casks): Nice bright red; cherry fruit bouquet; pleasing mouthful of summer fruits with soft tannins.

Pinotage 1994 (more wood used but maximum now): Darker colour than 1993; same cherry-fruit nose; lots of cherries and raspberries in the mouth, with soft tannins and some structure.

Merlot 1993 (some new wood): Deep colour; powerful black fruit nose with wet undergrowth; nice fruit in the mouth, well balanced with oak showing.

Merlot 1994: Colour slightly darker; soft black fruit bouquet; ripe fruit in mouth with soft tannins again and backbone.

Um Hap 1992 (named after a bushman village, to which some of the profit from the sale of this wine is donated, blend of 60% Cabernet and 40% Merlot): Dark red; open blackcurrant nose; some good fruit, but tannins dominate.

Muscadel 1992: Mid-deep gold; concentrated raisiny nose; very rich dried fruit concentration and a long aftertaste.

Muscadel 1995: Nice golden colour, fresh figgy nose; fuller than 1992, fat, rich, long.

Technical Notes

Co-operative: 130 members

Average production: 25,000 tons

Wines produced
WHITE: Chardonnay, Sauvignon Blanc, Chenin Blanc, White Muscadel, Riesling, Bukettraube, Stein, Late Vintage, Noble Late Harvest, Hanepoot Jerepiko
RED: Cabernet Sauvignon, Merlot, Pinotage, Um Hap, Nouveau
'PORT': Vintage (from 50/50 Pinotage/Tinta Barocca)
BON VINO RANGE (returnable screw cap 6 packs): Dry White, Semi-Sweet White, Dry Red

Useful Information

General Manager: Altus le Roux
Winemakers: Anthony De Jager, Jacques du Toit
Assistant Winemaker: Charl du Plessis
Address: Boland Wine Cellar, Box 7007, Noorder-Paarl 7645

Telephone: 021.872.1766 *Fax*: 021.872.3866
Also: Boland Wine Cellar, Box 2, Huguenot 7645
Telephone: 021.872.1766 *Fax*: 021.872.3866

Tasting/Sales: Weekdays 08.00 to 17.00 Saturday 08.30 to 13.00
Facilities: Cellar tours by appointment

DE LEUWEN JAGT

The name of this 360-hectare estate, 'The Lion Hunt', sandwiched between Fairview and Landskroon, dates back to the days before intensive farming drove most of the game from the Southern Cape. The previous owners became insolvent in 1990, and the estate was run by the liquidator until 1992, when it was bought by a Swiss company, African Farm Investments Limited, based in Jersey.

Day-to-day management is the responsibility of local director Leo Kimble, and winemaking is in the fresh and able hands of Frikkie Botes, late of the Wellington Wynboere and Bottelary Co-operatives. Frikkie finds that the most important advantage in being winemaker on a small estate, over working in a Co-op, is the control that he now has over the fruit that comes into the winery. The first radical change that he made here was to introduce whole-bunch pressing for the entire 1995 crop, which gives 10% more juice to the ton.

The first priority for the new owners was to increase production, particularly of the red wines. When they took over in 1992 there were 54 hectares in production – there are now 68, with an eventual target of 74. The cellar capacity also needed enlarging from 240 tons to 500 tons – they can currently cope with 350 tons, or around 290,000 litres. The aim here is to make South African style wine, and not to try to emulate any other wine country. Leo Kimble feels that their best red is the Cabernet Sauvignon/Merlot blend, and from their range of whites he singled out the Chardonnay, which they try not to over-oak. They are currently exporting about 2,500 cases of bottled wines, as well as a considerable quantity in bulk, mainly to the UK, Holland and Switzerland. Woolworths, the South African department store owned by Marks and Spencer, is also a very important customer, taking about 4,000 cases a year.

Tasting Notes

FROM TANKS/CASKS

Cape Riesling 1995: Tank-fermented, but smells distinctly oaky; good fruit, but finishes short and flat – harvested late.

Cape Riesling 1995: Different tank, earlier picking; a cleaner, crisper wine, more fruit, better acidity.

Sauvignon Blanc 1995: Pale gold; nice fruit on nose and in mouth, but not too up-front or typically Sauvignon, but quite normal for this part of Paarl, says Frikkie.

Chardonnay 1995 (unwooded): Nice, pale straw; ripe fruit nose; some nice weight, good fruit and length.

Chardonnay 1995 (fermented in mix of new and 3rd-fill casks, 8 months on lees and back to tank): Good pale gold; fruit and wood in balance on nose and in mouth, nice length.

Stein 1995 (some wood from oak chips): Young, fragrant wine, with quite a bit of complexity and dry elegance.

Weisser Riesling 1995: Palest straw; nose very spicy and grapey; same luscious grapiness on palate, more like a Hanepoot.

Merlot 1995: Dense, almost black colour; big, rounded fruit bouquet; concentrated, ripe mouthful, with good tannins and fruit and fine structure. A winner.

Cabernet Sauvignon 1995: Deep red; cassis and blackberry nose; well-made wine that needs time for fruit and tannins to come together.

Cabernet Franc 1995 (no wood): Dark, dense red; spicy, almost grassy nose; rich, ripe fruit, soft tannins and structured.

FROM THE BOTTLE

Merlot 1994: Fine, deep colour; black fruit nose; a fat and well-rounded mouthful of fruit with lovely, soft tannins – to drink in a couple of years, and will last.

Cabernet Sauvignon/Merlot 1993 (Veritas Double Gold): Deep red colour; plums and cassis nose; lots of ripe fruit, coffee and chocolate flavours, good structure and length.

Private Bin 1 1991 (100% Cabernet Sauvignon): Deep ruby colour; hayfield bouquet; lots of good fruit, a really well-made Cabernet Sauvignon with some class.

Technical Notes

Area under vines: 68 hectares, will be 74

Cultivars planted
WHITE: Chardonnay, Sauvignon Blanc, Chenin Blanc, Cape Riesling, Weisser Riesling
RED: Cabernet Sauvignon and Franc, Merlot, Cinsaut, Red Muscadelle

Wines produced
WHITE: Cape Riesling, Weisser Riesling, Chenin Blanc, Chardonnay, Sauvignon Blanc, Chenin Blanc/Chardonnay (Woolworths)
RED: Cabernet Sauvignon, Cabernet Franc, Merlot, Cabernet Sauvignon/Merlot

Useful Information

Owner: African Farm Investments Limited
Local Director: Leo Kimble
Winemaker: Frikkie Botes
Address: De Leuwen Jagt, Box 505, Suider-Paarl 7624
Telephone: 021.863.3495 *Fax*: 021.863.3797

Tasting/Sales: Weekdays 08.00 to 17.00, Saturday 09.00 to 13.00
Facilities: Lunches Monday to Friday 10.30 to 14.30

FAIRVIEW

Charles Back's grandfather, another Charles, came here as an immigrant from Lithuania in 1906, and bought his first wine farm, Klein Babylonstoren, now Backsberg, in 1916. It was not until 21 years later that he acquired Fairview. Charles the elder's son Sydney was fully committed to Backsberg, and when Charles died in 1954, it was his other son, Cyril, who took over the running of Fairview.

When Charles bought Fairview, the previous owner, one Mr Hugo, had only a few Cinsaut vines, from which he made a dry red wine, which was sold in barrel to the local merchants. Blessed with two decades of experience at Backsberg, Charles was not slow to recognize the potential at Fairview for the planting of noble grape varieties, and for the making of fine wine. Over the ensuing twenty years, he and Cyril gradually replaced all the old Cinsaut vines with low-yield, high-quality varieties such as Cabernet Sauvignon, Merlot, Shiraz and Pinotage for red wine and Chenin Blanc and later Chardonnay and Sauvignon Blanc for white.

In 1978 Cyril's son Charles finished his studies at Elsenberg, where he also completed an additional cellar-master's course, and joined his father as winemaker at Fairview. Charles is one of the Cape's *jeunes loups*, or Young Turks. He is undoubtedly a very able and talented winemaker, but is inclined to make some establishment figures raise their eyebrows with his novel and innovative blends and experiments. These include a Shiraz/Merlot, a Zinfandel/Cinsaut, a Shiraz/Gamay, a Gamay Nouveau, made with Beaujolais's traditional carbonic maceration, a Crouchen (Cape Riesling)/Chardonnay, a Sauvignon Blanc/Sémillon, a Sauvignon Blanc/Chenin Blanc and a Bouquet Blanc made from Rhine Riesling, Gewürztraminer and Bukettraube.

Charles Back is no loose cannon, however. He is very market-driven, and spends a prodigious amount of time, effort and money travelling, tasting and talking everywhere wine is made. He also listens attentively to the buyers, particularly those in the United Kingdom, who, he says, are especially aware of what the wine-buying public wants. In addition, he is continually sending off for samples, which arrive on an almost hourly basis at Fairview. On the day that I visited him, for example, there were five parcels containing different samples of Italian Shiraz for his consideration. All this research is put together, he then makes his blends, and after many trials launches them in the right direction, and they seem to work. Of the production from 180 hectares of Fairview, and 80 hectares of the leased vineyards of a neighbouring farm, 75% is now going for export, mainly to the UK, where his agent is Charles Hawkins. When I had the temerity to suggest that he was perhaps making too many different varietals and blends, and that surely the soil and micro-climate of Fairview could not be ideal for all of them, he said that he was certain that in a hot country like South Africa, the stamp of the winemaker was far more important than the *terroir*.

More than half the revenue at Fairview comes from the production of cheese from the farm's flocks of Saanen goats and German sheep, for which Charles is also responsible. Fairview produces 40% of all the exotic cheeses made in the Cape but, in spite of the importance of this enterprise, Charles finds that 90% of his time is taken up by wine. Recognition of the economic contribution of the cheese business is, however, given in the recent decision to put the famous Fairview goat tower on to all labels and stationery, bearing the legend 'Tower of Quality'.

Tasting Notes

Chenin Blanc 1995: Nice pale gold; floral bouquet; lots of good fruit with nice weight and length.

Chardonnay 1995 (barrel-fermented and 4 months in new oak): Pale gold; fruit open on nose, with vanilla of oak; fruit and wood nicely in balance on palate, with some fatness.

Sauvignon Blanc/Chenin Blanc 1995: Pale straw; good, if restrained Sauvignon nose; clean, crisp and dry, a good blend.

Crouchen (Cape Riesling)/Chardonnay 1995 (80% Crouchen, 20% Chardonnay, Crouchen tank-fermented with oak chips and left on lees): Pale straw colour; nice fruit nose, more Chardonnay than anything else; full, rich and fruity with a dry finish.

Sémillon 1995 (barrel-fermented, but all 2nd-fill casks): Pale, greeny gold; up-front fruit bouquet; big fruit in mouth, very woody.

Cinsaut 1995 Dry Rosé (carbonic maceration): Nice, deep pink; summer fruit bouquet; fine and elegant with raspberry, strawberry fruit and some tannins – a classy rosé.

Shiraz/Merlot 1993 (60% Shiraz, 40% Merlot aged 14 months in 2nd- and 3rd-fill casks): Very deep, brilliant red; powerful fruit on nose; well-balanced wine.

Shiraz 1993 (best parcels in new oak, all done malolactic): Deep, dense, blackish red; big, northern Rhône nose; a huge, concentrated mouthful of fruit and soft tannins, with excellent structure – a star.

Pinotage 1995 (very little use of wood): Bluey red; big, Pinotage fruit nose, very open; a pleasing mouthful of ripe and easy fruit, good now.

Tower Red 1994 (Fairview Estate's new red blend – Cabernet Sauvignon, Cabernet Franc, Malbec and Merlot): Very deep, almost black in colour; nose quite shy (just bottled); a big, concentrated mouthful of ripe and juicy black fruit, with soft tannins and good backbone.

Zinfandel/Cinsaut 1995 (fermented on skins with oak chips, 14.5% alcohol): Very dense, dark colour; a big and powerful wine, both on the nose and in the mouth. John Platter describes this as a 'thick of the scrum, front-row forward wine, for consumers similarly constructed'.

Cabernet Sauvignon 1994 (may have up to 10% Cabernet Franc and Merlot): Deep, dark red; up-front, minty new-clone Cabernet nose; ripe fruit and the right tannins, already good, but will keep well.

Technical Notes

Area under vines: 185 hectares with lease on 80 neighbouring

Cultivars planted
WHITE: Sauvignon Blanc, Chenin Blanc, Chardonnay, Crouchen, Sémillon, Weisser Riesling, Bukettraube, Pinot Gris, Gewürztraminer
RED: Cabernet Sauvignon, Cabernet Franc, Merlot, Malbec, Shiraz, Pinotage, Cinsaut, Pinot Noir, Gamay, Zinfandel

Wines produced
WHITE: Fairview Tower White, Crouchen/Chardonnay, Gewürztraminer, Chenin Blanc, Chardonnay, Sauvignon Blanc, Sauvignon Blanc/Sémillon, Sémillon, Sauvignon Blanc/Chenin Blanc, Chenin Blanc (barrel-fermented), Pinot Gris, Weisser Riesling, Bukettraube, Bouquet Fair, Special Late Harvest Chenin
RED: Fairview Tower Red, Cabernet Sauvignon, Shiraz/Merlot,

Cabernet Franc/Merlot, Merlot, Pinotage, Shiraz Reserve,
Shiraz, Zinfandel/Cinsaut, Pinot Noir, Shiraz/Gamay, Paarl Red
ROSÉ: Dry Rosé
SWEET DESSERT RED: Shiraz
SPARKLING: Charles Gerard, Brut

Useful Information

Owner/Winemaker: Charles Back
Assistant Winemakers: Piet Harris, Hennie Huskisson
Address: Fairview Estate, Box 583, Suider-Paarl 7625
Telephone: 021.863.2450 *Fax*: 021.863.2591

Tasting/Sales: Weekdays 08.00 to 17.30, Saturday 08.00 to 13.00,
December–March open Saturday 08.00 to 17.00, closed
Christmas Day, New Year's Day, Good Friday
Facilities: Wine, cheese, cold meats; watch Saanen goats being
milked, 4 p.m., except July–September

GLEN CARLOU

The name of the Glen Carlou estate comes, rather whimsically,
from the names of three daughters, Lena, Carol and Louise, of a
previous owner. There is, however, virtually no vinous history
attached to the property, whimsical or otherwise. Walter Finlayson,
formerly winemaker at Blaauwklippen, bought the estate in 1980,
at which time there were only a few old Chenin Blanc vines planted.
He built the imposing thatched cellar and reception building, which
sit well on the vine-clad slopes of the foothills of the Simonsberg.
An extensive programme of soil cultivation and preparation was
then embarked upon, and planting did not begin until 1985.
Including eight hectares of old Chenin Blanc, there is now a total
of just over 30 hectares down to vines, the balance of which are
mainly new clones of Chardonnay, Cabernet Sauvignon, Merlot,
Cabernet Franc, Petit Verdot and Pinot Noir.

Finlayson has an impressive record as a winemaker. Whilst
working at Blaauwklippen he received the Diners Club Winemaker
of the Year Award in two successive years. Since his solo debut
at Glen Carlou, he has produced a succession of startlingly

good wines, many of them medal-winners, including his Chardonnay 1994, the first South African example to score 90 in an American *Wine Spectator* tasting. Son David looks like following in his father's grape treading footsteps. He has experienced a vintage at Peter Lehmann's Barossa cellar, and helped with the 1995 vintage at Château Margaux, also gaining some Burgundian experience through the assistance of Amaury de Villard of Antonin Rodet at the Glen Carlou 1995 vintage. David trained at Elsenberg, and has now taken much of the work from his father's shoulders.

Tasting Notes

Chardonnay 1995: Pale, greeny gold; good fruit and oak a bit to the fore at the moment; pleasing citrus flavours, quite woody.

Chardonnay 1990: Deeper gold; rich, ripe fruit on nose, oak not there any more; very good Chardonnay, full of fruit and fatness. Well worth the high marks awarded by *Wine Spectator*.

Pinot Noir 1990: Brilliant deep red; fresh, summer fruit nose; cherries and strawberries in mouth, nice ripe tannins and some structure.

Les Trois 1994 (55% Cabernet Sauvignon, 20% Merlot, 25% Petit Verdot, 15 months in 2nd- and 3rd-fill barrels): Deep red colour; nice open nose of ripe black fruit; a big, generous mouth-filling wine with masses of fruit, but still very tannic – will make a fine bottle.

Grand Classique 1992 (70% Cabernet Sauvignon, 20% Merlot, 10% Cabernet Franc, 24 months cask ageing, with a good proportion of new wood): Very deep colour; rich fruit nose, lots of oak; an excellent Bordeaux-style blend, fine, ripe fruit, good soft tannins and well-structured.

Merlot 1993: Very deep colour; good blackberry nose with some vanilla; a big, rounded wine with some good backbone.

Merlot 1994: Deep colour, blue at edges; berry fruit nose, with lots of oak; very fat and ripe, with tannins very dominant at present – will make a very fine bottle in time.

Merlot 1990 (100% new oak): Fine, dense red; plummy fruit on nose; rounded fruit coming nicely into balance with the wood.

Chenin Blanc/Chardonnay 'Devereux' 1995 (named after the late Peter Devereux, the great SA wine promoter – an interesting barrel-fermented combination of 85% Chenin Blanc and 15% Chardonnay): Good, golden colour; rich, slightly asparagussy fruit nose; medium sweet, with rich, spicy fruit flavours and good length.

Cape Vintage 1993 ('vintage port', aged 30 months in 450-litre casks, made from Tinta Barocca, Tinta Roriz and Pinot Noir): Very deep, dense colour; nice nose of dried fruit; excellent mouthful of raisins, sultanas and figs, quite spirity – good.

Technical Notes

Area under vines: 35 hectares

Average production: 7,000 cases

Wines produced
WHITE: Chardonnay, Reserve Chardonnay, Devereux Chenin Blanc/Chardonnay
RED: Grande Classique, Les Trois, Cabernet Sauvignon, Mertlot, Cabernet-Franc Reserve, Pinot Noir
'PORT': Vintage

Useful Information

Owners/Winemakers: Walter and David Finlayson
Address: Glen Carlou, Box 23, Klapmuts, 7625
Telephone: 021.875528 *Fax*: 021.875314

Tasting/Sales: Weekdays 08.30 to 16.45, Saturday 09.00 to 12.30.

LANDSKROON

The de Villiers family were one of the first wine-farming settlers in the Cape. When Jacques de Villiers, a Huguenot *émigré*, arrived in the Cape on the packet boat *Zion* with his two brothers in

1692, he carried with him letters from the Lords XVII to Simon van der Stel commending their usefulness as winemakers. In the early eighteenth century, Jacques found himself established at Boschendal, where the family stayed until 1874. At the time the de Villiers sold Boschendal, there was one member of the family who was still making wine, and this was Paul de Villiers, who had just established himself at Landskroon. The first Paul set about enlarging his property, acquiring extra plots of land and buying the neighbouring farm called Schoongezicht. When he first arrived only a few old vines were planted, and his first plantings were of Cinsaut, Chenin Blanc and Muscadel, from which he made the sweet fortified wines that were so popular then, transporting them to Cape Town in small casks by ox-wagon, for sale either to local merchants or on the export market.

Each succeeding head of the family has taken the name of Paul. Paul the Second took the estate into the present century, and into the early days of the KWV, to whom virtually the entire production of Landskroon was sold until 1973. The third Paul was responsible for many innovations here. He was one of the pioneers of the South African 'sherry' industry, as it turned out that Landskroon was one of only a handful of farms in the Cape where the 'flor' yeast, essential for the production of fino, occurred naturally in the vineyard. He also planted a number of Portuguese varieties for the making of 'port', including Tinta Roriz, Tinta Barocca and Souzao, which are still at Landskroon today. The fourth Paul and his brother Hugo inherited the farm in 1963. They divided the activities of the estate into two parts, Paul taking charge of vineyards and wine, whilst Hugo established a magnificent Jersey dairy herd known as Fairseat.

The fifth generation of de Villiers is, not surprisingly, also called Paul. The Jersey herd is now gone, and its place has been taken by 120 head of beef cattle, assuring a continuing supply of organic fertilizer for the vineyard. There is a substantial 275 hectares under vines, 80% of which are red, and they also buy in grapes for their export contracts. The cellar vinifies an average of 1,500 tons of grapes each year, some of which is sold in bulk, but the majority is bottled at the estate. Half of their sales are on the export market, and United Kingdom supermarkets are strong customers: the range of red wines includes a Paarl Cabernet which is sold to Tesco, a Cinsaut/Shiraz blend available from Safeway and a Cabernet Franc made for Asda. White wine production is very much in the minority: Chenin Blanc, Sauvignon Blanc and Pinot Blanc are made, and it is rather a nice surprise to find an estate of this importance that does not produce a Chardonnay.

In common with most wineries in South Africa, 'sherry' is no longer made at Landskroon, but the 'port' tradition continues strongly. They make an excellent vintage wine, with fermentation stopped at 18.5% compared with the Portuguese 20%. Paul tells me that South Africa is starting to vinify its 'ports' drier, but it is a gradual process. He also still makes a very traditional fortified Jerepigo from Morio Muscat.

Tasting Notes

Chenin Blanc 1995: very pale golden; pleasing quincy nose; a clean, crisp, citrussy taste – lemon and grapefuit, long.

Pinot Blanc 1995: Good mid-gold colour; fruit and vanilla nose; fruit/acid balance good, but wood a bit dominant.

Sauvignon Blanc 1995: Pale straw; nose quite restrained; good balance, clean and crisp with nice length.

Cinsaut/Shiraz 1995 (export blend): Bright, cherry red; nose of summer fruits; a pleasant, easy-drinking red with a bit of soft tannin.

Pinotage 1994: Medium-dark ruby; open fruit, some banana on nose; a mouthful of round, easy fruit, with a little bit of structure there.

Cabernet Sauvignon 1990: Deep garnet colour; cassis nose; really nice blackcurrant fruit, with soft tannins and fine structure, ready now, and will keep well.

Shiraz 1994: Deep colour; ripe fruit and some mushroom on the nose; wood not too evident, good fruit and a bit of backbone.

Cabernet Franc 1992: Deep, bright ruby; cigar-box and cassis nose; mouthful of ripe fruit, slight green pepper finish.

'Port' 1992: Very deep colour; chocolate and coffee nose; rich, raisiny fruit and nice soft tannins, not over sweet.

Morio Muscat Jerepigo 1995: Bright golden; slightly dusty, Muscat bouquet; sweet, honeyed fruit, with trace of greenness in the middle palate – good.

Technical Notes

Area under vines: 275 hectares

Cultivars planted
WHITE: Chenin Blanc, Sauvignon Blanc, Pinot Blanc, Morio Muscat
RED: Cabernet Sauvignon, Cabernet Franc, Merlot, Shiraz, Pinotage, Pinot Noir, Cinsaut
'PORT': Tinta Barocca, Tinta Roriz, Sousao

Wines produced
WHITE: Chenin Blanc, Sauvignon Blanc, Pinot Blanc, Bouquet Blanc, Pinot Gris, Pinot Blanc/Chenin Blanc, Jerepigo Morio Muscat
RED: Cabernet Sauvignon, Shiraz, Merlot, Pinotage, Premier Reserve, Cabernet Franc, Cinsaut, Blanc de Noir
'PORT'

Useful Information

Owners: de Villiers family
Winemaker: Paul de Villiers
Vineyard Manager: Hugo de Villiers
Address: Landskroon Estate, Box 519, Suider-Paarl 7624
Telephone: 021.863.1039 *Fax*: 021.863.2810

Tasting/Sales: Weekdays 08.30 to 17.00, Saturday 08.30 to 12.30
Facilities: Tasting and sale of Simonsberg cheeses; light lunches served 11.30 to 14.30, November–April

NEDERBURG

Nederburg came under the Stellenbosch Farmers' Winery umbrella when SFW acquired fortified wine specialists Monis, then owners of Nederburg, in 1966. Nederburg is big: they are currently making

25% of all the HP (High Price) wines in South Africa, 50% of which comes from four farms totalling 650 hectares, and 50% from grapes bought in from carefully selected farms under regular contract. A mammoth three-quarters of a million cases of wine are produced each year from 13,500 tons of grapes.

The original farm was granted to a German immigrant by the name of Wolvaart in 1792, who named it Nederburgh in honour of the current Commissioner-General, Sebastian Nederburgh. The 'h' has disappeared from the end of the name over the years, possibly as a nod toward the Afrikaner language. Although there have always been vines on the estate, it was not until 1937 that Nederburg became the serious wine-producer that it is now. The property had been through many changes of ownership since Wolvaart's days, and it was curiously enough another German immigrant that then came upon the scene.

Johann Georg Graue, a successful managing director of a large German brewery, felt dark shadows building up over Europe, and decided to build a new life in the sun, especially for his beloved only son, Arnold. Full of hope, enthusiasm and excitement as he must have been, Johann undoubtedly had his work cut out. The setting was beautiful, the old Cape Dutch homestead enchanting, and the potential of the new wine venture enormous, but the vineyards were very run down and planted with all the wrong varieties. It has now become a cliché, but Graue was an ardent believer that good wine only comes from good grapes, and his first task was to reorganize the vineyards completely. This he did with formidable Teutonic thoroughness, keeping meticulous records of the performance of all his different varieties and rootstocks, and never hesitating to uproot anything that did not perform to his satisfaction.

The immediate post-war years were happy and successful ones for Nederburg and the Graues. Arnold had trained at the Geisenheim Wine School in the Rhineland, and became a skilled and dedicated winemaker. The process of cold fermentation for white wines, hitherto unknown in South Africa, and almost indispensable in such a hot climate, was first practised at Nederburg. In the midst of all this success and prosperity, tragedy struck when Arnold's private aeroplane collided in mid-air with a military training aircraft at Youngsfield near Cape Town. He was killed outright.

In his hour of need, the heartbroken Johann turned to his fatherland for help, which appeared in the form of Gunter Brozel, a graduate of Weinsberg and an inspired winemaker. He served Nederburg well for 33 years, going on to do great work at Stellenzicht and Neethlingshof. Under the German influence of Brozel, Nederburg was the first South African wine estate to produce botrytized dessert wines. These were not permitted under South African wine law, but Brozel obtained a special dispensation to make them. The wine was known as Nederburg Edelkeur, and was only sold at the Nederburg Auctions.

In 1956 Monis, the rapidly expanding Italian-owned fortified wine business, bought Nederburg, and Monis merged with Stellenbosch Farmers' Winery nine years later. Johann Graue died in 1959, having virtually withdrawn from Nederburg's activities following his son's death. Although his life ended so sadly, he left behind a living monument in the Nederburg complex, and, more importantly but less tangibly, in the enormous contribution that he and his son had made to the furtherance and improvement of fine wine in the Cape.

Today the enterprise is headed by Managing Director Ernst le Roux, one of South Africa's leading viticulturists. Winemaking is under the capable control of Newald Marais and his three assistants. Marais is a graduate of Elsenburg Agricultural College, and has travelled widely in pursuit of wine knowledge. Vineyards are the responsibility of group farm manager and viticulturist Hannes van Rensburg.

The Nederburg Wine Auction, now one of the most important dates on the world's wine calendar and probably the most prestigious social event in South Africa, was started in 1975. The purpose of the auction was four-fold: to serve as an incentive towards quality wines in South Africa; to increase world awareness of that quality; to ensure fair distribution of the best and rarest wines; and finally to raise money for charity. All of South Africa's estates, wineries and co-operatives are invited to submit a wide range of categories of their finest wines each year. These are carefully vetted and sampled by the tasting panel, whose strictly applied criteria ensure that only the Cape's finest wines are entered in the auction each year.

In a typical auction, between 120 and 150 different wines will come under the hammer of Patrick Grubb, former head of Sotheby's wine department. In 1992 this amounted to about 10,500 cases and a hammer value of R2,111,300, and R250,000 was raised for the Hospice Association of Southern Africa. The trade only are invited, but they may sometimes bring their top customers with them. Each year a top personality of the wine world is invited to speak, including people like Joseph Drouhin from Beaune, Paul Pontallier of Château Margaux, Robert Mondavi from California, Jean Hügel from Alsace and many others of that stature. Guests are entertained to a magnificent al fresco luncheon and, for any ladies who require diversion from the business of the wine auction, there is always a fashion show, where top couturiers strut their wares.

Not surprisingly the wines of Nederburg itself always feature strongly at the auctions, and these are normally labelled 'Private Bin' followed by a letter – D for dry white, S for sweet, C for sparkling and R for red – and a code number. In the early days of the Nederburg auctions, the wines were almost all white and sweet, often fortified, but the emphasis now has shifted very firmly towards quality red wines. For the wines of Nederburg, as indeed for those of any producer, selection for entry in the auction is a guarantee of quality.

Tasting Notes

Nederburg Sauvignon Blanc 1995: Pale straw; fruit good on nose, typical Sauvignon, but quite restrained; balance of fruit/acidity just right, good length.

Nederburg Prelude 1995 (75% Sauvignon Blanc, 25% Chardonnay): Pale gold; Sauvignon strong and dominates bouquet; clean, crisp and fruity, with some nice weight from Chardonnay.

Nederburg Chardonnay 1995 (30% oaked): Pale gold colour; good fruit bouquet, with some wood; Chardonnay fruit character a bit masked by wood at the moment, but everything there. Bottled a bit early because of demand!

Private Bin D270 1992 (Chardonnay 100% oaked, 40% of which was new): Mid-golden; very strong oak still on nose; huge weight and fatness, with some nice citrus tones, and oak just right.

Nederburg Lyric 1995 (50% Sauvignon Blanc, 30% Cape

Riesling, 20% Chardonnay): Medium gold; grapey fruit bouquet; pleasing grapey fruit, with touch of sweetness.

Nederburg Rhine Riesling 1995: Pale straw; open Riesling grape nose; fruit very much up-front in the mouth with citrus hints, very long.

Nederburg Rosé 1995 (Cinsaut and Gamay, one of Nederburg's biggest volume sellers): Raspberry pink; lovely, summery fruit nose; easy and refreshing, lots of strawberry, raspberry fruit.

Nederburg Baronne 1992 (60% Cabernet Sauvignon, 40% Shiraz, reduced to 30% Shiraz in later vintages, 18 months in large oak vats): Bright, medium red; nose good, with Shiraz tending to dominate; quite a light red, a bit peppery, with some nice Shiraz fruit, and quite long.

Paarl Cabernet Sauvignon 1992 (92% Cabernet Sauvignon, 6% Merlot, 2% Cabernet Franc, aged in mixture of large and small oak): Mid-red; good cassis fruit aroma; easy-drinking Cabernet with some nice tannins and a bit of structure.

Private Bin R161 1991 (Cabernet Sauvignon, 9 months in small oak, 25% new, 75% 2nd-fill): Bright, mid-red; rich, black fruit nose; full, fat fruit, soft tannin and good length.

Private Bin R161 1989 (same wooding as above): Beginning to brown slightly at edges; nose showing some age, a touch cooked; beginning to show some flabbiness.

Auction Reserve Cabernet Sauvignon 1984 (mixture of large and small oak): Deeper red than the 1989; ripe and lively fruit on nose; ready to drink now, excellent fruit with harmonious soft tannins – very fine.

Edelrood 1992 (60% Cabernet Sauvignon, 35% Merlot, 5% Shiraz, 75% wood-matured for 11 months): Darkish red; open, ripe bouquet, with Merlot and Shiraz rather than Cabernet; a big, mouth-filling wine with ripe tannins and a bit of spine.

Edelkeur, Noble Selection 1992 (100% Chenin Blanc, botrytized): Lovely treacle gold; rich, botrytis fruit, with beeswax and honey on the nose; a concentrated noble rot flavour, a touch cloying, lacking that essential degree of acidity.

Technical Notes

Area under vines: 650 hectares, plus bought-in grapes

Cultivars planted: Almost every variety and clone of variety

Wines produced
WHITE: Sauvignon Blanc, Chardonnay, Prelude, Lyric, Stein, Rhine Riesling, Noble Late Harvest, Paarl Riesling, Premier Grand Cru, Elegance, Gewürztraminer, plus all the Private Bin and Auction Reserve wines
RED: Paarl Cabernet Sauvignon, Edelrood, Baronne, Pinotage (Export), Duet, plus all the Private Bin and Auction Reserve wines
ROSÉ: Blanc de Noir, Rosé, Rosé Sec
SPARKLING: Blanquette, Premier Cuvée Brut, Cuvée Doux, Kap Sekt, plus Private Bin wine

Useful Information

Owners: Stellenbosch Farmers' Winery
Managing Director: Ernst le Roux
Winemaker: Newald Marais
Assistant Winemakers: Wilhelm Arnold, Stephan du Toit, Andries Burger
Production Manager: Louis van Wyk
Vineyard Manager: Hannes van Rensburg
Marketing: Schalk Burger
Public Relations: Clive Torr
Address: Nederburg, P/Bag X3006, Paarl 7620
Telephone: 021.862.3104 *Fax*: 021.862.4887

Tasting/Sales: Weekdays 09.00 to 17.00, closed Saturday, except 1 November–28 February, when open 09.00 to 13.00
Facilities: Cellar tours 10.30 and 14.30; picnic lunches by appointment only during season

PLAISIR DE MERLE

The total area of the Plaisir de Merle estate is 410 hectares, and is made up of four separate farms: Plaisir de Merle itself, Rust-en-

Vrede, Drostersnes and Rachelsfontein. The history up to the end of the nineteenth century is incredibly convoluted, and involves so many enormous families, with so much inter-marriage that only an Afrikaner genealogist would have the remotest chance of sorting it all out.

In precis, the first owners were the Marais family, Huguenots from the Ile de France, driven out of France by economic pressures and religious persecution, whose birthplace was Plessis-les-Marle, whence the name. Charles, the first Marais, lasted a very short time. Having been granted his 60-morgen farm in October 1688, he set about the task of clearing and planting his land and, of all the Huguenot settlers to be granted land, only he and one other managed to produce a crop in their first year. Sadly, hard work must usually be accompanied by a bit of good fortune before rewards are gained. In March 1689, only months after he had moved in, Charles Marais was inspecting his water-melons, when he was approached by a Khoikhoi native, who asked for a melon – Marais told him they were not ripe, but the native, either in disbelief or anger, plucked one of the fruit and hurled it at the unsuspecting Marais. The melon was followed by rocks, one of which hit Marais in the groin, causing internal bleeding and death four days later.

Four more generations of Marais were to follow the unfortunate Charles, culminating with Pieter, who died on the estate in 1831, having sold the property some 25 years earlier to his future son-in-law, Daniel Hugo, an experienced wine farmer from Worcester. The Hugo family were in charge until 1872, when Pieter Hugo died, leaving his son-in-law, Petrus Jacobus Retief in charge. He only held on to the property until 1877, when he sold it to one Jacobus Johannes Basson. The estate then passed through the hands of several owners, ending up in 1910 in the hands of the mort-gagors, the Norwich Union Life Insurance Society, who ran it until 1913, when a new owner and saviour appeared.

Lord John Henry de Villiers, created 1st Baron of Wynberg for his services in the establishment of the Union of South Africa, was an empire-builder. By the time he had completed all his agricultural purchases, he owned over 35,000 acres in the Paarl district, including Plaisir de Merle, and the part of neighbouring Vredenlust known as Rust-en-Vrede, which had always been linked by dynastic marriages with Plaisir de Merle. The de Villiers name had long been associated with the estate, as the Marais family had twice married de Villiers girls, and the de Villiers had also been owners of Vredenlust at the beginning of the eighteenth century.

Lord Wynberg, following a distinguished career as a barrister, and then as Chief Justice, became a conscientious and dedicated farmer, and learnt a great deal from H. E. V. Pickstone of the newly-formed Rhodes Fruit Farms. On his death in 1933, he was succeeded by his son, Sir Percy de Villiers, better known as Freddie, who only stayed in South Africa for ten years before selling up and leaving for New Zealand. The new owner was Nicholas Browse Gray, whose son Dougie took over the running of Plaisir de Merle on his return from the Second World War.

In the early 1960s wine farming in South Africa was very difficult: export was non-existent, and the only demand on the domestic market was for cheap fortified wine and wine for distilling into brandy, neither activity being profitable. Dougie Gray found himself in deep financial waters, and was forced to look around for a buyer. The giant Stellenbosch Farmers' Winery were themselves almost bankrupt, but had reached a policy decision that the only way forward was to buy land so that they could control and improve the quality of the wine that they made. An ambitious young employee, Ronnie Melck, later to become managing director of SFW, was charged with the task of looking for suitable vineyards, and it was he who was responsible for the company purchase of Plaisir de Merle in 1964 for £290,000.

Until very recently, Plaisir de Merle's 365 hectares of vines were used as a satellite vineyard for Nederburg, SFW's giant quality wine producing arm. Today the estate has its own identity, and is producing a limited range of very high-quality wines. A state-of-the-art winery and barrel-ageing cellar have been constructed. You enter by crossing a moat, stocked with trout, and once inside one is reminded of some of the newer vathouses in Bordeaux: the ranks of stainless-steel fermentation vats and row-upon-row of small oak casks can all be viewed from an overhead walkway by visitors without disturbing the flow of work. Meticulous planning and attention to detail at all stages of the development of Plaisir de Merle have resulted in a beautiful estate with a feeling of warmth and welcome from another age. There is even a working water-mill, where they grind wheat grown on the estate, from which they bake some of the best bread I have eaten.

Frenchman Paul Pontallier, the dynamic general manager from Château Margaux in Bordeaux, has been employed as consultant at Plaisir de Merle for some years. The quality of the estate's range of wine is certainly high, but Paul is now leaving more and more of the decisions to resident winemaker Niel Bester.

Tasting Notes

Chardonnay 1994: Very pale gold; nose quite lemony and restrained; nice balance of fruit/acidity, with some butteriness.

Paarl Sauvignon Blanc 1994: Pale straw; restrained fruit with touch of oakiness on the nose; pleasing, silky fruit with nice long finish – more white Bordeaux than New World.

Cabernet Sauvignon 1993: Deep ruby red; soft cassis bouquet; astonishingly easy-drinking, yet has lots of fruit, power and backbone, with lovely ripe tannins. (Pontallier, who was there when I did my tasting, said that ripeness of tannins was the most difficult thing to achieve when making red wine in a country as hot as South Africa, as over-ripeness can develop so quickly when the temperature is in the high thirties, and people tend to pick just before optimum ripeness to avoid this risk.)

Technical Notes

Area under vines: 365 hectares

Cultivars planted
WHITE: Sauvignon Blanc, Chardonnay
RED: Cabernet Sauvignon, Merlot, Shiraz

Wines produced
WHITE: Sauvignon Blanc, Chardonnay
RED: Cabernet Sauvignon, Merlot (not yet released)

Useful Information

Owners: Stellenbosch Farmers' Winery
Consultant: Paul Pontallier
Winemaker: Niel Bester
Address: Plaisir de Merle, Box 121, Simondium 7670

Telephone: 021.874.1027 *Fax*: 021.874.1488

Tastings/Sales: by appointment only (also picnic lunches)

PERDEBERG CO-OPERATIVE

Fifteen kilometres to the north-west of Paarl, surrounded by hundreds of hectares of wheatland, lie the cellars of the Perdeberg Co-operative. Named after the *perde*, or zebra that used to roam the land here, the co-operative was formed in 1942 under the chairmanship of S. F. Dreyer, and the cellar was built on a couple of hectares, sold to the co-operative for a nominal sum by one of the members, Jan Rossouw.

Pieter Dreyer, the chairman's brother, became the winemaker, and Jan Rossouw's brother, D. J. Rossouw, was the manager. Joseph Huskisson, formerly a pupil of Johann Graue at Nederburg, joined the co-operative as combined manager/winemaker in 1956, and remained there for 35 years until his retirement in 1990. The first harvest handled by the new cellar in 1942 amounted to 1,322 tons, and now the throughput is more than ten times this volume, and the workload has necessitated responsibility being shared once more. The manager today is Jacobus de Kock, and winemaking is in the hands of Pieter Verwey.

There are currently 45 members of the co-operative, owning between them 50 farms with a total of around 2,000 hectares of vineyards, all lying within a 35-kilometre radius of the cellars. Production is divided into 22% red wine and 78% white, but this is changing slowly in favour of red, as elsewhere in the Cape. Of the 15,000 tons of grapes being processed, only a tiny 0.1% goes into bottle, the rest being sold in bulk to SFW, Distillers, Douglas Green and to the KWV for making into wine, for distillation, rebate (for brandy) and for processing into grape concentrate.

Tasting Notes

Vin Blanc 1995 (80% Sauvignon Blanc, 20% Chardonnay): Clear, pale straw; restrained fruit on nose; a bit dumb at first impression, but some nice gooseberry fruit comes through on the backtaste.

Chenin Blanc 1995 Dry: Greeny gold; quince and guava bouquet very marked; excellent, clean and citrussy white, totally dry and great value.

Chenin Blanc 1995 Off-dry (15 g/l sugar): Slightly darker colour than the dry; mango bouquet; a heavier and more concentrated style – good Chenin Blanc.

Chenin Blanc 1994 Dry: Mid-gold colour; slightly dusty nose; clean, but fruit beginning to fade a bit.

Chenin Blanc 1994 Off-dry: Darker colour than the 1995 off-dry, but lacks the lusciousness and fruit concentration.

Cape Riesling 1993: Greeny gold; muted fruit nose; almost dry, still has some nice fruit and length.

Cinsaut 1992: Bright, cherry red; cherries and strawberries on nose; easy drinking, light and fruity, finishes dry.

Pinotage 1994: Deep red; good fruit on nose, some banana; cherry and plum fruit in mouth, easy drinker, but some nice, soft tannins there.

Pinotage 1995: Deep red; strong Pinotage fruit bouquet; more fruit and body than the 1994, but this could just be the age difference.

Vin Rouge 1995 (50% Cabernet Sauvignon, 20% Shiraz, 20% Merlot, 10% Cinsaut): Good ruby red; open and ripe fruit bouquet; very ready, rounded easy drinker.

Noble Late Harvest 1990 (made in celebration of Huskisson's 35th year as winemaker): Very deep golden colour; rich nose of dried apricot; concentrated dried fruit flavours, figs, apricots and raisins, tremendous length.

Technical Notes

Co-operative: 45 members/50 farms

Area under vines: 2,000 hectares

Cultivars planted: No data, but mainly Chenin Blanc, Sauvignon

Blanc, Chardonnay, Cape Riesling; Cinsaut, Pinotage and
Cabernet

Wines produced: Mainly various varietals and blends for bulk
sales, plus for bottle sales: Vin Blanc, Chenin Blanc Dry, Chenin
Blanc Off-dry, Cape Riesling, Chenin Blanc Noble Late Harvest,
Muscat Noble Late Harvest; Cinsaut, Pinotage, Vin Rouge

Useful Information

Winemaker: Pieter Verwey
Manager: Jacobus de Kock
Address: Perdeberg Wynboere Co-op, Box 214, Paarl 7621
Telephone: 021.863.8112 *Fax*: 021.863.8245

Tasting/Sales: Weekdays 08.00 to 12.30, 14.00 to 17.00

SIMONSVLEI CO-OPERATIVE

Simonsvlei is certainly one of the most forward-thinking, market-
driven and successful of the many co-operatives in the Cape. Established in 1945, there are now 84 farms within the membership of
Simonsvlei. These are located on a wide variety of soils, at several
different altitudes, from the cooler districts like Klein Drakenstein
to the gravelly soil of Muldersvlei, allowing the co-operative to
produce a wide range of wines from a huge variety of cultivars.

The first winemaker at Simonsvlei was Sarel Rossouw, who held
the job for 34 years, to be succeeded in 1982 by his son Johan,
who was in turn followed in 1985 by his brother Kobus. All have
been and are highly skilled and dedicated winemakers, and have
consistently produced prize-winning wines for Simonsvlei. Kobus,
the current Rossouw at the winemaking helm, is producing 32
different wines for Simonsvlei, but would prefer to limit the range
to ten or twelve in order to concentrate even more on quality.

In 1991 the co-operative appointed Philip Louw as manager, and
he plays a very active and successful role in the marketing of
Simonsvlei's range on a worldwide basis. Annual throughput aver-
ages a considerable 16,000 tons of grapes, of which about 40% is
exported, 70% going to the United Kingdom, and the rest to
Holland, Denmark and Germany. Philip Louw tries to visit all

his overseas markets at least twice a year, and the co-operative participates regularly in wine shows and fairs all over the world. It is little wonder that Simonsvlei has twice received President Mandela's Award for Export Achievement.

Tasting Notes

Chenin Blanc 1995 (Premier Range): Pale golden colour; typical quince and guava bouquet; clean, crisp fruit, well-balanced with long aftertaste.

Chardonnay/Sauvignon Blanc 1995 (Premier Range): Medium deep gold; both varieties distinct on nose; a good balance, with the weight of the Chardonnay offset by the springy fruit of the Sauvignon.

Cabernet Sauvignon/Merlot 1995 (50/50 blend): Deep red; open fruit nose; an easy-drinking, fruit-driven wine with some nice soft tannins – good value, shows New-World influence.

Pinotage Reserve 1993 (Veritas Gold, wine developed for UK market): Cherry red; powerful cherry/banana fruit on nose; nice rounded fruit in mouth, with some good tannins and structure.

Premier White Muscadel 1993 (fortified to 17.5% by volume): Golden syrup colour; raisins, sultanas and tropical fruits on nose; very rich, fruit-cake taste, with nice touch of acidity.

Technical Notes

Co-operative: 84 farms

Average production: 16,000 tons, 200,000 cases

Wines produced
RESERVE RANGE (top of the market, export only): Chardonnay, Cabernet Sauvignon, Shiraz, Pinotage
PREMIUM RANGE: Cabernet Sauvignon/Merlot, Chardonnay/ Sauvignon Blanc
LIFESTYLE RANGE: Classique Reserve, Premier Grand Cru, Special Late Harvest, White Muscadel, Rouge Classique (red sparkler)
WHITE: Grand Cru, Blanc de Blancs, Premier Chenin Blanc, Sauvignon Blanc Reserve, Riesling, Chardonnay, Chardonnay/

Sauvignon Blanc, Blanc de Noir, Stein, Bukettraube, Late Vintage, Special Late Harvest, Hanepoot, Premier Wit Muskadel
RED: Simonsrood, Shiraz, Cabernet/Merlot, Cabernet Sauvignon
SPARKLING: Vin Sec, Vin Doux
'PORT': Non-vintage, Vintage
FIVE LITRES: Premier Grand Cru, Stein, Late Harvest, Simonsrood, Hanepoot

Useful Information

Manager: Philip Louw
Winemaker: Kobus Rossouw
Address: Simonsvlei Winery, Box 584, Suider-Paarl 7624
Telephone: 021.863.3040 *Fax*: 021.863.1240

Tasting/Sales: Weekdays 08.00 to 17.00, Saturday 08.30 to 14.00
Facilities: Lunches during Christmas season, or by special arrangement

VILLIERA

Originally a de Villiers property, as one would guess, Villiera does not have a long winemaking history. When the Grier family bought the estate in 1983, there were not many vines planted, and very few of those were noble varieties, nor was this obvious wine land. There are no hills, and the soil is sandy, with a little loam and some pebbles and chalk. These topsoils form a layer of between one and three metres, on a clay subsoil, which means that the vines have to put their roots well down to just above the clay to get their moisture and the all-important trace elements. The farm is very exposed, and the soils not very fertile, resulting in low yields of grapes with a high concentration of flavour.

This is a real family business, with two Grier brothers in the background, and their sons Jeff the winemaker, and Simon, who looks after the vineyards, in the front line, ably backed by Jeff's sister Cathy, who is the marketing and export whizz-kid. The first priority on arrival here was to find a flagship wine on which to build their reputation. The Griers knew the Denois family of Champagne, and were encouraged by them, and by the terroir of Villiera, to enter into an agreement with the Denois for a joint venture in the production of Méthode Champenoise sparkling wine. The first Tradition, Charles de Fère was produced in 1984, and has met with consistent success. The French name has now been dropped, and the range increased to four different wines.

There is a non-vintage wine called Carte Rouge, which is 45% Pinot Noir, 15% Chardonnay, 20% Pinotage and 20% Chenin Blanc; a non-vintage Tradition Rosé, made from 50% Pinot Noir, 35% Chardonnay and 15% Pinotage for local colour; and top of the range, also a non-vintage wine, is Grande Cuvée Tradition, made from 50/50 Pinot Noir and Chardonnay, and retailing in SA at R25 a bottle. Villiera also brings out a Vintage Tradition, Première Cuvée in occasional years when conditions are exceptionally good. This is made from 65% Pinot Noir and 35% Chardonnay, part of which is oak-fermented. From these early beginnings, Villiera rapidly became the largest producers of Méthode Cap Classique in the country.

It is now part of South African wine folklore that the talented but always modest Jeff Grier only escaped becoming a chicken farmer by a set of happy circumstances, but the poultry industry's loss is definitely a gain for the world of wine. The Griers soon turned their attention to the making of still wine, in which they have succeeded in their usual understated style. White wine came first. Two blended wines are made – Sonnet, which is off-dry, and the dry Blue Ridge Blanc – and five varietal wines: Sauvignon Blanc, Blanc Fumé, which is the wooded version of the Sauvignon, Chenin Blanc, Gewürztraminer and Rhine Riesling. The Villiera range is now complete with four red wines. Again two blended wines are made, Blue Ridge Rouge, a lightly wooded, fruity wine at the lower end of the price spectrum, and Cru Monro, a classic Bordeaux-style blend at the top of the range. The two varietal reds are Cabernet Sauvignon and Merlot, the latter being Jeff Grier's, and many of his clients' favourite.

Tasting Notes

Tradition, Carte Rouge, Brut N. V.: Pale straw colour, with persistent, largish bubbles; attractive bouquet, slight pear-drops; clean, crisp fruit, nice and creamy, with good length.

Vintage Tradition, Brut 1989: Same pale straw, with good long mousse; slight biscuity flavour, good fruit with nice bit of bottle-age.

Blue Ridge Blanc 1995 (70% Chenin Blanc, 30% Sauvignon Blanc): Very pale colour; good up-front fruit on nose; clean and crisp in mouth, Sauvignon dominates, as on nose.

Chenin Blanc 1995 (30% barrel-fermented): Mid-gold colour; open guava and quince nose; medium-dry, nice guava and quince aromas released in mouth, long aftertaste, will keep.

Rhine Riesling 1995: Bright, mid-gold; lovely Riesling fruit on nose; clean, dry, fruit/acidity in balance, another class act that will improve with keeping.

Sauvignon Blanc 1995: Pale colour; herbaceous and fruity nose; good, clean slightly gooseberry fruit, dry and quite long.

Chardonnay 1995 (first vintage of still Chardonnay – barrel-fermented, with three months on lees and regular batonage. Jeff says next year will pick riper): Mid-gold colour; nose has more Sauvignon character than Chardonnay; nice, rather green fruit, with some wood, but not over-stated.

Blanc Fumé 1995 (100% Sauvignon Blanc, fermented in cask, two months on lees): Very pale colour; good fruit on nose, with some vanilla; all very nicely in balance, fruit, acidity and just a touch of oakiness.

Blue Ridge Rouge 1994 (Shiraz, Gamay and Pinotage): Bright scarlet colour; open bouquet of ripe summer fruits; easy-drinking, with cherry flavours, some nice soft tannins.

Merlot 1993: Deep ruby red; good fruit on nose, with some pepperiness; really ripe fruit with a touch of spices, very long, with good tannins and some backbone. A good Merlot.

Cru Monro 1993 (60% Cabernet Sauvignon, 40% Merlot, some new wood): Deep red colour; open nose, with Cabernet cassis dominant; mouthful of ripe fruit, soft tannins and considerable structure.

Technical Notes

Area under vines: 170 hectares

Cultivars planted
WHITE: Chardonnay, Sauvignon Blanc, Chenin Blanc,
Gewürztraminer, Rhine Riesling
RED: Pinot Noir, Cabernet Sauvignon, Merlot, Pinotage, Shiraz,
Gamay

Wines produced
WHITE: Blue Ridge Blanc, Sonnet, Chenin Blanc, Sauvignon Blanc,
Blanc Fumé, Rhine Riesling, Chardonnay, Gewürztraminer
RED: Blue Ridge Rouge, Merlot, Cabernet Sauvignon, Cru Monro
SPARKLING: Tradition Carte Rouge, Tradition Rosé Brut, Vintage
Tradition Brut, Tradition Carte d'Or Brut

Useful Information

Owners: Grier family
Winemaker: Jeff Grier
Vineyard Manager: Simon Grier
Marketing/Export: Cathy Grier
Address: Villiera Estate, Box 66, Koelenhof 7605
Telephone: 021.882.2002 *Fax*: 021.882.2314

Tasting/Sales: Weekdays 08.30 to 17.00, Saturday 08.30 to 13.00
Facilities: Champagne breakfasts, winter lunches occasionally;
telephone for dates and details

WELGEMEEND

The Hofmeyr family used to own the last vineyard within the city
boundaries of Cape Town: it was situated where the Jan van Riebeeck High School stands today, and was called Welgemeend. So
when writer and wine-lover Billy Hofmeyr bought a wine farm
called Monte Video at Klapmuts in 1974, he renamed it Welgemeend, and set about planting it with noble varieties. Hofmeyr
was always a lover of the great wines of Bordeaux, as well as those
of the southern Rhône, so his plantings were the two Cabernets,
Merlot, Petit Verdot and Malbec for his Bordeaux blend, plus

198

Shiraz, Grenache and a little experimental Pinotage for the Rhône style. This was a bold and pioneering move in South Africa at that time, as the vast majority of winemakers only grew high-yield varietals like Chenin Blanc and Cinsaut.

The first vintage to be made was 1979, and the two wines were the Welgemeend Estate Wine – which was and still is the estate's flagship Bordeaux blend – and Amade, the Rhône-style red which also carries on today. The range has now been increased to include a second label Bordeaux blend named, unpronounceably for foreigners, Soopjeshoogte, which means 'the little hill where you stop for a drink', and Douelle, also a mix of Bordeaux varieties, with a high 27% of Malbec.

When Billy Hofmeyr fell ill in the early nineties, his daughter Louise stepped into the breach. She was a Fine Arts graduate, and had no experience whatever of winemaking. 1996 was her fifth vintage at Welgemeend, and she has made a marvellous success of her new career. She is small, determined, intelligent and highly articulate, and the artistic sensitivity acquired during her university years shows clearly in her approach to wine. Louise's mother, Ursula Hofmeyr, is, and has been for twenty years, in charge of the vineyards, and the two make a formidable team on the still male-dominated winemaking scene in the Cape.

Tasting Notes

Amade 1993 (50% Shiraz, 40% Grenache, 10% Pinotage, aged in shaved casks, as well as 2nd- and 3rd-fill): Brilliant red; lots of ripe, up-front fruit on the nose; very easy, pleasing taste of strawberries, raspberries and cherries, with some nice soft tannins.

Soopjeshoogte 1993 (2nd label since 1991, 39% Cabernet Franc, 36% Merlot, 25% Cabernet Sauvignon, all aged in small wood, no new casks): Luscious deep red; blackcurrant bouquet; an easy-drinking blend, with plenty of nice fruit, but no great pretensions.

Douelle 1992 (30% Merlot, 27% Malbec, 26% Cabernet Sauvignon, 17% Cabernet Franc): Fine, deep colour; some pleasing fruit on the nose, but still quite closed; nice balance – a well-put-together wine, with fruit and wood in harmony.

Welgemeend Estate Wine 1992 (41% Merlot, 34% Cabernet Sauvignon, 24% Cabernet Franc, 1% Petit Verdot, 26% aged in new oak): Brilliant red, due to reduced skin-contact; ripe fruit nose; a lean, elegant wine, racy with some nice structure, will age well.

Technical Notes

Area under vines: 13.4 hectares

Cultivars planted
RED: Cabernet Sauvignon, Merlot, Cabernet Franc, Malbec, Petit Verdot, Shiraz, Grenache, Pinotage

Wines produced
RED: Welgemeend Estate Wine, Soopjeshoogte, Douelle, Amade

Useful Information

Owners: Hofmeyr family
Winemaker: Louise Hofmeyr
Vineyard Manager: Ursula Hofmeyr
Address: Welgemeend Estate, Box 69, Klapmuts 7625
Telephone: 021.875.5210 *Fax*: 021.875.5239

Tasting/Sales: Saturdays 09.00 to 12.30; no tastings on weekdays, except by appointment; no credit cards

UNVISITED

Estates and Wineries: Alan Nelson, Belcher Wine Farm, Berghof, Brenthurst Winery, Diamant, Hoopenberg, Laborie (KWV's estate), Rhebokskloof, Sonop, Veenwouden, Windmeul, Zabdwijk (Kosher winery)
Co-operative: Simondium Winery

8

Wellington

Wellington is a small town to the north of Paarl and, although it is officially part of the Paarl wine region, it has its own Wine Route and its own character. The soils are similar to those of the rest of the Paarl region, and the vineyards lie mainly on the banks of the Berg river to the west of Wellington, and south of the Kromme river, which flows in from the north-east to join the Berg.

WELLINGTON WYNKELDER

The first co-operative to be established in the Cape in the early 1900s, Wellington Wynboere experienced various problems in its early days, and was reconstituted in 1934 with only ten members. Today, having undergone a name change to the Wellington Wynkelder, there are 52 members. The cellar, modernized in 1986, processes about 12,500 tons of grapes a year from farms, which are mostly monocultural, along the banks of the Berg river and on the slopes of the Groenberg mountain.

This is a hot, dry-land area, and irrigation is necessary on all the farms. Originally Wellington was a fortified wine district, and the co-operative still supplies SFW with its brown and ship sherries. The land is well suited to the production of red wine, but production is still 85% white – this is changing rapidly, and soon the percentage will be up to 30% red.

Winemaker/manager Gert Boerssen, here since 1981, is keen and optimistic about the future. On the day of my visit he was eagerly awaiting the delivery of a new pneumatic press, for which the roof had had to be partly removed, and there will be a new red wine cellar constructed next year. Grapes are carefully inspected and analyzed on arrival at the winery, and the farmers are paid strictly according to the quality of their crops. Boerssen plans to carry out this classification of the noble varieties in the vineyards in the future, and the co-operative is considering employing the services of a full-time viticulturist.

Only about 2% of the total production goes into bottle at present, the remainder being sold in bulk to the likes of SFW, Distillers and the KWV on the home market, and for export through a company called South African Dry Foods, which is also used by three Wellington wineries and the Bolandse Co-op.

Tasting Notes

Chenin Blanc 1995: Very pale colour; clean, quite shy bouquet; crisp, clean elegant fruit, nice balance.

Sauvignon Blanc 1995 (Veritas Gold award): Pale, greeny gold; up-front Sauvignon nose of elder-bark; fresh, ripe, gooseberry fruit, nice balance with long finish.

Pinotage 1992 (Veritas Double Gold): Deep red; rounded Pinotage fruit nose; pleasant mouthful of cherries and other red berries, with some nice tannin and structure.

Cabernet Sauvignon 1991: Very dark, dense red; cassis, cigar-box and slight farmyard aromas; good fruit and non-aggressive tannins, some backbone, a good Cabernet.

Special Late Harvest 1995 (13% alcohol, 43.6 g/l sugar, Chenin and Hanepoot): Pale golden colour; nose quite closed up, but some tropical fruit aromas coming through; rich, concentrated and ripe, but no botrytis, very long aftertaste.

'Port' 1992 Vintage (made from Ruby Cabernet): Deep red; prunes and figs on nose; rich, dried fruit taste and good length.

Technical Notes

Co-operative: 52 members

Average production: 12,500 tons, of which 2% bottled

Wines produced
WHITE: Sauvignon Blanc, Chenin Blanc, Blanc de Blancs, Riesling, Stein, Late Vintage, Special Late Vintage, Hanepoot Jerepigo
RED: Cabernet Sauvignon, Merlot, Pinotage
'PORT': Vintage

Useful Information

Winemaker: Gert Boerssen
Address: Wellington Wynkelder, Box 520, Wellington 7657
Telephone: 02211.31163 *Fax*: 02211.32423

Tasting/Sales: Weekdays 08.00 to 12.30 and 14.00 to 17.00, Saturday 09.00 to 12.30

UNVISITED

Estates and Wineries: Jacaranda, Napier Winery, Onverwacht, Claridge, Welvanpas (Retief Family Cellar)
Co-operatives: Bovlei, Wamakersvallei

9

Worcester

Worcester is a large area, centred around the town of that name, which lies about 50 kilometres north-east of Stellenbosch as the crow flies. In the first part of the eighteenth century, however, the only access to the Breede river valley lay to the north from Tulbagh, via the Roodezand pass. It was not until the completion of the Bain's Kloof road in 1853 that a viable commercial route was established between Worcester and Cape Town. By the 1860s, the area under vines had increased enormously, though the main part of the crop was dried for raisins – as it remained until after the Second World War, when world demand for raisins dropped away. At this point the vineyard owners turned to winemaking, which led to the establishment of a large number of co-operatives. These dominate the Worcester region to this day and, with only a handful of estates, they contribute about 25% of South Africa's total wine production, making Worcester the largest wine producing area in the Cape in terms of volume.

The Breede river valley, where most of the vineyards are situated, is bounded to the north, west and south by mountains, and to the east by its boundary with Robertson. Rainfall varies greatly, from 1,500 millimetres in the east around Slanghoek, to as low as 300 millimetres around Nuy in the west. Vineyards are mainly along the banks of the Breede. In the area of lower rainfall to the west of the region, irrigation is necessary and is drawn principally from the Brandvlei Dam south of Worcester.

The majority of Worcester's production is sold in bulk to the merchants, for export, or for the making of brandy. The estates, however, are producing some fine wines from the noble grape varieties; and most of the co-operatives are bottling a small proportion of their output in response to the increasing demand for

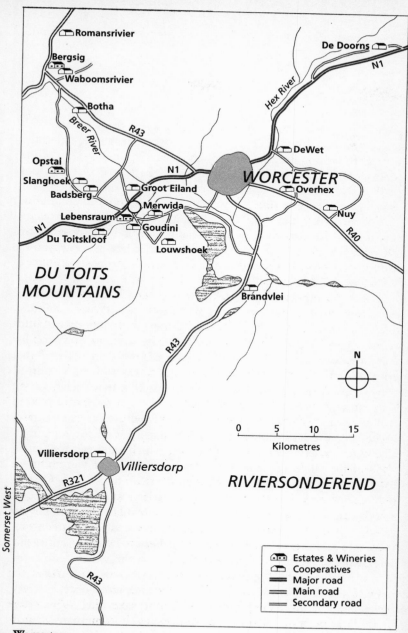

good South African wines on both the domestic and export markets.

BERGSIG

Although the quickest way to reach Worcester from Stellenbosch or Paarl is now by the N1, by far the most scenic route, especially if you are visiting Bergsig, is through the mountains by way of the spectacular Bain's Kloof pass from Paarl. Bergsig lies at the foot of the pass, and its 320 hectares of vines grow mostly along the banks of the Breede river and on the foothills of the mountains. Irrigation is necessary most years from the river, while the growing of vines on the lower slopes of the mountains is made possible by the relatively high rainfall – 1,000 millimetres, against only 300 in Worcester. Cold winters and cool springs mean less pests, less need for spraying and an even bud-break.

Willem Hendrik Lategan settled here to farm back in 1843, and the family have grown grapes at Bergsig in an unbroken line for over a century and a half. 'Prop' Lategan is the present owner, and his son, De Wet, makes the wine, aided by his two brothers. In common with most Worcester wine farms, the main part of the crop until the 1920s was for raisins, but demand fell off after the Second World War, and the Lategans, like their neighbours, concentrated their efforts on winemaking.

A very large number of cultivars are grown at Bergsig, mainly white, but the lesser-known ones are usually used for blending. The main variety here is Chenin Blanc, which accounts for up to 30% of the vineyard, and 10,000 cases of the 1995 were bottled for the Sunday Times Wine Club under their own label. Of the reds Cabernet Sauvignon is the main variety, and Tinta Barocca and Touriga Nacional are used to make a regular prize-winner of a 'port'. Prizes are the norm at Bergsig: in recent years the 1990 Pinotage, and the 1989 Hanepoot won Veritas Double Golds, the 1992 Ruby Cabernet was Wine of the Year at the Worcester Young Wine Show, and the 1994 was Wine of the Month on SAA.

Only about 5% of the huge production goes into bottle, the rest being sold in bulk to the wholesalers. Export sales have begun only recently, and are handled by the Cape Vineyards Company.

Tasting Notes

Chenin Blanc 1995: Bright, medium gold; quincy Chenin nose; lovely, crisp and dry with great length, a charmer.

Sauvignon Blanc 1995: Good, brilliant gold; nose good, but quite restrained; excellent fruit, but quite weighty for Sauvignon, with long aftertaste.

Cabernet Sauvignon 1994: Deep, dark red; minty, blackcurrant aromas; a medium-bodied wine, with nice minty tones, already very drinkable, and will keep.

Pinotage 1993: Very deep colour; lovely ripe-fruit nose, plums and cherries, with hint of banana, good tannins and a slight dry finish, good.

Gewürztraminer 1995: Pale, greeny gold; very intense grapey, spicy, almost Muscat bouquet; concentrated, spicy and tropical, with tremendous length – a star.

DE WET CO-OPERATIVE

The De Wet Co-operative winery is just on the outskirts of Worcester on the right of the N1 as you head towards Touw River. I called without an appointment, and winemaker Zakkie Bester was on the forecourt of the cellar, changing a wheel for a lady customer. This is typical of his kindness. He is a very busy man, especially at the time of my visit, having lost his right-hand man, assistant winemaker Kobus de Wet, who had recently died after 30 years at the cellar. In spite of being so pressed, and my not having telephoned in advance, he gave me a lot of his time and a comprehensive tasting of the co-operative's wines.

Founded in 1946, this is the oldest winery in Worcester. There are 55 members, some of them father-and-son teams, farming 42 farms. Average throughput is around 17,000 tons of grapes. This would add up to about 15.5 million cases if all the wine were bottled, but only 1% is sold this way, the rest going in bulk to merchants and for export.

Currently around 40% of the vineyards are planted with Chenin Blanc, most of which is used for brandy, for which Worcester is the main region. Palomino is also grown for 'sherry'. In 1994 a decision was made to increase plantings of the noble cultivars up to 30% of the whole, and many red varietals, mostly Shiraz, Cabernets, Merlot and Pinotage will soon come on stream.

Each member farm is treated as a single producer; grapes are tasted and analyzed, and farmers are paid according to quality, and their wines are vinified separately. A viticulturist is available for advice on soils, planting and plant material, though each member is free to buy vines independently. 1995 saw the first 'Vintage port' from the co-operative, made mostly from Shiraz, but with a little Touriga Nacional included, and it has won a Gold at the Young Wine Show.

Tasting Notes

Cape Bay Chenin Blanc 1995 (export only): Pale straw; up-front guava bouquet; lovely, clean and dry, with tropical fruit flavours and good length.

Cape Riesling 1995: Pale straw; good fruit nose; well balanced, ripe fruit with acidity just right and long on the aftertaste.

Sauvignon Blanc 1995: Pale gold; some nice elderflower and Sauvignon grassiness on the nose; clean, crisp and lean, not typical of the variety, but a good dry white.

Clairette Blanche 1995: Very pale colour; shy but nice bouquet; fresh, clean and fruity, with low acidity and low alcohol at 10.9% (screw cap).

Fernao Pires 1995: Pale gold; smells very spicy, almost like Gewürztraminer; nice fruit, quite spicy with a touch of sweetness and good length.

Blanc de Noir 1995 (50/50 Merlot/Pinotage): Pale pink; faint but pleasing summer fruit nose; light, nice fruit on palate, quite sweet.

Special Late Harvest Gewürztraminer 1995: Nice golden hue; luscious bouquet of fruit and spices; lovely, concentrated sweet grapiness and good length, very good.

Petillant Fronte (carbonated Muscat de Frontignan): Pale colour, light bubbles; fresh Muscat nose; light in body and alcohol at 8.5%, approved by Heart Foundation, and by me.

Petillant Bouquet (carbonated Gewürztraminer and Fernao Pires): Very similar to Fronte, but more fruit, body and alcohol.

Merlot/Shiraz 1995 (includes 24% of oaked 1994): Good mid-red; nice blackberry nose; easy drinker with a bit of structure.

Hanepoot Jerepigo 1993 (17% alcohol): Syrup gold; lovely Muscat bouquet; tremendous concentrated fruit, raisins and apricots. Deserves its Veritas Gold.

'Port 1995' (cask sample): Deep, purplish colour; rich, figgy fruit bouquet; lots of nice dried-fruit taste, rather sweet, a good SA-style 'port'.

Technical Notes

Co-operative: 42 farms

Average production: 17,000 tons, 1% bottled

Wines produced
WHITE: Sauvignon Blanc, Cape Riesling, Chenin Blanc, Clairette Blanche, Fernao Pires, Blanc de Noir, Gewürztraminer Special Late Harvest, Vin Doux, Sweet Hanepoot
RED: Droe Rooi, Cabernet Sauvignon, Merlot/Shiraz, Red Muscadel
SPARKLING (carbonated): Fronte Petillant, Bouquet Petillant
'PORT': Vintage

Useful Information

Winemaker/Manager: Zakkie Bester
Address: De Wet Co-op Wine Cellar, Box 16, De Wet 6853
Telephone: 0231.92710 *Fax*: 0231.92723

Tasting/Sales: Weekdays 08.00 to 17.00, Saturday 09.00 to 12.00

NUY CO-OPERATIVE

One of the smallest co-operatives in South Africa, Nuy – pronounced Nay – has only twenty members, several of whom are father-and-son partnerships, with thirteen farms. It is quite easy to find if you look at the map, but I took the scenic route by a very long dirt road which leads off the N1 close to the De Wet Co-op winery, and began to wonder if I would ever get there.

Small though it is, and however arduous your journey, the visit is very worthwhile. The overriding impression at the winery is of order and spotless cleanliness. I think this is the only place I have ever been, including the world's best hotels, restaurants and private houses, where there are fresh roses in the Gents' lavatory. This sets the tone for a welcoming and professionally run establishment, where quality is the order of the day.

Winemaker/Manager Wilhelm Linde has been in charge here since 1971. He is a highly skilled vintner, and is dedicated to producing wines of maximum possible quality. To this end, only 3% of the annual production is bottled, the rest being sold in bulk to merchants, by far the biggest customer being SFW. Four-fifths of the throughput is white wine, including a sparkler made from Sauvignon Blanc, 8% is fortified Muscadel Jerepigo, both red and white, and only 10% is red table wine – there are plans afoot, however, to increase this to up to 18%.

All the farms are fairly close, within eight kilometres of the winery, and the soils and micro-climates are very similar. All irrigate as necessary, but always after harvesting. As with most co-operatives, members are paid according to the quality of their grapes. The grapes are tasted and analyzed by Linde, as well as by the KWV's consultant viticulturist, two-fifths of whose time is bought by the co-op each year. He is also available to give advice to members on soil treatment, selection of varietals and supply of plant material.

The Nuy name is now well-established as one of the premier quality producing co-ops. Wines are regularly entered in the wine shows, and pick up many prizes. Linde has twice been awarded the coveted Diners Club Winemaker of the Year award, the last time being in 1991, when he and four of the Directors went to Australia.

Tasting Notes

Riesling 1995: Very pale colour; good, Riesling fruit nose; excellent ripe fruit with some nice weight.

Sauvignon Blanc 1995: Pale gold; definite asparagus aromas; cross between Old- and New-World styles, with loads of up-front fruit, but some weight as well.

Colombard 1995: Pale gold; nose not giving much, but nice fruit there; completely dry, but lots of clean fresh fruitiness.

Chardonnay 1995 (no wood used): Greeny-golden colour; nice Chardonnay fruit nose; ripe, full and fat, with good weight and length.

Chant de Nuit 1995 (45% Colombard, 45% Chenin, 10% Ferdinand de Lesseps): Bright, pale gold; very individual bouquet, like a cross between Gewürztraminer and Muscat; concentration of delicate, grapey fruit, but with some weight too, very long.

Sparkling Sauvignon Blanc (carbonated): Pale colour, good mousse; good fruit nose; medium-dry, with nice Sauvignon fruit.

Fernao Pires 1995: Pale gold; spicy, grapey bouquet; medium-dry, with good fruit and a persistent aftertaste.

Bukettraube 1995: Greenish gold; quite shy on nose; rich, semi-sweet fruit with a long, slightly metallic aftertaste.

Colombard Semi-Sweet 1995: Mid-gold; again quite closed up on nose; loads of rich, ripe fruit, not at all cloying, and good length.

Steen Late Harvest 1995: Pale gold; lovely white peach bouquet; the same luscious taste of ripe white peach in the mouth, a bit short.

Dry Red 1992 (mainly Pinotage, some Cabernet Sauvignon, very little wood used): Medium red, browning a bit; good Pinotage nose of cherries; delicious taste of summer fruit, some soft tannins, to drink now with pleasure.

Red Muscadel 1992 (17% alcohol): Pale, browny colour; nose of apricots and raisins; a full, rich, ripe mouthful of fruit, excellent.

White Muscadel 1993 (17% alcohol): Treacle colour; grapey smell, slightly hot and dusty; amazing richness of dried fruits, apricots and figs.

Technical Notes

Co-operative: 20 members/13 farms

Average production: 10,000 tons, 3% bottled

Wines produced
WHITE: Riesling, Colombard Dry, Sauvignon Blanc, Chardonnay, Chant de Nuit, Fernao Pires, Bukettraube, Colombard Semi-Sweet, Steen Late Harvest, White Muscadel
RED: Rouge de Nuy
SPARKLING (carbonated): Sauvignon

Useful Information

Winemaker/Manager: Wilhelm Linde
Address: Nuy Wine Cellar Co-op, Box 5225, Worcester 6850
Telephone: 0231.70272 *Fax*: 0231.74994

Tasting/Sales: Weekdays 08.30 to 17.30, Saturday 08.30 to 12.30; sales at stall on R60 turn-off, and by mail order

ROMANSRIVIER CO-OPERATIVE

When this co-op was founded in 1950, practically all the wine was rebate for distilling, but now there is a strong move towards the production of quality table wines, of which 20% are red. The 48 members enjoy a wide range of soil types and micro-climates, but the best grapes for table wine come from farms near Wolseley and Ceres, where nights are cooler and yields lower. The area is split roughly half and half between fruit and wine, and the cool climate in the shadow of the Langeberg mountains gives wines of a definite New-World style.

Young winemaker Eben Sadie, a graduate of Elsenburg, has only had one vintage here, although he has had a year's experience in Germany, and will do a vintage in France in 1996. He is keen and passionate about his chosen career, and should have a great future. Only 8,000 cases of bottled wines are sold of the average 8,000-ton production, representing about 5% of the total. The rest is sold in bulk, with a high proportion going for export.

Tasting Notes

Grand Cru White 1995 (50% Colombard, 25% Chenin, 25% others): Pale, greeny gold; clean, limey fruit bouquet; same nice citrus fruit flavours in mouth, with refreshing acidity.

Chenin Blanc 1995: Deeper colour than Grand Cru; guavas and slight cat's pee nose; fruit good, acidity on the high side, but nice enough.

Sauvignon Blanc/Chardonnay 1995 (75%/25%): Pale straw; nose good, but not over-Sauvignon; nice fruit, Sauvignon very much to the fore, but some Chardonnay weight.

Ceres Colombard 1994: Medium-deep greeny gold; good fruit nose; clean, pleasant fruit, high acidity, alcohol 13%, a good Colombard, Diners Club Selection.

Ceres Chardonnay 1994 (unwooded, whole-bunch pressed, 2 months on lees): Nice mid-gold; ripe Chardonnay nose; fat, buttery Chardonnay, with almond tones.

Ceres Chardonnay 1992 (barrel-fermented, a third in new oak, two thirds in 2nd-fill): Deep golden colour; some good fruit on nose, but also a distinct wet sawdust smell as well; big and buttery, wood very strong, good length.

Ceres Chardonnay 1993 (barrel-fermented in same mix of wood): Shade lighter colour than 1992; good, rich fruit on nose, oak marked; lovely, fat and buttery, a fine Chardonnay.

Ceres Chardonnay 1994 (same barrel treatment): Bright gold with green tinge; fine fruit and vanilla nose; very ripe, open fruit in mouth, with oak nicely harmonized.

Cabernet Sauvignon 1991 (in tank, volatile acidity was developing, wood chips added): Black colour; ripe fruit bouquet; full, rounded berry fruit – to be bottled next month.

Cabernet Sauvignon 1992 (part wood-aged): Quite good colour; slightly stalky nose; some good fruit in mouth, but some greeny bitterness from unripe tannins.

Cabernet Sauvignon 1993 (part wood-aged): Same deep colour as 1991; cassis nose; softer and riper, with good fruit, less aggressive tannins and a bit of backbone.

Cabernet Sauvignon 1995 (no wood yet, picked at optimum ripeness): Dark, almost black colour; nose closed; soft, sweet fruit, not too full-bodied, will all go in oak.

Technical Notes

Co-operative: 48 members

Average production: 8,000 tons, 8,000 cases bottled

Wines produced
WHITE: Colombard, Chenin Blanc, Blanc de Blancs, Riesling, Grand Cru, Blanc Fumé, Sauvignon Blanc/Chardonnay, Special Late Harvest, Sweet Hanepoot, Chardonnay Ceres Vin Blanc Special Reserve, Ceres Colombard, Ceres Chardonnay
RED: Cabernet Sauvignon, Vino Rood, Ruby Nektar Rooi Jerepiko
SPARKLING: Vin Doux, Chiffon Pienk
'PORT'

Useful Information

Winemakers: Olla Olivier, Eben Sadie
Address: Romansrivier Co-op Wine Cellar, Box 108, Wolseley 6830
Telephone: 0236.311070 *Fax*: 0236.311102

Tasting/Sales: Weekdays 08.00 to 17.00, Saturday 08.30 to 10.30

UNVISITED

Estates and Wineries: Lebensraum, Opstal
Co-operatives: Badsberg, Botha, Brandvlei, De Doorns, Du Toits-

kloof, Goudini, Groot Eiland, Louwshoek, Merwida, Overhex, Slanghoek, Villiersdorp, Waboomsrivier

10

Robertson

The wine region of Robertson is situated between those of Worcester and the Klein Karoo. Its western boundary marches with the eastern limit of Worcester and is about 120 kilometres east of Cape Town. The bulk of the vineyards lie along the banks of the Breede river, which runs through the district in a south-easterly direction, and in the foothills of the mountains to the north and south of the river valley.

Farming in Robertson did not really begin until the early part of the nineteenth century, at which time it was largely confined to the raising of sheep and cattle in the wild grassland of the valley. It was, and still is, a hot region with a very low average annual rainfall, and in high summer the Breede river often ran dry. It was not until the construction of the Brandvlei dam and the irrigation canal that runs through the valley that vine growing became a viable proposition. In the early days, wine production was almost entirely for the making of fortified wines and brandy.

The understanding of cold fermentation, mainly learnt by winemakers who went to Germany to study winemaking, saw the beginning of table wine production in Robertson. All of the estates and many of the co-operatives are now producing some excellent dry whites from Chardonnay and Sauvignon Blanc; a few good reds are made, such as the Shiraz from Zandvliet, and some respectable Cabernets from Springfield and Weltevrede, but the region is better suited to the white varieties.

ASHTON CO-OPERATIVE

One of the Cape's younger co-operatives, Ashton was established in 1962. There are currently 94 members, owning about 60 farms. This differential between the number of members of a co-operative and the number of farms is explained in two ways. If, as in the case of Ashton, there are more members than farms, this is because there are a number of father-and-son partnerships; on the other hand, you may have more farms than members when certain members have more than one farm. The Ashton farms all lie around Ashton, and total about 1,000 hectares, giving the cellar an annual throughput of around 25,000 tons of grapes.

The majority of the wines made at Ashton are white, and most are sold in bulk to big merchants like SFW and Distillers. Some goes as grape concentrate to the wine industry for making semi-sweet wines, and to the confectionery trade. About 10,000 cases are bottled, and are sold directly by the co-operative. Management is in the hands of Willem Joubert, and winemaking, following the retirement of Kas Huisamen in 1995, is the responsibility of young Marna Mans, assisted by André van Dyk. In common with many of South Africa's co-operatives, Ashton employs the services of one of the KWV's consultant viticulturists, who advises members on what varieties and which clones are best suited to their different plots, optimum harvesting times, soil treatments, etc.

Tasting Notes

Colombar 1995: Very pale straw; not much nose; clean, crisp fruit with correct acidity. Astonishing value at R4.50.

Sauvignon Blanc 1995: Pale, greenish gold; classic Sauvignon bouquet of elder bark; a clean, elegant wine with no faults.

Chardonnay 1995 (30% barrel-fermented, 3 weeks on lees): Medium greeny gold; ripe fruit and no wood on nose; good fruit with some weight on the palate, wood coming through at the end.

Gewürztraminer 1995: Very pale, almost colourless; typical, spicy Traminer nose; same spicy fruit in the mouth, quite surprisingly dry, and finishes a little short.

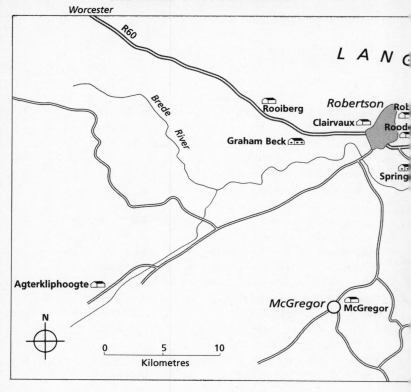

Robertson

Dry Red 1995 (Cabernet Sauvignon, Merlot, Ruby Cabernet):
Bright, medium red; agreeable fruit bouquet; an easy, highly
gluggable red.

Satin Red 1994 (Shiraz, 6–7 months in 3rd-fill French oak): Deep
red; nose a bit peppery; ripe fruit with peppery notes like the
nose, some nice tannins, ready to drink.

Special Late Harvest 1995 (Muscat de Frontignan): Pale gold;
rich, ripe Muscat nose; good, ripe table grape flavour, lacks
complexity, but an enjoyable grapey wine.

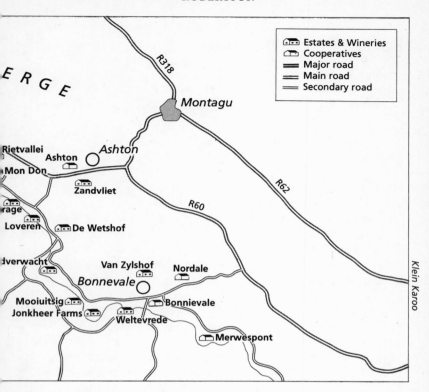

Technical Notes

Co-operative: 60 farms/94 members

Average production: 25,000 tons, only 10,000 cases bottled.

Wines produced
WHITE: Colombard, Riesling, Sauvignon Blanc, Chardonnay, Gewürztraminer, Bukettraube, Petillant Blanc, Late Harvest, Special Late Harvest, Hanepoot, White Muscadel
RED: Dry Red, Satin Red, Red Muscadel
'PORT'

Useful Information

Manager: Willem Joubert
Winemaker: Marna Mans
Assistant Winemaker: André van Dyk
Address: Ashton Kooperatiewe Wynkelder, Box 40, Ashton 6715
Telephone: 0234.51135

Tasting/Sales: Weekdays 08.00 to 12.30 and 13.30 to 17.00,
Saturday 08.30 to 12.30

GRAHAM BECK WINES, MADEBA

Coal magnate Graham Beck bought this 1,850-hectare estate in 1983. The previous owners named the property Madeba after a town on the old King's Highway in Jordan. It is aptly named, for Madeba means 'place of running water', and the valley in which the land lies is bisected by two rivers, the Breede and the Finch. There are currently 140 hectares planted with vines, an area that will be increased to 180 by 1998. Other farming activities include citrus fruit and the rearing of sheep and game, and Graham Beck also owns a large racing stud here, as the high pH content in the soil is particularly well-suited to the breeding of horses.

Graham Beck is a major player in the South African wine game, as he is in everything that he touches. As well as the Madeba farm, he also acquired the 117-hectare Bellingham winery in the Franschhoek valley in 1990, and in 1991 merged his wines and spirits interests with those of Sol Kerzner's Kersaf, and the two businesses now trade as Douglas Green Bellingham.

Soon after the purchase of Madeba, it was considered that although the soils of the valley were well-suited to the growing of the noble varieties, there were certain areas that could be better aspected. In typical Beck fashion, some of the giant plant used in the mining business was shipped in, and a few million tons of earth were moved around to form new hills, with slopes facing the right way. The same big thinking was applied to the construction of the cellar. The first building, completed in 1990, was created specifi-cally for the making of Méthode Cap Classique, which accounts for about a third of the estate's production. Cellar 1, as it is called, is also used for fermentation and maturation in oak casks. Cellar

2, finished a year later, has the same rather startling architectural style and colour scheme, and is used for making still wine in bulk.

In the vineyard, which is all irrigated by a highly sophisticated computerized system, there are currently fourteen varieties planted, but this will be scaled down to nine by 1998. Because of the emphasis on Cap Classique, there is a slight preponderance of Chardonnay and Pinot Noir. Although most of the wine of Madeba is made from the estate's own grapes, some are bought in as well.

The range of wines made at Madeba is relatively limited. Two Cap Classiques are produced, a Brut Non-Vintage and a Blanc de Blancs Vintage, and only four still wines. A barrel-fermented Chardonnay is at the top end of the range, with two white blends, one, Waterside White, from Colombard and Chardonnay, and the other, Bouquet Blanc, made from three grapes, at the lower end. The one red wine of Madeba is called Railroad Red, and is a blend of Cabernet and Shiraz, which sees 7 months in 2nd-, 3rd- and even 4th-fill French oak.

General management of Madeba is in the very able hands of Gary Baumgarten, ex-KWV technical guru, who is also Chairman of the Cape's Oenology Research Committee. Cellarmaster is ex-Clos Cabrière Pieter Ferreira who, not surprisingly, is the Cap Classique specialist. He is helped by Cellar Manager Manie Arendse, who assumes responsibility for still wine production. Pieter's wife, Ann, is in charge of public relations.

Production in 1995 totalled 55,000 cases, but this will increase in 1996 to 72,000. Sales emphasis is strongly on export, and the Cap Classique is doing well in the United Kingdom: Sainsbury's took 6,000 cases of the N. V. Cap Classique in 1995, and the same wine is also taken by Marks and Spencer and Tesco. Packaging and presentation of the whole range of wines is of an exceptionally high standard, typifying an operation where quality and attention to every detail are the watchwords.

Tasting Notes

Graham Beck, Brut N. V. (50% Chardonnay, 50% Pinot Noir, with 20% of the blend barrel-fermented in Pièce Champenoise casks from Seguin-Moreau): Pale straw colour, with small and persistent bubbles; very Champagne biscuit on nose; smooth and creamy in the mouth, with nice fruit and a bit of bottle age.

Graham Beck, Brut, Blanc de Blancs 1991 (100% Chardonnay, of which half is fermented in cask, and half in stainless steel; 40 months yeast contact after bottle fermentation before disgorgement): Slightly paler colour than the N. V., with a finer mousse; biscuity again, with touch of vanilla on nose; lovely fruit, very dry and smooth.

Graham Beck Chardonnay 1993 (barrel-fermented, 6 months on lees): Greeny gold colour; vanilla and citrus nose; elegant, limey fruit on palate, with some Chardonnay butteriness, oak perfectly in balance.

Waterside White 1995 (70% Colombard, 30% Chardonnay): Light straw colour; fresh, citrus bouquet; clean, crisp fruit, with just the right level of acidity – good.

Bouquet Blanc 1995 (55% Cape Riesling, 35% Weisser Riesling, 10% Muscat de Frontignan): Pale, greenish gold; big, up-front fruit bouquet; very grapey and spicy in the mouth, with a nice touch of sweetness.

Railroad Red 1994 (60% Shiraz, 40% Cabernet, 7 months barrel ageing in old casks): Brilliant mid-red; good summer berry nose; ripe, accessible fruit, with some nice soft tannins, an easy-drinking red.

Technical Notes

Area under vines: 140 hectares, increasing to 180

Cultivars planted
WHITE: Chardonnay, Colombard, Cape Riesling, Weisser Riesling, Chenin Blanc, Sauvignon Blanc
RED: Pinot Noir, Shiraz, Cabernet Sauvignon, Merlot, Cabernet Franc

Wines produced
WHITE: Bouquet Blanc, Waterside White, Chardonnay
RED: Railroad Red
SPARKLING: Graham Beck Brut N. V., Graham Beck Brut, Blanc de Blancs Vintage

Useful Information

Owner: Graham Beck
General Manager: Gary Baumgarten
Cellarmaster: Pieter Ferreira
Cellar Manager: Manie Arendse
Public Relations: Ann Ferreira
Address: Graham Beck Winery, Box 724, Robertson 6705
Telephone: 02351.61214 *Fax*: 02351.5164

Tasting/Sales: October–April, weekdays 09.00 to 17.00, Saturday 09.00 to 13.00; Sunday and public holidays by appointment. May–September, weekdays 10.00 to 17.00, Saturday, Sunday and public holidays by appointment

BON COURAGE

Jacques Bruwer is the third generation of his family to make wine at Bon Courage. His grandfather bought the farm in 1927, and his father, André, took over in 1965. Up to that time, production of wine had been restricted to ports and sherries for the KWV, but André was more interested in making quality table wines, and set about replanting the vineyard with suitable varieties, which were mainly white. Today there are 130 hectares under vines, still mostly white varieties, with a little Cabernet Sauvignon, Merlot and Ruby Cabernet for a blended red called Grand Vin Rouge, plus a couple of hectares of Shiraz and some Pinot Noir for Cap Classique.

The original name of the farm was Goedemoed, but when André registered it as an estate in 1983 he was obliged to rename it, because the original property was much larger, and this could have led to confusion. Bon Courage was chosen, as it is an almost exact French translation of Goedemoed. In addition to the wine business, the Bruwers also grow apricots and peaches.

André turned out to be a gifted winemaker, and was also some-thing of an innovator. On taking over from his father, he installed cold fermentation equipment, and concentrated his efforts on making dry white wines, something that was unheard of for Robertson at that time. He was one of the first people in South Africa to experiment with a mechanical harvester, and in 1986 was one of the first to introduce night harvesting, realizing that the quality of the grapes, particularly the flavours taken from the skins, is much better if the fruit is cool. His wines have been consistent prizewinners, and André himself gained the signal honour of being named South African Estate Winemaker of the Year for three consecutive years in 1984, 1985 and 1986. In 1990 he won the coveted Diners Club Winemaker of the Year award.

Jacques, André's son, has now taken over the vinous reins, although he says his father still keeps an eye on things. He certainly looks like following in his father's footsteps, having won a new trophy at the 1995 SA Young Wine Show for the best marks scored with five wines, a remarkable achievement for his first solo vintage.

Only 25% of the farm's production is sold in bottle, the greater part being bought in bulk by the likes of Stellenbosch Farmers' Winery, and of the bottled wines, about 30% is exported, mainly to the United Kingdom and Canada.

Tasting Notes

Jacques Bruère, Brut Reserve 1993: Pale straw, good and persistent mousse; pleasing fruit and some yeastiness on the bouquet; fresh and fruity with some nice Champagne biscuit.

Sauvignon Blanc 1995: Pale, greenish gold; open fruit nose; fruit attack good, with nice middle palate and good length.

Chardonnay 1994 (50% barrel-fermented and 4 months in new oak, 50% in tank): Pale golden colour; slightly citrussy fruit nose with some vanilla; good weight, soft fruit with wood there, but not too much.

Gewürztraminer Special Late Harvest 1995: Medium-dark gold; pronounced, spicy Gewürz bouquet; a rich mouthful of spicy, sweet fruit, but quite dry on finish.

Shiraz 1994 (8 months aged in 2nd-fill Nevers oak): Medium-deep colour; powerful, ripe raspberry bouquet; very good, mouth-filling, ripe fruit, with some nice tannins and enough backbone to keep it going for three or four years.

White Muscadel (16.7% alcohol): Treacle gold; dried apricots and sultanas on nose; delicious, complexity of rich, ripe fruit, smoothed by alcohol.

Technical Notes

Area under vines: 130 hectares

Cultivars planted
WHITE: Chardonnay, Sauvignon Blanc, Colombard, Chenin Blanc, Cape Riesling
RED: Pinot Noir, Cabernet Sauvignon, Merlot, Ruby Cabernet, Shiraz

Wines produced
WHITE: Riesling, Sauvignon Blanc, Chardonnay, Rhine Riesling, Bouquet Blanc, Gewürztraminer, Blanc de Noir, Late Harvest, Gewürztraminer Special Late Harvest, Noble Late Harvest, Muscadel
RED: Grand Vin Rouge, Shiraz, Red Muscadel
SPARKLING: Chardonnay Vin Sec, Blush Vin Doux, Jacques Bruère, Brut Reserve, Jacques Bruère, Blanc de Blancs

Useful Information

Owners: Bruwer family
Winemaker: Jacques Bruwer
Address: Bon Courage Estate, Box 589, Robertson 6705
Telephone: 02351.4178 *Fax*: 02351.3581

Tasting/Sales: Weekdays 09.00 to 17.00, Saturday 09.00 to 12.30

GOEDVERWACHT

Jan du Toit's father bought the first part of this low-lying farm back in 1961. Jan succeeded him on his death in 1987, and has since bought a neighbouring farm, and this, together with a few smaller parcels he has acquired, brings the total area under vines to 110 hectares. He has built a large new winery, equipped with modern stainless steel equipment, and processing in excess of a million litres of wine each year. There are many varieties planted, and the vast majority of the wine goes for bulk sales to the merchants.

Jan's future lies in the bottling of his own wines, and he will do well. His first bottling, a mere 500 cases of the 1993 Colombard, was a great success, gaining him a Gold medal at the Robertson Young Wine Show. In 1994 his Sauvignon Blanc won a Silver Veritas award, and his Colombard got a Bronze. He increased his range of bottled wines in 1995 to include an unwooded Chardonnay, and his Colombard achieved a Veritas Gold. At the moment his bottled wines are sold about 20% locally, and 80% on the export market, mostly going to Germany and the United Kingdom.

Unfortunately his sales are going so well that, on the day that I called on him, he was only able to produce one bottle, and that was the Chardonnay 1995. He gave me a card from his UK agent so that I could taste the other wines on my return to England. Sadly I mislaid it – judging from the quality of the Chardonnay, its loss was my loss also.

Tasting Notes

Chardonnay 1995 (unwooded): Lovely, pale limey-gold; open, Chardonnay, citrus fruit bouquet; nicely rounded, ripe fruit, with surprising weight and breadth for an unwooded Chardonnay.

Technical Notes

Area under vines: 110 hectares

Cultivars planted
Details not given for bulk wines, but for bottled wines:
WHITE: Colombard, Sauvignon Blanc, Chardonnay

Wines produced: Colombard, Sauvignon Blanc, Chardonnay

Useful Information

Owner/Winemaker: Jan du Toit
Address: Goedverwacht Estate, Box 128, Bonnievale 6730
Telephone: 02346.2845 *Fax*: 02346.3430

McGREGOR CO-OPERATIVE

Established in 1948, the McGregor co-operative now has 41 members with 43 farms, covering about 550 hectares. It is situated about eighteen kilometres from Robertson, just outside the small town of McGregor, which has changed little since its foundation in the nineteenth century. The farms are all around McGregor, but there is a wide variety of soils and exposures, as some are mountain farms, and some lie along the banks of the Breede river. There is also a certain amount of red Karoo soil, which puts it apart from most of the Robertson area.

The atmosphere of the town of McGregor may be old-fashioned, but the approach to winemaking of Danie Marais at the co-operative is bang up to date. Since his arrival here in 1993, the standard of wine produced has taken great leaps forward. Of the 10,000 tons of grapes that pass through the winery each year, only about 3,000 cases are bottled, the vast majority being sold in bulk to the merchants and wholesalers. Bottled wines are sold through wine clubs like the Oaks, by mail-order and direct from the cellar to callers.

Bottling is done at the large bottling plant in Worcester, which is used by many smaller wineries all over the Cape, and the presentation is very smart, with each label showing the McGregor tartan. Like most co-operatives, McGregor employs the services of one of the KWV's viticulturists, who will give help and advice to any of the members who need it. Planting decisions are shared between the members, Danie Marais and the viticulturist according to a ten-year master plan, and it is Danie who decides what will be picked and when. From 1996 onwards, members will be paid according to quality for their 'good wine' cultivars.

Tasting Notes

Chardonnay/Colombard 1995 (80% Chardonnay, 20% Colombard, no wood used): Pale, greeny gold; Colombard stronger than Chardonnay on nose; crisp, clean and elegant, with nice fruit and good length.

Sauvignon Blanc 1995: Pale straw; slight asparagus whiff; clean, crisp and dry with good fruit and some length.

Colombard 1995: Lovely, greenish gold; beautiful nose of tropical fruits; lean, clean and long, with same tropical fruit flavour promised by nose. A class act. (McGregor's flagship, class winner at SA Wine Show, and rightly so.)

Rhine Riesling 1995: Very pale straw colour; honeyed, grapey smell; pleasing, off-dry Riesling fruit in the mouth, with good long aftertaste.

White Muscadel 1994: Pale golden; Muscatty nose; rich honey and fruit, but not too cloying.

Red Muscadel 1993: Pale, pinkish red; raisiny, figgy nose; same rich, Christmas pudding flavours on the palate, a nice winter warmer.

Technical Notes

Co-operative: 41 members/43 farms

Area under vines: 550 hectares

Average production: 9,500 tons, of which only 3,000 cases bottled

Wines produced
WHITE: Sauvignon Blanc, Chenin Blanc, Colombard, Rhine Riesling, Late Vintage, White Muscadel, Colombard/Chardonnay
RED: Cabernet Sauvignon, Red Muscadel
SPARKLING WINE: Demi-Sec

Useful Information

Winemaker: Danie Marais
Address: McGregor Koop, Private Bag X619, Robertson 6705
Telephone: 02353.741 *Fax*: 02353.829

Tasting/Sales: Weekdays 08.00 to 12.00, 13.00 to 17.00

ROBERTSON CO-OPERATIVE

The Robertson Kooperatief Wynmakery was first established in 1942, and now has 35 members with 40 farms covering about 1,300 hectares, processing some 25,000 tons of grapes a year, and providing a living for over a thousand families.

The first winemaker at the co-operative, Pon van Zyl, became a legend in his own lifetime, for he was the first to recognize that the Colombard grape was capable of better things than being made into rebate for brandy distillation. The story goes that a local farmer, one Wouter de Wet, ordered a supply of St Emilion vines from a nursery in the Klein Karoo, and it was not until the vines were bearing fruit that he realized that he had been supplied with Colombard in error. Since both vines were equally suited to the making of rebate wine, he proceeded to press the grapes. It was Pon van Zyl, wandering through the co-operative's winery, who noticed a wonderful, heady perfume of the Koekmarka flower emanating from a vat of fermenting wine. When he discovered what the grape was, he decided there and then that he would make a fine wine from the Colombard. He was very successful in this enterprise, and won countless prizes for the co-operative's Colombard, and many other wines. To this day the Robertson co-operative is known for the very high quality of its Colombard.

Pon van Zyl's mantle was assumed in 1984 by Bowen Botha, another dedicated and innovative winemaker. In 1993 he introduced the Vinipak, a packaging idea borrowed from the fruit juice industry, and from a target of 1 million litres, he sold over double that amount. Four different wines are offered in these 250 and 500 ml cartons – Smooth Dry Red, Dry White, Stein and Late Harvest – representing 10% of the Co-operative's total annual output.

Since 1987, the Robertson Co-op has been doing all its own marketing, and in the first year they sold more wine than they had previously been selling to all the merchants in bulk. They are now in a position where they are obliged to buy in wine from other co-operatives in order to satisfy demand. Only 10% of production is exported, as they feel that they must look after their faithful domestic market first.

A KWV viticulturist is employed, and plantings are carried out on a pool basis: in other words a pool is opened when the winery has a need for a certain variety – when that need is filled, the pool is closed, say for Cabernet Sauvignon, and one for Chardonnay may be started.

Tasting Notes

Colombard 1995: Pale gold; fresh, ripe fruit bouquet; clean, crisp and easy to drink, with perfect fruit/acid balance.

Sauvignon Blanc 1995: Shade darker than the Colombard; nose not at all floral, slight asparagus; clean, with nice fruit, some weight and good length.

Chardonnay 1995 (10–15% barrel-fermented with three months on lees): Greeny gold colour; Chardonnay fruit nose with some oakiness; wood just a little dominating at the moment, but good fruit there, and will be good in time.

Pinotage 1994 (no wood): Brilliant scarlet; nose quite shy, and slightly dusty; easy-drinking, light and fruity, good of its type.

Cabernet Sauvignon 1994 (some ageing in used barrels, tannins muted because of CO_2 bubbling remontage method employed): Good, medium deep colour; fruit and slight acetone on nose; easy-drinker Cabernet with not much structure and very soft tannin.

Red Muscadel 1994 (17% alcohol): Pale, almost onion-skin colour; smells of roses and Muscat; delicate flavour of raisins and dried apricot, alcohol giving soft, dry finish.

Technical Notes

Co-operative: 35 members/40 farms

Area under vines: 1,300 hectares

Average production: 23,000 tons, of which approx. 120,000 cases are bottled or sold in Vinipaks or 5-litre packaging

Wines produced
WHITE: Colombard, Sauvignon Blanc, Chardonnay, Chardonnay/Sauvignon Blanc, Bukettraube, Late Harvest, Rheingold. 5-litre packs: Rob Roy Late Harvest, Rob Roy Stein. 500/250-ml Vinipaks: Late Harvest, Stein, Dry White

RED: Cabernet Sauvignon, Pinotage, Red Muscadel. 5-litre packs: Baron du Pon Red Muscadel, Baron du Pon Cabernet Sauvignon, Rob Roy Grand Cru, Rob Roy Dry red. 500/250-ml Vinipaks: Dry Red

SPARKLING WINE: Santino Vin Sec, Santino Vin Doux, Santino Spumante, Santino Rouge, Sauvignon Blanc

Useful Information

Winemaker: Bowen Botha
Address: Robertson Kooperatief Wynmakery, Box 37, Robertson 6705
Telephone: 02351.3059/3566 *Fax*: 02351.61415

Tasting/Sales: Weekdays 08.00 to 12.30 and 13.00 to 17.00; Saturday during school holidays only, 09.00 to 12.30

ROOIBERG CO-OPERATIVE

Rooiberg is another relatively young co-operative, founded in 1964. It now boasts 34 members, owning 50 farms. These are fairly widespread, giving many different terroirs and the possibility of making many different wine types, which is fully exploited by Dassie Smith, winemaker here for 25 years. The wines for which Rooiberg receives the most plaudits, and Veritas Golds and Double Golds, are the fortified Rooi Jerepiko and Muskadel. These come from the farms with rich alluvial Karoo soils in the Eilandia, Goree and Riverside areas along the banks of the Breede and Vink rivers.

The huge winery processes around 15,000 tons of grapes annually, 20% of which is bottled and sold on both the home and export markets, the balance being sold in bulk to the merchants and for export. A proportion of the bottled wine is sold with special labels for clubs and the Lions, and Rooiberg supplies two-thirds of the Chenin and Colombard sold by the Woolworths chain.

Winemaker and Manager Dassie Smith has an impressive record: since he became winemaker in 1970, his achievements have included the nomination of Rooiberg as champion co-operative in 1978, 1982, 1983, 1984 and 1986. He also made the champion Cabernet Sauvignon for the 1979 Cape Wine Show; was joint winner, with Sydney Back of Backsberg, of the General Smuts Trophy for best winemaker in 1982; and outright winner in 1984. In the 1995 Veritas awards, Rooiberg scored 29 awards, including two Double Golds and ten Golds, a sterling performance for a co-operative in Robertson, an area about which the Stellenbosch establishment tend to be sniffy.

Thirty-six different wines are bottled, including a barrel-fermented, *sur lie* Chardonnay and some respectable oak-aged reds. In common with many Robertson wineries, all bottling is done at the Worcester bottling plant.

Tasting Notes

Chardonnay 1995: Nice golden colour; ripe Chardonnay fruit bouquet; broad palate with some butteriness, a good barrel-fermented Chardonnay.

Riesling 1995: Medium gold; nice Riesling whiff; shortish, but has some nice fruit.

Rhine Riesling 1995: Pale gold; classy Riesling fruit, with a touch of asparagus; half dry, with some good fruit and length.

Rooiberg Roodewyn 1992 (Cabernet Sauvignon, Cabernet Franc, Merlot and Ruby Cabernet): Deep red; soft, ripe nose; good fruit with coffee flavours, and some soft tannins.

Shiraz 1991: Very deep, young colour; ripe fruit bouquet; fresh, berry fruit, soft tannins and some structure, with good length.

Pinotage 1993: Dark red; distinct Pinotage nose with echoes of banana; fruit and wood nicely balanced, high alcohol at 14.5%.

'Vintage Port' 1991: Rich, plummy colour; concentrated dried fruit nose with raisins and figs; a bit sugary, with lots of Christmas pudding fruitiness.

Rooi Jerepiko 1994 (Pinotage only): Ruby red; plummy fruit and coffee bouquet; added spirit lends smoothness to rich ripe, dried apricot and raisin taste, excellent of its type.

Hanepoot Jerepiko 1993: Deep, treacly gold; lovely wafts of Muscat on nose; rich and luscious with concentration of dried fruits, and very long.

Technical Notes

Co-operative: 34 members/50 farms

Average production: 15,000 tons, of which 20% bottled

Wines produced
WHITE: Colombard, Chardonnay, Chardonnay Sur Lie, Blanc de Noir, Riesling, Rhine Riesling, Premier Grand Cru Selected White, Sauvignon Blanc, Chenin Blanc, Bukettraube, Late Vintage Selected Stein, Hanepoot, Muskadel Rooi, Special Late Harvest Chenin, Vintage Reserve
RED: Cabernet Sauvignon, Pinotage, Shiraz, Roodewyn, Selected Red Wine, Rooi Jerepiko
SPARKLING: Brut Sparkling Wine, Demi-Sec Sparkling Wine, Vin Doux, Flamingo – all carbonated
'PORT': Vintage

Useful Information

Winemaker/Manager: Dassie Smith
Address: Rooibergse Co-op Winery, Box 358, Robertson 6705
Telephone: 02351.3124/3146 *Fax*: 02351.3295

Tasting/Sales: Weekdays 08.00 to 17.30, Saturday 08.00 to 13.00

ROODEZANDT CO-OPERATIVE

The offices and winery of the Roodezandt Co-op may be in the centre of Robertson town, but the name, Red Sand, tells you of the alluvial red soil from which the grapes come. Formed in 1953, there are now 52 members, some of them father-and-son partnerships, with some 1,200 hectares of vines on 42 farms. Like most of the co-operatives, Roodezandt pays for the services of a KWV viticultural consultant: the viticulturist's recommendations are only a guideline, but if the member decides to plant something else, he risks his harvest being turned away should the grapes not meet standards. It is also the function of the consultant to say when harvesting will take place, and members are paid according to the sugar content, pH level and acidity of their fruit. Between 30% and 50% is paid on delivery, and the balance over a series of monthly payments. Approximately 25% of harvesting is done by mechanical harvesters, which are either owned, loaned or rented.

Of the massive 25,000 tons of grapes handled annually at the winery, only 5% is bottled, and only a fifth of this is sold on the domestic market, the rest going for export on the European market. The vast majority of the co-op's production is sold in bulk to the merchants, as well as to the Scandinavian countries. Management and marketing are in the capable hands of Abe Rossouw, and the winemaker is Christie Steytler.

Tasting Notes

Colombard 1995: Very pale colour; pleasing fresh fruit nose; lots of nice, up-front fruit, fresh and crisp, good value at R5.95 per bottle.

Sauvignon Blanc 1995: Even paler colour than Colombard; nose slightly herbaceous; clean, crisp fruit, elegant Sauvignon with the correct fruit/acid balance.

Chardonnay 1995: Medium deep gold; rounded Chardonnay fruit on nose; nice weight and fruit in mouth, good, uncomplicated Chardonnay and value at R7.75.

Roodeshuiswyn N. V. (Cabernet Sauvignon, Merlot, Ruby Cabernet and Tinta Barocca): Deep, ruby red; rounded, soft fruit nose; a round, soft easy-drinker.

Cabernet Sauvignon 1994 (12 months in used oak casks): Good, deep red; cassis on nose; clean fruit, not particularly exciting, but quite correct.

Technical Notes

Co-operative: 42 farms/52 members

Area under vines: 1,200 hectares

Average production: 25,000 tons, of which 5% bottled

Wines produced
WHITE: Colombard, Cape Riesling, Chardonnay, Sauvignon

Blanc, Late Harvest, Special Late Harvest, White Muscadel, Vino Zante (500ml)
RED: Roodeshuiswyn, Cabernet Sauvignon, Red Muscadel
SPARKLING: Brut, Demi-Sec
'PORT'

Useful Information

Manager: Abe Rossouw
Winemaker: Christie Steytler
Address: Roodezandt Ko-op Wynmakery, Box 164, Robertson 6705
Telephone: 02351.2912 *Fax*: 02351.5074

Tasting/Sales: Weekdays 08.00 to 13.00 and 14.00 to 17.30, Saturday 09.00 to 14.30

SPRINGFIELD

The afternoon that I arrived at Abrie Bruwer's farm, there was an almighty storm of thunder, lightning, hail and rain, and within the space of twenty minutes Robertson had more than half of its average annual rainfall. Luckily Abrie did not suffer much damage, though several of his Robertson colleagues fared less well. Danie de Wet lost several hectares of soil and newly planted vines when the irrigation canal burst on the high ground above de Wetshof, and Paul de Wet at Zandvliet suffered extensive hail damage. The vine growers of Robertson are not accustomed to worrying about excess of rain, rather the reverse.

Up to the end of the nineteenth century, the cultivation of the vine was virtually unknown in this region, due to the very hot summers and lack of rain. Irrigation at that time could not be relied upon, as the main source of water, the Breede river, often dried up. In the late 1800s, an enterprising Scottish entrepreneur acquired large tracts of land along the river, and proceeded to construct the Brandvlei dam, and the long irrigation canal, rendering the land workable and, one imagines, making a large fortune.

The Springfield Estate is a new name on the Robertson scene, but vines have been grown here for a long time. The Bruwers bought the farm in 1902, and for many years have been selling their wines in bulk to SFW and the Distillers Corporation. Since 1995, however, following an argument about prices, they have registered Springfield as an estate and are bottling under their own label.

Abrie Bruwer is an open and likeable man and, in a very laid-back way, an ambitious and skilled winemaker. His favourite French wine region is Sancerre – he goes there every year and has many friends among the Sancerrois winemakers. This explains the very high and untypically Robertson quality of his Sauvignon Blanc. Although the accent at Springfield is mainly on white wine, Abrie also produces a very creditable Cabernet Sauvignon, and plans to increase his planting of this varietal in 1997, when he will also be planting two or three hectares of Sémillon. He currently has 145 hectares under vines, 20 of which are down to Clairette Blanche and Raisin Blanc for the grape juice market. By the end of 1997, his total area of vines will be increased to 185. The farm also produces peaches, apricots, nectarines and easy-peel satsumas.

Abrie, who likes to give the impression that he is a fisherman who makes a bit of wine in his spare time, is doing well with his own label wines. He is already exporting to Benelux, Norway and Sweden, and has his eye on the UK supermarkets like Waitrose and Marks and Spencer. But he is cautiously wary of putting too many eggs in one buyer's basket, and feels that he might be better placed with a good agent who supplies the restaurant business and private customers.

The Bruwers are a kind and hospitable family. They kindly put me up on my Robertson pilgrimage, and I very much enjoyed meeting Abrie's English wife, who is a doctor, and their two angelic Goldilocks daughters, as well as Abrie's father, who still takes a very active part in the running of the farm.

Tasting Notes

Colombard/Chardonnay 1995 (80% Colombard, 20% Chardonnay, partly oak-fermented): Pale straw; fruit good on nose, but neither grape dominant; clean, dry and crisp, slight peardrops.

Sauvignon Blanc/Chardonnay 1995 (70% Sauvignon, 30% Chardonnay): Pale, greeny gold; lovely nose of citrus and grassiness from Sauvignon; clean crisp fruit, dry and pleasing, with low acidity.

Sauvignon Blanc 1995: Very pale, greenish gold; very Sancerre style bouquet of elder-bark and grass; clean and fruity with asparagus notes, a fine Sauvignon.

Chardonnay 1995 (30% barrel-fermented): Pale straw colour; citrussy, fresh nose; soft, rounded Chardonnay fruit, again with low acidity.

Cabernet Sauvignon 1993 (30% oak-aged for 6 months): Medium-deep red; cassis and hazelnuts on nose; good fruit, no harsh oakiness, a very pleasant Cabernet with no great pretension.

Technical Notes

Area under vines: 145 hectares, increasing to 180 in 1997

Cultivars planted
WHITE: Sauvignon, Chardonnay, Chenin Blanc, Colombard, Gewürztraminer, Muscadel, plus Clairette Blanche and Raisin Blanc for juice
RED: Cabernet Sauvignon

Useful Information

Owner: Bruwer family
Winemaker: Abrie Bruwer
Address: Springfield Estate, Box 770, Robertson 6705
Telephone: 02351.3661 *Fax*: 02351.3664 or *Tel/Fax*: 02351.4712

Tasting/Sales: Weekdays 09.00 to 13.00, Saturday 09.30 to 13.00

VAN LOVEREN

John Platter's guide informs the reader that the Retief family are renowned for their hospitality, and I was warned by more than one winemaker that they were 'dangerous'. I can vouch for the truth of both statements. Having spent an instructive and enjoyable visit, and having tasted their entire range of excellent wines, a long session drinking very generous gin and tonics with brothers Nico and Wynand, joined by Danie de Wet, impaired my navigation to such an extent that I was over an hour late for my next appointment.

Van Loveren was originally part of a much larger farm called Goudmyn, belonging to the Potgieter family. The fortunes of the estate were based on the boom in ostrich farming, which collapsed after the First World War. The property had to be divided up between the nine Potgieter children, and in 1937 Nicholaas Retief bought a 28-hectare piece of the estate for his son Hennie, whose wife Jean was a van Zyl by birth. The farm had been named rather uninspiringly 'Goudmyn F', and Jean persuaded her husband to rename the property van Loveren – the family name of the wife of Guillaume van Zyl, founder of the van Zyl dynasty, who settled in the Cape in 1692.

Since the original purchase, a further four farms have been added to the Retief empire. Hennie bought Schoemanskloof for son Nico on his marriage in 1964, whose brother Wynand bought Jacobsdal in 1968. In 1980 a part of the Goedemoed estate was acquired, and the fifth farm, Spes Bona, was bought in 1988. Altogether, the two brothers, who have farmed in partnership since Hennie's death in 1982, have 125 hectares under vines, to be increased to 150 in the next couple of years, as well as 30 hectares of apricots and 10 of vegetables. General management is in the hands of Nico, while Wynand and Nico's son Bussell are the winemakers, and the vineyards are the responsibility of Nico's other son, Hennie. Wynand's skill and delicacy as a winemaker are remarkable, for he had no formal training. He is the first to recognize that he owes much to the help and advice he has received from other Robertson winemakers, notably Danie de Wet. This spirit of friendship and co-operation is especially strong in Robertson, and could serve as a model for the rest of the wine world.

In the early days of van Loveren's existence, the emphasis, as elsewhere in the Cape, was on the making of fortified sweet wines, particularly red Muscadel, which were invariably sold to SFW. In 1972 cold fermentation equipment was installed, prompting the Retiefs to plant more of the natural white varieties like Steen (Chenin) and Colombard; Sauvignon Blanc followed in 1980 together with the innovative Harslevelu, a Tokay varietal of Hungarian origin, and the Fernao Pires from Portugal, both of which have had remarkable success. They have now added Chardonnay to their repertoire, and about five years ago planted fifteen hectares of red varietals – Cabernet, Merlot, Shiraz and Pinotage – from which they make a blend called River Red.

The total capacity of the van Loveren cellar is now 2,500 tons, about half of which is bottled, and half sold in bulk. Half of their wine is sold on the domestic market, and half is exported, mainly to the United Kingdom, but also to the Scandinavian countries, Holland, Germany and Canada.

It is impossible to write about van Loveren without mentioning Nico and Wynand's mother Jean, or the garden, and one cannot mention one without the other. The garden tells a story, for Jean made a lifetime habit of planting trees, shrubs and roses to commemorate special events in history, as well as to mark births and marriages in the family. One of her favourite stories was of the Rhus Lancea she ordered from Carters in Natal as a young bride. The price was one shilling and sixpence, a not inconsiderable sum in those days. When her husband Hennie collected it from the station, his fellow farmers roared with laughter, for they insisted that it was exactly the same tree that grew prolifically along the Breede river, known locally as the Karee. Jean would not have it, so to prove his point, Hennie fetched a cutting of a wild Karee and planted it alongside his wife's Rhus Lancea. The two identical trees stand together today, with their branches inextricably entwined, a symbol of Hennie and Jean's marriage, and proof of one of the very few arguments she ever admits to having lost. In later years, as the garden grew more and more densely planted with trees, Jean took to planting commemorative rose bushes instead. When Nelson Mandela and F. W. de Klerk were jointly awarded the Nobel Peace Prize, Jean marked the occasion by planting a Black Madonna and a Peace of Vereeniging.

Tasting Notes

Sauvignon Blanc 1995: Pale greenish colour; nice fruit bouquet; clean and crisp, with refreshing fruit and good length.

Harslevelu 1995: Pale greeny gold; fresh, spicy nose; an easy drinking white with nice grapey fruit and a refreshing touch of sweetness.

Fernao Pires: Medium straw; nose of spice and Muscat; drier than the Harslevelu, but with the same spicy fruitiness.

Colombard 1995: Very pale colour; fresh guava nose; light, fresh and clean, with good fruit and some sweetness.

Pinot Gris 1995: Medium pale gold; nose good, with spicy fruit; light, citrussy fruit with good balancing acidity.

Colombard/Chardonnay 1995 (80% Colombard, 20% Chardonnay): Pale golden; attractive fruit on nose; lots of up-front Colombard fruit, with the weight of Chardonnay behind it.

Spes Bona Chardonnay 1995 (not fermented in oak, but 2 months in cask): Pale greeny colour; light, elegant nose; delicate, easy Chardonnay, very light wooding shows.

Chardonnay 1995 (fermented in 40% new oak, and aged 5 months in cask with regular batonage): Slightly darker than the Spes Bona; nose good, with vanilla from wood; heavier, more buttery Chardonnay, with the right balance between fruit and oak. Good.

Blanc de Noir, Red Muscadel 1995: Pale, onion-skin colour; aromatic Muscadel nose; a nice, semi-sweet summer drinker, with refreshing fruit.

Special Late Harvest Gewürztraminer 1994: Fine mid-gold colour; spicy whiffs of Gewürztraminer; excellent fruit, with same spiciness and some delicacy.

River Red 1995 (40% Merlot, 20% each Cabernet Sauvignon, Shiraz and Pinotage): Good, deep red; ripe, berry fruit nose; lovely, ripe and fruity, uncomplicated quaffer, with little structure and only a touch of soft tannin.

Red Muscadel 1994: Brilliant red; nose powerful, more like dry red wine than Muscadel; rich, dried fruit sweetness, with high alcohol, an excellent Muscadel.

Technical Notes

Area under vines: 125 hectares, increasing to 150 in 2–3 years

Cultivars planted
WHITE: Sauvignon Blanc, Chardonnay, Colombard, Pinot Gris, Gewürztraminer, Pinot Blanc, Cape Riesling, Rhine Riesling, Muscat de Frontignan, Harslevelu, Fernao Pires
RED: Cabernet Sauvignon, Merlot, Pinot Noir, Shiraz, Pinotage, Red Muscadel

Wines produced
WHITE: Sauvignon Blanc, Chardonnay, Spes Bona Chardonnay, Blanc de Blancs, Vino Blanc, Cape Riesling, Blanc de Noir Shiraz, Pinot Gris, Pinot Blanc, Colombard/Chardonnay, Rhine Riesling, Harslevelu, Fernao Pires, Blanc de Noir Red Muscadel, Bouquet Blanc, Special Late Harvest Gewürztraminer, Noble Late Harvest Pinot Gris
RED: River Red, Red Muscadel
SPARKLING: Papillon Brut, Papillon Demi-Sec, Papillon Vin Doux (pink)

Useful Information

Owners: Retief family
Manager: Nico Retief
Winemakers: Wynand and Bussell Retief
Vineyard Manager: Hennie Retief
Address: Van Loveren Estate, Box 19, Klaasvoogds 6707
Telephone: 0234.51505 *Fax*: 0234.51336

Tasting/Sales: Weekdays 08.30 to 13.00 and 14.00 to 17.00, Saturday 09.30 to 13.00

VAN ZYLSHOF

Andri van Zyl is a big man, he has a big dog, and he serves very big steaks. He also has a big heart, and welcomes visitors with traditional Afrikaans hospitality. I stayed with him, his wife and his beautifully behaved children, as well as one very large dog and one very small Jack Russell at their home in Bonnievale before setting off for the Klein Karoo. Their warm welcome, their kind hospitality and the good behaviour and manners of their children left a lasting impression that typifies so many of their countrymen.

Andri's grandfather started here in 1934, and was followed by Andri's father and uncle, who farmed the land in partnership until 1991, when the partnership was dissolved and the land split in two. Andri now farms his father's portion of the land, which took his family name to become Van Zylshof. Historically the farm has always grown vines, mainly Colombard and Chenin Blanc for the production of brandy, or rebate wine. These varieties are still grown on the low-lying land near the Breede river and for the making of rebate wine they can be exceptionally heavy croppers. Andri will continue growing them both, for they are very useful cash crops. He plans to make wine from them as well, but doubtless there will be some pretty heavy pruning, and consequently lower yields for the vines intended for winemaking. The chief interest in the Van Zylshof estate for Andri lies in making fine dry white wine from Sauvignon Blanc and Chardonnay, and to this end he has already cultivated an incredibly rocky plot on the south-facing slope near his house, and planted it with Chardonnay. The back-breaking labour involved in the preparation of this piece of land, previously thought untillable, can only be imagined when you look at the vast piles of rock, some as big as small houses.

I had the opportunity of sampling the first fruits of Andri's labours in the two wines that resulted from the 1995 vintage. He is at present bottling only two wines under the Van Zylshof name, a Chardonnay/Sauvignon blend which he calls Riverain, and a pure Sauvignon Blanc. His plan for the future is to concentrate on a pure Chardonnay as soon as his new plantings come on stream, when he may abandon the blend. He will also continue with the Sauvignon Blanc, as he feels that his terroir is well suited to both these varietals. This is a name to watch. Van Zyl is hardworking, ambitious and a very gifted winemaker, and deserves every success.

Tasting Notes

Van Zylshof Sauvignon Blanc 1995: Very pale colour; delicious open nose of fruit, asparagus and elder bark; clean, crisp and delicious, long, with the perfect balance of fruit and acidity, a classy Sauvignon that could hold its head up in Sancerre or Pouilly.

Riverain 1995 (51% Chardonnay, 49% Sauvignon Blanc, no wood used, with 80 days on lees in stainless steel): Very pale greeny gold; Chardonnay certainly dominates the bouquet, and on the palate, but the Sauvignon fruit shines through at the end.

Technical Notes

Area under vines: 26 hectares

Cultivars planted
WHITE: Chenin Blanc, Colombard, Chardonnay, Sauvignon Blanc

Wines produced
WHITE: Sauvignon Blanc, Riverain

Useful Information

Owner/Winemaker: Andri van Zyl
Address: Van Zylshof Estate, Box 64, Bonnievale 6730
Telephone: 02346.2940 *Fax*: 02346.3503

Tasting/Sales: By appointment

WELTEVREDE

Klaas Jonker, grandfather of Lourens, bought a scrubland farm just outside Bonnievale in 1912, and was certainly among the first to plant vines in the area. These were probably only for growing table grapes, or possibly for turning into brandy. It was his son, Japie, who started serious wine farming here in 1933, and the tradition is now carried on by the third generation, Lourens Jonkers. Lourens, having obtained a degree in viniculture, spent most of 1962 touring and studying in the vineyards of California and Europe before settling down to help his father at Weltevrede. He took the reins on his father's death in 1969, enlarging the estate to its present 150 hectares by buying first a farm called, appropriately, Muscadel in 1969 and then another, Riversedge, in 1981.

Weltevrede, for the Jonker family, is aptly named, for it means 'well satisfied', and they have every right to feel so. They have been pioneers in the area, and have notched up a number of important 'firsts'. In 1976 they became the first wine producers to market wine under their own label with their Colombard 1975, and in the same year produced South Africa's first certified Red Muscadel. This was followed in 1977 by the first Muscat de Hambourg, and in 1979 they made the first certified Wine of Origin in Bonnievale, as well as making Privé du Bois, one of South Africa's first white wines to be matured on the lees in small French oak casks. In 1983 came another Breede River valley first in the Weltevrede Gewürztraminer and they were also pioneers in 1986 with South Africa's first Therona, a wine made from the Riesling hybrid developed by Professor Theron at Stellenbosch University.

There is a strong family involvement at Weltevrede. Lourens's wife Annamarie is a talented artist, and her flair – and her paintings – are evident in the guesthouse, tasting-room and the restaurant, which was the first to be opened on a wine estate in the Breede River valley. Son Philip was, at the time of writing, studying for his Oenology B.Sc. at Stellenbosch, and daughters Annien and Eza have both done wine courses at the KWV, and are often to be seen helping out at wine shows. Lourens himself, in typical Robertson tradition, gives much of his time to the general service of the wine industry. He is currently Chairman of the Veritas awards committee, and is the present Chairman of the KWV, the first estate owner to head an organization whose function is to represent the interests of the thousands of small grape growers, demonstrating his considerable diplomatic skills.

From a throughput of 2,000 tons of grapes, some 30,000 cases are bottled, 25% of which are sold on the export market, principally to the UK, and 75% on the home market – the rest is sold in bulk.

Tasting Notes

Sauvignon Blanc 1995: Greeny gold; elder-bark nose; clean with good fruit, and bone dry, fruit and acidity in balance.

Blanc de Blancs 1995 (mainly Colombard and Chenin Blanc):

Pale straw colour; spicy nose, redolent of Muscat; easy and very quaffable, lean and clean with a spicy fruitiness.

Privé du Bois 1994 (70% Sauvignon Blanc, 30% Chardonnay, tank-fermented, and then 5 months on lees in French oak casks): Greeny gold; nose quite shy; lovely, citrussy fruit on palate, with weight and length, and vanilla note from oak.

Chardonnay 1993 (all tank-fermented, and then a third matured on the lees in a mix of new and used French oak casks): Quite deep, golden colour; good fruit with oakiness on nose; fat, buttery fruit, oak quite strong.

Colombard 1995: Very pale; curious, limey bouquet; dry, with good citrus fruit attack and good length.

Gewürztraminer 1995: Greenish gold; typical spicy Traminer bouquet; lots of same spiciness in mouth, clean with nice grapey fruit and long.

Blanc de Noir 1995 (Muscat de Hambourg and Red Muscadel): Pale onion-skin pink; strong Muscat aromas; not a great deal of complexity, but some nice, sweetish fruit.

Oupa se Wyn 1994 (Red Muscadel, some of which comes from a carefully preserved patch of vineyard, planted by Klaas Jonker in 1926 and called Oupa se Wyngerd, the rest from other old vines on the farm): Deep rose pink; rich, Muscat nose, with strange trace of onion; concentrated sweet fruit, spirity.

Special Late Harvest 1994 (mix of Therona, Cape Riesling and Ugni Blanc): Medium deep gold; strange bouquet, very ripe fruit; curious, overripe tropical fruit flavours.

Muscat de Hambourg 1994: Dark, bricky red; spicy, ripe and tropical aroma; rich and concentrated, fortified to 18.8%, but not overly spirity, delicious.

Technical Notes

Area under vines: 150 hectares

Cultivars planted
WHITE: Sauvignon Blanc, Chardonnay, Chenin Blanc,

Gewürztraminer, Colombard, Ugni Blanc, Chardonnay, Cape
Riesling, Therona, Rhine Riesling
RED: Muscat de Hambourg, Red Muscadel

Wines produced
WHITE: Sauvignon Blanc, Blanc de Blancs, Privé du Bois,
Chardonnay, Colombard, Gewürztraminer, Blanc de Noir,
Special Late Harvest
RED: Oupa se Wyn Red Muscadel, Muscat de Hambourg

Useful Information

Owner: Lourens Jonker
Winemaker: Simon Smith
Address: Weltevrede Estate, Box 6, Bonnievale 6730
Telephone: 02346.2141 *Fax*: 02346.2460

Tasting/Sales: Weekdays 08.00 to 17.00, Saturday 09.00 to 15.30
Facilities: Cellar tours by prior arrangement, December/January
and March/April school holidays; light lunches available 11.30
to 14.30, weekdays October–April and Saturdays all year

DE WETSHOF

The name of de Wet is part of South African wine history and
Danie is a tough and able scion of this family that came over with
the first settlers in the seventeenth century. A typical, tall and
strongly-built Afrikaner, Danie, ably assisted by his attractive wife
Lesca, is the locomotive force of the Robertson community.
Nothing is too much trouble when it comes to assisting neighbours
with any kind of problems or winemaking difficulties, and I am
especially grateful to both of them for the time, help, information
and generous hospitality which they gave without stint.

De Wetshof was bought in 1952 by Danie's father, Johann, who
had previously farmed near McGregor. At that time the farm was
only 70 hectares, but subsequent purchases have given de Wetshof
140 hectares under vines. As a young man, Danie was exempted
from military service due to high blood pressure, and his father
sent him to Germany to study winemaking under Wolf Erben, after
which he studied at Geisenheim. On his return to Robertson two

years later, Danie found that when he went to parties, he was the only one who drank wine. At that time de Wetshof, in common with most of the wine farms in the area, was producing almost entirely sweet fortified wines which were sold to the KWV. Danie was convinced that the soil, with its very high lime content, combined with the micro-climate and the possibility of irrigation from the Breede river, made his farm well-suited to the production of elegant, light, dry white table wines.

His first move was to install cold fermentation equipment, and then he began to plant the appropriate varieties, such as Rhine Riesling, Pinot Gris and later Sauvignon Blanc and Chardonnay in addition to the traditional Chenin Blanc and Colombard. He carried out many experiments with different clones of the noble varieties, particularly Chardonnay, and he determined that those used for making white Burgundy gave far better results than the higher yielding clones used in Champagne. So, Danie, along with one or two other young thrusters, managed to get the ridiculously stringent quarantine regulations for the importation of new plant material relaxed. The way that they achieved this is neither explained nor recorded, but it is amazing how many vine cuttings you can get into a suitcase. He was also, and still is, one of the leading winemakers in the study of the effects of different oaks on the vinification and maturation of white wines.

In addition to all this hard work and innovation on his own farm, which resulted in de Wetshof being the first Robertson property to be granted estate status, Danie has been a prime mover in achieving higher recognition for the region. He started the Robertson Wine Trust in 1983 to monitor and improve the quality of the region's wines and to promote its image. All producers, including the co-operatives, participate and the funding came half from the KWV and half from a levy on grape juice. Activities of the Trust include a Food and Wine Festival, a Young Wine Show, a Road Show, and various promotional and advertising campaigns. In addition the Trust has undertaken a scientific study of the area, including an intensive look at the Sauvignon Blanc, which has involved gathering weather statistics, a five-year soil analysis profile, and regular tastings to establish minimum acceptable quality.

It is only comparatively recently that Robertson has been making more dry white than fortified wines and rebate wine and, due to the initial poor plant material and canopy management, Danie reckons that it will take ten years for the region to realize its full potential as a quality table wine producer. De Wetshof itself is well into its stride, as witnessed by the innumerable awards and SAA listings Danie's wines have achieved, to say nothing of the seven four-star ratings notched up in the 1996 John Platter guide.

De Wetshof's flagship grape is the Chardonnay, which accounts for a third of the estate's vineyard area, but watch out for Danie's Sémillon wines in the future – although the grape has been grown in the Cape from the earliest days, the Green Grape has gained an unjustifiably poor reputation due to sub-standard plant material. Danie is a firm believer in the potential of this variety, both as a single-cultivar wine, and as an ingredient for blending with Chardonnay, Sauvignon Blanc and Colombard.

De Wetshof used to be a member of the Bergkelder, but since rather bravely cutting the commercial umbilical cord, Danie and Lesca are now successfully marketing the 35,000 cases that the estate produces off their own bat.

Tasting Notes

Blanc de Wet 1995 (Chardonnay, Sauvignon Blanc and Cape Riesling): Greeny gold; strong nose of mainly Sauvignon; clean, crisp fruit, good length and perfect balance.

Rhine Riesling 1995 (clone 100 gives best quality, less kerosene than some others): Very pale colour; nice Riesling fruit nose; loads of grapey fruit, acidity just right.

Blanc Fumé 1995: Pale straw; nice Sauvignon bouquet, quite muted; good, clean fruit, well balanced, very little wood.

Chardonnay Bon Vallon 1995 (unwooded, 4 months on lees in stainless steel): Very pale straw colour; yeasty fruit nose; a well-made Chardonnay with some breadth and length and elegant fruit.

Chardonnay Lesca 1995 (also sold as Finesse; barrel-fermented and aged on lees): Greeny gold; pleasant, lemony nose with vanilla from cask; fine, sweetish cirtus fruit attack, with some weight and length, an excellent Chardonnay.

Chardonnay Bateleur 1995 (single vineyard wine, light toast barrel-fermented and aged): Darker, greeny gold than Lesca; sharpish, zesty fruit bouquet; lovely, clean, citrus fruit in mouth with some wood and good weight.

Chardonnay d'Honneur 1995 (top of the de Wetshof Chardonnay range, also barrel-fermented and aged): Greenish straw, not yet 100% bright; ripe Chardonnay fruit, with strong vanilla; oak quite dominant at this stage, lovely, limey, grapefruit fruit flavours, and considerable weight, good in 1–2 years.

Mine d'Or 1993 (late-harvested Rhine Riesling, only 8% alc.): Lovely lime-green colour; good fruit bouquet, but with slight paraffin hints; light, with high acidity, good concentration of peachy fruit, with some citrus as well, appears quite dry in spite of 71.5 g/l sugar.

Edeloes 1993 (botrytized Rhine Riesling): Deep, orangey gold; rich bouquet of raisin and apricot; concentrated, rich and raisiny fruit, high acidity hides very high sweetness.

Technical Notes

Area under vines: 140 hectares

Cultivars planted
WHITE: Chardonnay, Sauvignon Blanc, Rhine Riesling, Cape Riesling, Sémillon

Wines produced
WHITE: Blanc de Wet, Rhine Riesling, Blanc Fumé, Chardonnay Bon Vallon, Chardonnay Lesca/Finesse, Chardonnay Bateleur, Chardonnay d'Honneur, Mine d'Or, Edeloes

Useful Information

Owner/Winemaker: Danie de Wet
Assistant: Herman Erasmus
Marketing and P. R.: Lesca de Wet
Address: De Wetshof Estate, Box 31, Robertson 6705
Telephone: 0234.51853/7 *Fax*: 0234.51915

Tasting/Sales: Weekdays 08.30 to 16.30, Saturday 10.00 to 13.00

ZANDVLIET

Paul and Cuckoo de Wet live in an attractive, low Cape Dutch farmhouse on their 917-hectare Zandvliet estate. They kindly had me to stay for the night, and I found them both charming and very friendly. Paul is a man of few but wise words, whilst Cuckoo is exceedingly vivacious, and chatters away like a bird. Paul, in accordance with being the quiet type, is also strong.

On 14 July 1994 he was driving into the village before breakfast and, whilst temporarily distracted in the course of adjusting his car-clock, he inadvertently crossed the level-crossing at the same time as a goods train which was travelling at 70 kph. This was unwise, as he discovered when he found himself 350 metres up the line, encased in the almost totally unrecognizable heap of twisted metal that had been his car. The only damage sustained in an accident that would kill most people was a few broken ribs, a chipped tooth or two and a small scar on his forehead. After only a few days in hospital, he was back at work on the farm. 'I tend to keep my eyes open at that time of the morning now,' he commented drily.

Paulie de Wet Snr took over Zandvliet farm in 1947. It was the lime-rich soil with high pH that attracted Paulie, for this is ideal land for raising horses, and the Zandvliet stud became famous for its thoroughbreds. A combination of circumstances have caused a severe dip in the South African bloodstock business: the economic slump slowed domestic purchasers down; the export of bloodstock has become extremely difficult due to a disease carried by the fruit-fly, requiring a costly quarantine in the disease-free Western Cape; and the tax loophole for horse ownership has been closed. Moreover, the improvement of bloodlines by the importation of stallions has now become a virtual impossibility due to the weakness of the rand.

Fortunately for Zandvliet and the other Robertson stud farms, the same lime-rich soils are equally good for the cultivation of the vine, and both activities have developed together. The stud still struggles on under the management of Paulie's son Dan, and vineyards and fruit are the responsibility of brother Dan.

The Robertson district has always been noted for its sweet fortified wines, and more lately for its dry whites. Zandvliet, however, stands apart, in that the de Wets were convinced that its soils, combined with rigorous pruning, organic fertilizers and minimum cultivation, were suitable for making red wine, especially from the Shiraz. Since the first Shiraz, produced in 1975, they have enjoyed considerable success with this variety, and brought out their first Cabernet Sauvignon in 1985. There is also a little Merlot planted, as well as Pinot Noir, though this last is used in a 90% Pinot Noir, 10% Chardonnay Cap Classique. Paul is planning to plant some Pinotage, but only intends this for use in blending his reds.

After nineteen years as part of the Bergkelder, Zandvliet is now very much open to visitors, both private and trade, and is actively pursuing the marketing of its wines. A new label has been introduced to market a slightly less expensive range under the name of Astonvale, but the Zandvliet name will still adorn the best wines of this highly individual estate.

Tasting Notes

Astonvale Chardonnay 1995 (unwooded): Pleasing mid-gold; fat Chardonnay fruit, with some citrus, long aftertaste, good.

Zandvliet Chardonnay 1995 (barrel-fermented): Same mid-gold colour; Chardonnay fruit with some vanilla on nose and in mouth, fat, buttery and long with nice citrus fruit.

Astonvale Sauvignon Blanc 1994: Well developed colour; some herbaceous, asparagus aromas; long, with nice lime juice fruit.

Astonvale Fumé Blanc 1995: Greeny gold; good, grassy Sauvignon fruit bouquet; wood gives breadth to Sauvignon fruitiness, nice length.

Astonvale Colombard 1995: Pale greeny colour; fresh, up-front limey fruit in mouth, dry with good length.

Astonvale Creme 1995 (80% Colombard, 20% Sauvignon): Pale straw colour; nose slightly grassy; clean, crisp, dry fruit, with excellent length.

Astonvale Shiraz/Cabernet Sauvignon 1994 (75% Shiraz, 25% Cabernet, Shiraz 6 months in 2nd- and 3rd-fill casks.): Scarlet colour; fresh, summery fruit nose; raspberry fruit on palate, easy drinker, nice.

Astonvale Cabernet Sauvignon/Shiraz 1993 (75% Shiraz, 25% Cabernet): Same scarlet colour; strawberry fruit aroma; nice summer fruit on palate, with soft, easy tannins.

Astonvale Shiraz 1994: Bricky red; open fruit bouquet; fresh, ripe fruit, tannins give smooth, long finish.

Zandvliet Shiraz 1991 (18 months in 2nd-fill casks): Much deeper red than the Astonvale; rounded, ripe fruit on nose; good mouthful of evolved fruit, nice, easy tannins with some structure.

Zandvliet Shiraz 1990: Colour a shade lighter than 1991; lovely, Rhôney nose; good, soft mouth-filling ripe fruit, soft tannins and some backbone.

Zandvliet Cabernet Sauvignon 1987: Brilliant mid-red; very ripe fruit bouquet; everything together now, fruit and tannins in harmony. At its peak.

Zandvliet Cabernet Sauvignon 1989: Colour still quite dark; classic cassis nose; fruit and structure good, with tannin still quite dominant.

Technical Notes

Area under vines: 137 hectares, 22 planned for 1996

Cultivars planted
WHITE: Chardonnay, Sauvignon Blanc, Colombard
RED: Shiraz, Cabernet Sauvignon, Merlot, Pinot Noir

Wines produced
WHITE: Astonvale – Chardonnay, Colombard, Creme, Sauvignon Blanc, Blanc Fumé. Zandvliet – Chardonnay
RED: Astonvale – Shiraz, Cabernet Sauvignon/Shiraz, Shiraz/Cabernet Sauvignon. Zandvliet – Shiraz, Cabernet Sauvignon
SPARKLING: Zandvliet Méthode Cap Classique

Useful Information

Owners: de Wet family
Winemaker: Paul de Wet
Address: Zandvliet, Box 36, Ashton 6715

Telephone: 0234.51146 *Fax*: 0234.51327

Tasting/Sales: Weekdays 09.00 to 17.00, Saturday 09.00 to 13.00

UNVISITED

Estates and Wineries: Jonkheer Farms Winery, Mooiuitsig, Mon Don, Rietvallei

Co-operatives: Agterkliphoogte, Bonnievale, Clairvaux, Merwespont, Nordale

11

Klein Karoo

Karoo derives from a Hottentot word meaning dry, arid and sparsely covered, and it fits the region well. Although the average rainfall is only around 300 millimetres, and the summers very hot, the Swartberg mountains to the north and the Langeberg and Outeniqua ranges in the south afford some shelter, and the vine can flourish on river banks where there is water for irrigation. The Karoo stretches about 250 kilometres from Montagu in the west to Oudtshoorn in the east, and only about 50 kilometres from north to south.

BARRYDALE CO-OPERATIVE

I started my trek through the Klein Karoo from the western end, crossing the spectacularly scenic Tradouw pass through the Swartberg mountains from Swellendam, emerging at Barrydale. The small Barrydale co-operative, founded in the early 1940s, started its life as a producer of brandy, all of which was sold to the Distillers Corporation. It was then, and still is, the only co-operative in South Africa to distil brandy.

Since the early 1980s the attention of the members of the co-operative has been turned more towards the making of good table wines, mainly white. The rich alluvial soils along the bottom of the Tradouw valley are well-suited to growing the noble varieties and, surprisingly, this small valley has a cooler micro-climate than that enjoyed by Stellenbosch. All the bottled wines come from a single farm on the Barrydale-Montagu road, belonging to Kobus Joubert, current President of the Co-operative Association and a leading light in the South African wine world. The majority of the sales of Barrydale's bottled wines is through Australian Robin Day of Orlando's Long Mountain range, as well as through the co-operative's retail outlet.

Brandy distillation still accounts for 60% of the 5,000-ton throughput, which gives members delivering five tons or more the attractive perk of being able to drink duty-free brandy. Of the remaining 40%, about a quarter is bottled and the rest sold in bulk.

Barrydale is fortunate in its choice of Bob de Villiers as wine-maker, who started here in 1988. He was instrumental in gaining Young Wine Champion awards in both 1989 and 1991 for Barry-dale. His white wines are of more than average quality, though the red still has a way to go. In 1991 he produced the first Méthode Cap Classique to be made by a co-operative, which I found to be of excellent quality.

Tasting Notes

Chardonnay Tradouw 1995: Pale golden; fruit good on nose with vanilla; clean, lemony fruit, a nice, long Chardonnay.

Chardonnay, Sur Lie 1991 (80% fermented in new oak casks, matured on lees for 3 months): Deep gold; lovely, ripe Chardonnay bouquet; a fine Chardonnay, full of ripe, buttery fruit flavours, with benefit of a few years in bottle.

Sauvignon Blanc 1995: Very pale colour; nice, up-front fruit bouquet; good, clean and crisp, excellent fruit and length.

Colombard 1995: Same very pale straw as Sauvignon; nose still quite dumb, normal for SA Colombards; good citrus fruit attack, acidity quite high, finishes a little short.

Tradouw Tradeaux Reserve 1993 (Bordeaux blend of 75% Cabernet Sauvignon, 25% Merlot, aged 12 months in small oak): Quite deep colour; slightly closed up on nose and in mouth, where the fruit has slight cooked quality.

Tradouw Cap Classique 1991 (100% Chardonnay): Pale straw, with fine, long mousse; yeasty fruit bouquet; clean and creamy, with nice Champagne biscuit taste.

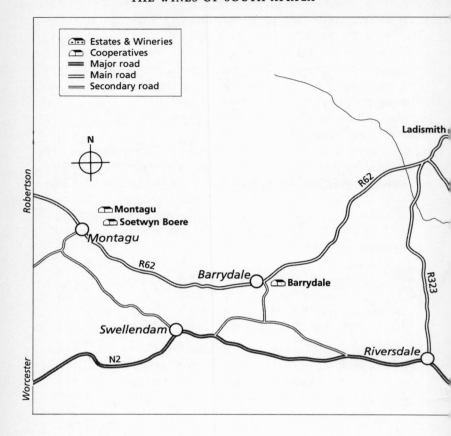

Klein Karoo

Technical Notes

Average production: 5,000 tons, bottling 5,000 cases

Cultivars planted: Details not given, but mainly white varieties like Colombard and Chenin for brandy, Sauvignon Blanc, Chardonnay, Colombard for still whites, Chardonnay for Cap Classique, Cabernet Sauvignon and Merlot for reds

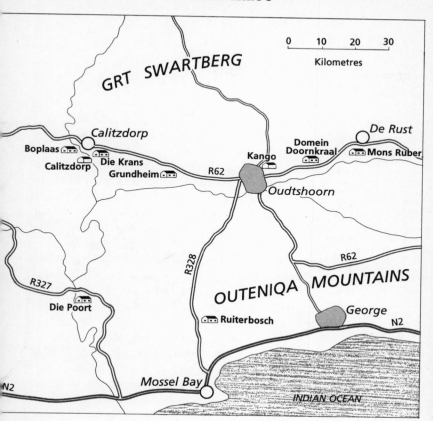

Wines produced

WHITE: Chardonnay, Sauvignon Blanc, Colombard, Blanc de Noir, Late Harvest Colombard, Hanepoot Jerepiko, Tradeaux Blanc
RED: Dry Red, Tradeaux Reserve
SPARKLING: Cap Classique, Vonkelwyn Sec

Useful Information

Manager/Winemaker: Bob de Villiers
Address: Barrydale Winery, Box 59, Barrydale 6750

Telephone: 028.5721012 *Fax*: 028.5721541

Tasting/Sales: Weekdays only 08.30 to 13.00 and 14.00 to 17.00

BOPLAAS

After a 150-kilometre drive from Barrydale through the arid, featureless Karoo, relieved only by the sight of the odd ostrich, and the equally featureless town of Ladysmith (not the one that was relieved), I arrived in Calitzdorp. This town is the capital of South African 'port'. Apart from one or two really good 'port' makers in the Stellenbosch area, like J. P. Bredell and Overgaauw, this is without doubt where the serious 'ports' originate. The ruling family, the Symingtons of the Cape, if you like, are the Nels. The patriarch of the family, Oom Danie Nel of Boplaas, sadly died whilst I was in South Africa. He was, by all accounts, a larger than life character, and will be greatly missed by his large family, and by all who knew him. It is one of the big regrets of my stay in the Cape that I did my Klein Karoo trek at the end of my visit, thus missing the chance of meeting Oom Danie.

The story goes that he knew fairly accurately when his death was coming. He had a marvellous cellar of fine wines from all over the world, and when this was inspected soon after he died, following a superb dinner with some of his best friends, it was found to be practically empty. His place at the helm, however, is far from empty: the Boplaas torch is now carried by Danie's son Carel who was the winemaker for some years prior to his father's death, and is more than capable of taking the estate's produce to new heights of excellence. Although his prime interest lies in the excellent range of Boplaas 'ports', the estate also produces some very good table wines, both red and white and, since 1989, a fine potstill brandy. In 1985 they bought a farm called Ruiterbosch in the mountains to the south, about ten kilometres from Mossel Bay and the Indian Ocean. This enjoys a far cooler climate than Calitzdorp, and they have planted the seventeen hectares with mainly Chardonnay, Sauvignon Blanc and some Pinot Noir. Sadly time prevented me from visiting Ruiterbosch, but I was able to taste some of the wines at Boplaas.

Carel's first love is his 'port'. He uses principally Tinta Barocca, but recently-planted Touriga Nacional is now coming on stream, and promises wonderful things for the 1994, a year which will definitely see a Vintage Reserve from Boplaas, and will, says Carel, be the best yet. The grapes are trodden in open lagares, exactly as in Portugal, and see two years in 500-litre barrels before bottling, and the tendency is towards a drier style, with alcohol pushing up to 20%. The Nel family are frequent visitors to the Douro, where the Symington family are good friends and have made reciprocal visits to Calitzdorp. Carel is, however, no mean maker of table wines and – apart from the excellent range of white and reds made both at Boplaas and Ruiterbosch – he has embarked on a new range of table wines under the Carel Nel label, for which he buys in grapes from carefully selected vineyards, rather in the manner of Neil Ellis.

Four different 'ports' are made at Boplaas, and all win prizes, both locally and overseas, with consistent regularity. Two wood 'ports', a White and a Ruby, are produced, as well as a Vintage, which spends two years in cask, as does the Vintage Reserve, which comes only from older, low-yielding vines and is only made in the best years. The 1989, which I tasted and found extremely Portuguese in style, was one of only two South African wines that featured in the latest Italian guide to the world's top 50 wines. I managed to slip a bottle of this wine into a dinner with three Portuguese 'port' shippers present, and only one of them spotted the ringer.

Tasting Notes

Ruiterbosch Méthode Cap Classique 1992 (50/50 Chardonnay/Pinot Noir, on lees in bottle after second fermentation until July 1995): Pale straw colour, fine mousse; yeasty, biscuit nose; creamy, biscuity taste with fine fruit.

Ruiterbosch Sauvignon Blanc 1995: Very pale greeny gold; lovely, elder-bark cool climate bouquet; classic Sauvignon, with gooseberry fruit and asparagus, excellent.

Chardonnay 1994 (100% barrel-fermented, of which a third were new, 30% went through malolactic, and all 4 months on lees): Mid-gold colour; good lime/lemon fruit aromas; well in balance, with nice, fat fruit and wood coming through on the long finish.

Blanc de Noir 1995 (18 g/l sugar, Pinotage, Cabernet Sauvignon, Cabernet Franc and Merlot): Rose-pink colour; summer berries on nose; same fresh summer fruit in mouth, a cooling, fruity summer quaffer.

Pinotage 1993 (8 months barrel aged, 25% new): Dark, dense red; good Pinotage fruit smell, plummy with banana hints; a big, mouth-filling wine with nice fruit, tannins a bit to the fore, but will be super in a year or two.

Merlot 1992: Deep, bluey red; St Emilion nose, with slight farmyard and leather; loads of lovely fruit, nice soft tannin and well structured for ageing.

Carel Nel Cabernet Sauvignon 1994 (grapes from Stellenbosch): Lovely dense colour; cassis and undergrowth bouquet; fine, ripe Cabernet blackcurrant fruit, with non-aggressive tannin and big backbone.

Boplaas Vintage Reserve 1987: Deep red, browning at edges; rich, pruney, plummy nose; full, complex mouthful of Christmas pudding fruit and soft tannin.

Boplaas Vintage Reserve 1989: Deep, dense, blackish red; nose still quite closed up; very big mouth-filling wine, lots of complex, rich tannic fruit, drier and more alcoholic than the 1987, will go 10 to 15 years with no problem.

Boplaas Estate Brandy (100% potstill, aged 5 years in wood): Golden colour; smooth, grapey but fiery nose; tremendous!

Technical Notes

Area under vines: 60 hectares, plus 17 at Ruiterbosch

Cultivars planted
WHITE: Sauvignon Blanc, Chardonnay, Colombard, Muscat, Chenin Blanc, Hanepoot, White Muscadel
RED: Cabernet Sauvignon, Cabernet Franc, Merlot, Pinotage, Pinot Noir
'PORT': Tinta Barocca, Touriga Nacional

Wines produced
WHITE: Vin Blanc, Sauvignon Blanc, Blanc Fumé, Chardonnay,

Late Harvest, Special Late Harvest, Golden Harvest, Sweet
Hanepoot, Sweet Muscadel, Blanc de Noir
RED: Cabernet Sauvignon, Carel Nel Cabernet Sauvignon, Merlot,
Grand Vin Rouge, Pinot Noir, Dry Red, Red Dessert
SPARKLING: Ruiterbosch Méthode Cap Classique, Sparkling Pinot
Noir, Vonkelwyn Soet, Vonkelwyn Rooi
'PORT': White, Ruby, Vintage, Vintage Reserve

Useful Information

Owners: Nel family
Winemaker: Carel Nel
Address: Boplaas Estate, Box 156, Calitzdorp 6660
Office/Cellars/Tastings: 2 Saayman Street, Calitzdorp 6660
Telephone: 04437.33326 *Fax*: 04437.33750

Tasting/Sales: Weekdays 08.00 to 17.00, Saturday 09.00 to 16.00,
Sunday 11.00 to 16.00
Facilities: Home-cooked traditional Cape lunches in December
school holidays; book ahead for groups of 25 and over

CALITZDORP CO-OPERATIVE

Established in 1928 by a group of fifteen farmers who needed the
strength of numbers to build an export business for Hanepoot
table grapes. There are now 68 members making red and white
wines, as well as a good 'ruby port'. About two-thirds of the 2,500
to 3,000 tons of grapes processed by the winery, however, are still
Hanepoot. The main portion of the wines made has always gone
to the KWV for distillation, and only about 3,000 cases are bottled.

Winemaker Alwyn Burger is especially proud of the winery's
'Ruby Port', which is aged for 7 months in a mixture of 500-litre
KWV brandy casks, and other used 300- and 225-litre oak. Of the
table wine range, pride of place must go to the Welgevonden
Chardonnay, made from a plot of about one hectare in the garden
of local lawyer Rheenen Barry's guesthouse of that name.

Tasting Notes

Welgevonden Chardonnay 1995 (50% barrel-fermented, 7 months in cask, of which 3 on lees, the rest in tank with wood chips): Mid-gold colour; oak quite strong on nose, but good fruit as well; a broad palate with some fat fruit, oak nicely tuned.

Colombard 1995: Pale straw; fresh fruit nose; easy-drinker, clean, crisp fruit with good length.

Merlot 1993 (3 months wood chips): Brownish colour; blackberries and oak nose; soft and easy, not much structure.

Pinotage 1994 (also aged on wood chips): Colour good, but starting to brown; Pinotage fruit nose; delicious *fraise des bois* fruit palate, with some structure and soft tannin.

Cabernet Sauvignon 1993 (15 months in used French casks): Good, bright scarlet; strange pruney nose; some fruit, but short. (Winemaker not happy with vines, old clones.)

'Ruby Port': Deep plummy colour; raisin nose; simple, fruity mouthful, with some nice, soft tannin, easy drinking.

'Vintage Port' 1994: Colour more tawny; Christmas pudding nose; fruit nice, spirity, finishes dry, needs time.

Technical Notes

Co-operative: 68 members

Average production: 2,500–3,000 tons, approx. 3,000 cases bottled wines

Wines produced
WHITE: Welgevonden Chardonnay, Colombard, Vin Blanc, Blanc de Noir, Late Harvest, White Muscadel, Golden Jerepigo
RED: Pinotage, Merlot, Cabernet Sauvignon, Red Muscadel
SPARKLING: Vin Doux
'SHERRY': Cream
'PORT': Ruby, Vintage

Useful Information

Winemaker: Alwyn Burger
Address: Calitzdorp Winery, Box 193, Calitzdorp 6660
Telephone: 04437.33301 *Fax*: 04437.33328

Tasting/Sales: Weekdays 08.00 to 13.00 and 14.00 to 17.00,
Saturday 08.00 to 12.00

DIE KRANS

The history of Die Krans dates back to 1890, when Boets Nel's great-grandfather bought the farm. At that time the main emphasis was on ostriches and fruit, and what wine was made was either used for sweet, fortified wine or distilled into brandy, both of which were exported to London in the 1890s. When the ostrich boom ended in 1914 with the beginning of the First World War, Die Krans concentrated all its efforts into the cultivation of the vine and other fruit crops.

The original owner's grandsons, Chris and 'Oom Danie' Nel, were farming in partnership until Boets' father, Chris, died in 1981, when Danie decided to split the property. Boets and his brother Stroebel kept the Die Krans name and about 60 hectares of the original farm, whilst the late Oom Danie's portion became the present Boplaas estate, currently in the able hands of Danie's son Carel.

The present cellar was built in 1964, and Die Krans became the first property to be registered as an estate in 1979. There are presently 45 hectares under vines, producing an average of 550 tons of grapes each year, about 30% of which goes into bottled wines, 10% is sold in bulk for export, and the remaining 60% in bulk to the merchants and wholesalers. Of the bottled wines, 25% is 'port', 60% white wine and the rest red. As at Boplaas, 'port' is the passion here. The first bottlings were in 1976, and again like his cousin Carel, Boets produces a fine ruby, a vintage, and, in exceptional years a Vintage Reserve. The quality of the Die Krans table wines is exceptionally good for the area and for the youth of the vines – planting of the noble varieties only dates from 1983.

Tasting Notes

Chardonnay 1995 (80% barrel-fermented with 2 months on lees, rest in tank): Good, mid-gold colour; strong vanilla with ripe fruit nose; a broad, quite weighty fruit palate, oak a bit strong at present, but will soon integrate.

Cabernet Sauvignon 1994 (10 months wood-ageing, 15% new, rest 2nd- and 3rd-fill casks): Deep red with bluey edges; ripe berry fruit smell; no great structure, but rounded, ripe fruit and agreeable, soft tannin.

White Muscadel 1994: Brilliant gold colour; rich, ripe fruit bouquet, not dried; fresh, concentrated ripeness of fruit, very long.

White Muscadel 1988: Deep, treacle gold; tropical fruit, but still very fresh; delicious, evolved lychee fruit, very rich and persistent finish.

Ruby Port: More tawny than ruby; ripe fruit nose with chocolate hints; soft, easy style of 'port', with quite a dry finish.

Vintage 1993: Full, deep red; nice, plummy fruit nose; fruit, tannins and spirit all coming together, will be delicious in a year or two.

Vintage Reserve 1991: Dark, dense red; rich cooked-fruit smell of prunes and figs; big, strapping wine, lots of Christmas pudding fruit and structure, drink in 5 years, and then keep on for another decade or two.

Technical Notes

Area under vines: 45 hectares

Cultivars planted
WHITE: Chardonnay, Chenin Blanc, Sauvignon Blanc, Gerwürztraminer, Muscat d'Alexandrie
RED: Cabernet Sauvignon, Shiraz, Pinotage
'PORT': Tinta Barocca, Sousao, Tinta Roriz, Touriga Nacional

Wines produced
WHITE: Chardonnay, Sauvignon Blanc, Grand Vin Blanc,

Gewürztraminer, Bouquet Blanc, Muscat d'Alexandrie, Late Harvest, Golden Harvest, White Muscadel Jerepigo, Heritage Collection
RED: Cabernet Sauvignon, Pinotage, Vin Rouge
SPARKLING: Spumante
'PORT': Ruby, Vintage, Vintage Reserve

Useful Information

Owners: Boets and Stroebel Nel
Winemaker: Boets Nel
Address: Die Krans Estate, Box 28, Calitzdorp 6660
Telephone: 04437.33314/33364 *Fax*: 04437.33562

Tasting/Sales: Weekdays 08.00 to 16.00, Saturday 09.00 to 16.00
Facilities: Vintners platters 12.00 to 14.00, December holidays only, except Sunday; rest of year, groups of 10 or more require prior appointment

DOMEIN DOORNKRAAL

Swepie le Roux is one of the people that I most enjoyed meeting in South Africa. Although he is the Klein Karoo's regional director for the KWV, he is very definitely not an establishment figure, as is clearly demonstrated by his approach to winemaking, his unusual range of wines, and his dry, sometimes rather wicked sense of humour. I was due to meet him at Domein Doornkraal on my last night in the Klein Karoo. A message reached me at my previous visit, asking me to meet him for dinner at his daughter and son-in-law's excellent restaurant, Bernard's Taphuis, in Oudsthoorn. He installed me in the bar, bought me a large and very welcome whisky and soda and, apologizing profusely, left me there for an hour while he went off to an unavoidable and unexpected meeting. On his return, all apologies, he asked me a few careless questions about my life, what I did, my family and what they did. A few minutes later, he presented me to his lovely daughter, who owns the restaurant. 'This is Mr Seely,' he said, 'I think he is a bit of a cad. His wife works her fingers to the bone, running a Christmas Hamper business in England, while he swans off to South Africa for two months, having a marvellous time.' All of this was true, but it is not quite as black as it sounds.

The town of Oudsthoorn is fascinating. Its prosperity was entirely founded on the farming of ostriches for their feathers in the late nineteenth century, when an unbelievable 400,000 kilograms of plumes were being exported annually to the fashion centres of the world, like Paris, London and New York. The wonderful black and white cocks' plumes sold for R420 a kilogram. The entre-preneurs of this profitable trade were the Jewish immigrant brokers, many of whom came here with nothing, made enormous fortunes, brought culture to the desert and built vast 'Ostrich Palaces', many of which survive today along the broad streets of Oudsthoorn. Like many industries based upon fashion, the boom was relatively short-lived. The First World War, coupled with the advent of the motor-car, which precluded the wearing of delicate plumage, put an almost instant brake on sales in 1914, and many fortunes were lost as quickly as they had been made. The industry has had a recent renaissance but the tall, rather stupid looking birds, with their beautiful Walt Disney eyes, are now farmed in their thousands again, not for their plumage, nor even for their meat, which is a delicious by-product – but for their leather, which is used for the most expensive shoes, ladies' bags and luggage that you can buy.

Swepie's farm, where he is now the third generation to make wine, is typical of the area. The house is large and grand, built on boom-time ostrich money – now vines, winemaking and ostriches flourish side by side. Sweet wines are le Roux's speciality, and he firmly believes that even his dry wines need a touch of Muscat to set them apart from those of the western winelands. Everything about the Domein Doornkraal wines is slightly eccentric, from the blends of grapes, through the bright, attractive labels down to the names themselves. Many of his excellent dessert wines bear army ranks as names: there is a fortified wine made from Zante raisins called Luitenant; a blend of red Muscadel, Pinotage and Chenin named Kaptein; a golden Jerepigo made from Chenin under the title of Majoor; and a blend of red and white Muscadel from 1973 labelled Generaal. There is also a sparkling pink wine called Tickled Pink, which comes with a shocking-pink ostrich-feather attached. The only completely normal names in the Doornkraal range are the Merlot – a smooth, easy-drinking wine with plummy fruit and some soft tannins, which went well with an ostrich steak in Bernard's Taphuis – and Port, a very drinkable ruby wine.

Swepie's son Piet helps his father with the winemaking. He has spent some time at the California winery of Robert Mondavi, and his particular responsibility is with the dry white wines.

Tasting Notes

Serenade Droog 1995 (60% Sauvignon Blanc, 30% Colombard, 10% Hanepoot): Pale gold; grassy, gooseberry fruit nose from Sauvignon; clean, crisp, dry fruit in mouth, with good acid balance.

Tinta Bianca Effe-Droog 1995 (Colombard, Pinotage, Red Muscadel): Pale pink colour; summer fruit bouquet; fresh and light, an easy summer quaffer.

Kannaland N. V. (Merlot/Pinotage blend): Nice mid-red; ripe, soft fruit nose; easy drinking red with good fruit.

Merlot 1994: Good, deep red; rounded fruit bouquet; ripe and smooth, easy-drinking red with soft tannin.

Pinta 1990 (dessert wine from Tinta Barocca/Pinotage): Brilliant colour; syrup and fruit bouquet; cassis and nutty flavours, luscious.

Technical Notes

Area under vines: 35 hectares

Cultivars planted
WHITE: Sauvignon Blanc, Colombard, Chenin Blanc, Hanepoot, Muscat d'Ottonel, White Muscadel
RED: Merlot, Pinotage, Tinta Barocca, Red Muscadel

Wines produced
WHITE: Serenade Droog, Tinta Bianca Effe Droog, Kuierwyn Effe Droog
RED: Merlot, Kannaland
DESSERT WINES: Luitenant, Kaptein, Majoor, Generaal, Hanepoot, Jerepigo, Pinta
SPARKLING: Tickled Pink

'PORT': White Port, Port

Useful Information

Owner: Swepie le Roux
Winemakers: Swepie le Roux and Piet le Roux
Address: Domein Doornkraal, Box 14, De Rust 6650
Telephone: 04439.6715 *Fax*: 04439.2548

Tasting/Sales: Weekdays 09.00 to 17.00, Saturday 08.00 to 13.00, school holiday weekdays 08.00 to 18.00
Facilities: Wine sales on De Rust/Oudsthoorn road; farm/cellar visits and meals at Tante Marie's for groups by appointment

UNVISITED

Estates and Wineries: Die Poort, Grundheim, Mons Ruber, Ruiterbosch (see Boplaas)

Co-operatives: Kango, Ladysmith, Montagu, Soetwyn Boere

12
Tulbagh

A group of men first clapped eyes on the mountain-girt valley that is now Tulbagh in 1658, whilst journeying in search of new land for the ever-increasing number of settlers on the orders of Jan van Riebeeck. Although there was a river running through the valley, the surveyor, Pieter Potter, thought it looked too barren and infertile for farming, and went to look elsewhere. It was not until 1699 that Wilhem Adriaen van der Stel, newly appointed Governor after his father, Simon, and eager to make his mark, came to the valley and opened it up for settlement.

Early farming did not include the growing of vines, and the land was mainly used for grazing. In 1743 the church was built, and a small, necessarily self-sufficient community developed. Until the beginning of the nineteenth century, the area was known as Waveren, named after influential relations of the van der Stels back in Amsterdam. In 1804 the Commissioner General annexed the area from Stellenbosch, giving it its own measure of self-administration, and renaming it Tulbagh after an earlier Governor, Ryk Tulbagh.

Early winemaking was perforce only for local consumption because of transport difficulties, and probably quantities of both wine and brandy made were small, as there was only a handful of families living there. Life went on undisturbed in this isolated farming community well into the twentieth century until, on 29 September 1969, the valley was rocked by the most severe earthquake ever recorded in South Africa. Not a building was untouched, and many of the lovely old houses of Church Street were completely demolished. The whole town of Tulbagh was restored with tremendous care to its original form, apart from the incorporation into every building of special reinforcements against

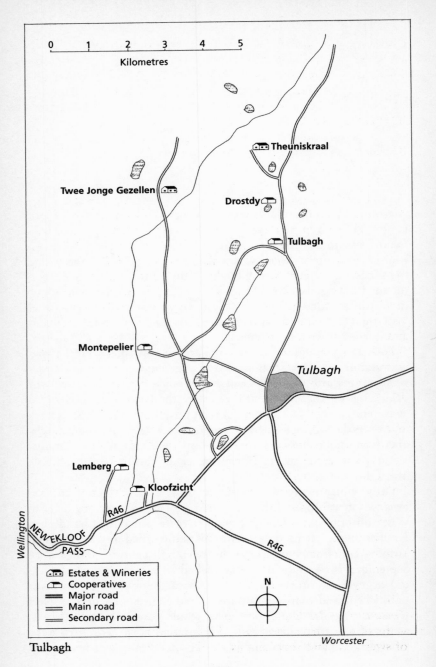

0 1 2 3 4 5
Kilometres

Theuniskraal

Twee Jonge Gezellen

Drostdy

Tulbagh

Montepelier

Tulbagh

Lemberg

Kloofzicht

R46

Wellington

NEW EKLOOF PASS

R46

Estates & Wineries
Cooperatives
Major road
Main road
Secondary road

N

Worcester

Tulbagh

future tremors. Today the town is an almost exact copy of how it must have looked a hundred years ago, and in December Main Street and Church Street are a lovely sight, lined with the dazzling blue of rows of jacaranda trees.

THEUNISKRAAL

Theuniskraal is perhaps the best known of the five estates producing wine in Tulbagh. The farm has been in the hands of the Jordaan family since Kobus's mother bought it back in 1927. Although vines have been grown here since the nineteenth century, there was no winery until 1905. When the Jordaans first came to Theuniskraal, they had no winemaking experience. The vines that they found here were Palomino, presumably for 'sherry', Green Grape (an early and unsatisfactory variety of Sémillon), and Cape Riesling. Early efforts with this unpromising cocktail were not very successful, as cold-fermentation was unheard of. Kobus's father received much help from Frank Myburgh of the Drostdy Co-op, and the first blend of the three varieties, labelled simply 'Theuniskraal', was an instant success. It is Theuniskraal Riesling, however, first appearing in 1948, upon which the estate's reputation is founded.

There are currently 130 of the total 289 hectares under vines, and twelve different varieties, all of them white, are grown. The main contender is the Cape Riesling with 30 hectares, which is used for the flagship Theuniskraal Riesling. For years this has been the only wine to be bottled under the Theuniskraal label, the rest of the wine going to the Bergkelder for use in their blends. Since 1994, however, there has been another Theuniskraal wine on offer in bottle, the Sémillon/Chardonnay blend. Kobus and his son Andries are the winemakers, and Kobus's brother, Rennie, is in charge of the vineyards. Theuniskraal was one of the first estates to join the Bergkelder group in 1947, along with Alto, and they still market their wines today.

Tasting Notes

Theuniskraal Riesling 1995: Lovely, pale greenish gold; delicate wafts of limey fruit; mouthful of ripe citrus fruit flavours, touch of sweetness, and very long finish. Great.

Sémillon/Chardonnay 1995 (66% Sémillon, 34% Chardonnay, no casks used): Good, greeny gold, brilliant; quite closed on nose, but some pleasing nectariney fruit coming through; dry, with rather appley fruit, this is an unostentatious but elegant wine of some complexity that will improve with a year in bottle.

Technical Notes

Area under vines: 130 hectares

Cultivars planted
WHITE: Cape Riesling, Sauvignon Blanc, Sémillon, Chardonnay, Rhine Riesling, Chenin Blanc, Colombard, Pinot Gris, Gewürztraminer, Bukettraube, Muscat d'Ottonel, Muscat de Frontignan

Wines produced
WHITE: Theuniskraal Riesling (Cape), Sémillon/Chardonnay, rest in bulk to Bergkelder

Useful Information

Owners: Jordaan family
Winemakers: Kobus and Andries Jordaan
Vineyards: Rennie Jordaan
Address: Theuniskraal, Tulbagh 6820
Telephone: 0236.300688/9/0 *Fax*: 0236.301504

Tasting/Sales: Wines are marketed by the Bergkelder, but tours and tasting can be arranged by appointment

TWEE JONGE GEZELLEN

The name of this estate has always held a fascination for me, and I have wrongly thought it to mean Two Young Gazelles, whereas the correct translation is Two Young Bachelors which, though interesting enough, is somehow less romantic. It in fact refers to two gentleman to whom the farm was first granted in 1710, and who subsequently returned to their native Holland. N. C. Krone, the present owner, is the current generation of a family that have held this estate on the western edge of the Tulbagh valley since 1745. The first Krone, all of whose sons have borne the initials N. C., came to Twee Jonge Gezellen in 1916 after spending fourteen years in the wine trade in Holland, and married the daughter of the then owner, thus keeping alive the family line (for his father-in-law, Christian Theron, had no male heir).

N. C. Krone the First did a great deal in establishing the name and fame of Twee Jonge Gezellen, but it was N. C. the Second, now 78 years old and still active, who took the estate through the most formative years of South Africa's wine history, and established the name as a prime producer of quality white wines. He took over the reins in 1939, having studied viticulture and winemaking at Stellenbosch University. At that time all the vines were concentrated on the low-lying alluvial soils near the Klein Berg river, but he knew from his studies that the poorer soil and cooler air of the lower slopes of the Obiqua mountains would produce grapes of higher quality, although the yield would be much lower; he knew that in Tulbagh, just as much as in Bordeaux and Burgundy, the key to making good wine lies always in sacrificing quantity on the altar of quality, and quality was his goal.

Gradually N. C. the Second extended his plantings of classic white varieties like Sauvignon Blanc, Sémillon and Cape Riesling on to the higher ground, and replaced the high-yield Palomino and Green Grape vines on the lower ground with the same nobler stock. The high-ground vineyards proved themselves very quickly in terms of quality, but the ground is so steep and rocky that the vineyards have to be terraced like the Douro valley, which is highly labour-intensive and extremely expensive.

When Nicky, the third N. C., started on the farm, all his father's hard work and investment had given him an estate bursting with potential. Innovations since his arrival have included the introduction of night picking, the introduction of very fine Méthode Cap Classique and the construction of an excellent cellar specifically designed for the production of sparkling wines. The first vintage released of the Krone Borealis Brut, a blend from Chardonnay, Pinot Noir and Pinot Blanc was the 1988. The name is a clever corruption of the constellation Corona Borealis, supposedly, according to Greek mythology, the crown of the Greek god of wine Bacchus. So successful has this Méthode Champenoise been that the Champagne house of G. H. Mumm selected the 1992 vintage for their Cuvée Cap label. Vintages are released for sale not always in chronological order, but according to their readiness for drinking. A new style was made in 1994 which will have shorter lees contact and a higher dosage, and will therefore be slightly less dry; for release in 1996, it was called Krone Borealis Celestial.

There are now three generations of N. C. Krones at work at Twee Jonge Gezellen. Nicky's father now chiefly occupies himself with the growing of proteas, Nicky himself is the general wine supremo, whilst his son, aged 25, is the farm manager. Nicky's second son, Graham works on the financial side of the business, and Matthew, now aged 18, has ambitions to become a writer. There is also a 'late lamb', Luke, aged 4, who has not yet decided what he will do.

Twee Jonge Gezellen is a jewel in a beautiful setting. The reception and tasting room, built over the new cellar, are reached by an outside staircase, with a rivulet of water cascading down a channel which forms the bannister rail. Visitors can taste on the terrace, whilst enjoying a magnificent view over the vines to the slopes of the Obiqua mountains. A large flock of white ducks, which is kept for snail control, can often be seen amongst the vines.

Tasting Notes

Krone Borealis, Brut 1990: Pale straw, with long, fine mousse; creamy, with yeasty, biscuity taste, dry and very long.

Krone Borealis, Brut 1993: Same appearance; very Champenois bouquet, yeasty and fragrant; very similar in taste, without the smoothness of the bottle-age of the 1990.

Chardonnay/Weisser Riesling 1995: Pale gold; Riesling very much to fore at the moment on the nose, and in the mouth; lovely, rich, ripe Riesling fruit and good length.

T. J. 39 1995 (named for a clone of the Weisser Riesling, which is blended with mainly Chenin Blanc and Sauvignon): Pale straw; Riesling dominant on nose; spicy, dry with loads of ripe fruit, long.

T. J. Light 1995 (blend of Müller-Thurgau, Pinot Gris, Gewürztraminer and others, 8% alcohol. Recommended by Heart

Foundation!): Pleasing, grapey and very perfumed, with a pale gold colour; lots of nice fruit, finishes short.

T. J. Schanderl 1995 (a blend named after Professor Hugo Schanderl, Nicky's teacher and mentor at Geisenheim): Very pale colour; fine Muscatty grape bouquet; rich and spicy fruit from main ingredient Gewürztraminer, quite dry, and long.

T. J. Night Nectar 1995 (semi-sweet blend of mainly Chenin, Furmint and Sémillon, 27 g/l sugar): Palish, greeny gold; nose a bit shy, but honeyed and tropical; ripe, grapey flavour with low acidity and a shortish finish.

Technical Notes

Area under vines: 274 hectares

Cultivars planted
WHITE: Chardonnay, Sauvignon Blanc, Pinot Blanc, Pinot Gris, Gewürztraminer, Furmint, Sémillon, Muscat d'Ottonel, Rhine Riesling, Sylvaner
RED: Pinot Noir (for MCC)

Wines produced
WHITE: Sauvignon Blanc, T. J. Chardonnay/Rhine Riesling, T. J. Night Nectar, T. J. Grand Prix 39, T. J. Light, T. J. Schanderl, T. J. Engeltjiepipi, Gewürztraminer Special Late Harvest
SPARKLING: Krone Borealis Brut, Krone Borealis Celestial

Useful Information

Owners: Krone family
Winemaker: Nicky Krone
Assistant Winemaker: Henry Links
Farm Manager: N. C. Krone, Jnr
Marketing: Mary Krone
Address: Twee Jonge Gezellen Estate, Box 16, Tulbagh 6820
Telephone: 0236.300680 *Fax*: 0236.300686

Tasting/Sales: Weekdays 09.00 to 12.30, Saturday 09.00 to 12.00
Facilities: Cellar tours weekdays 11.00 and 15.00, Saturday 10.30; large groups by appointment

UNVISITED

Estates and Wineries: Drostdy, Kloofzicht, Lemberg, Montpelier
Co-operatives: Tulbagh

13
Olifants River

The vineyards of the Olifants River are the most northerly and the hottest in the Cape. They stretch from Citrusdal, which is about 200 kilometres north of Cape Town, 120 kilometres north to Lutzville. The vines cannot grow successfully, especially at the northern end, without intensive irrigation, so all the farms are concentrated along the banks of the river. Apart from the Cederberg cellars, all the wine is made by co-operatives, of which there are seven.

With the possible exception of Cederberg, the whole area is really unsuited to the making of good table wine. Until the advent of cold fermentation for white wines, virtually the entire production from the Olifants River vineyards went for distillation. By and large, this is still the case, though a certain amount of table wine is sold in bulk to the merchants and for export, and a small percentage is sold in bottle by the co-operatives.

CEDERBERG

When I set off from Stellenzicht on my Olifants River expedition, André van Rensburg insisted that I take his assistant winemaker, Herman (known as Buller) Gerber with me. 'It's wild country up there, man, and half the buggers only speak Afrikaans.' Buller proved a good companion, and his muscular frame promised well in the event of attack by marauding elephants or bushmen. In fact we met neither, both species having long disappeared from the area, and I met nobody who was more difficult to understand than Buller himself, who has an Afrikaans accent that you could cut with an assegai.

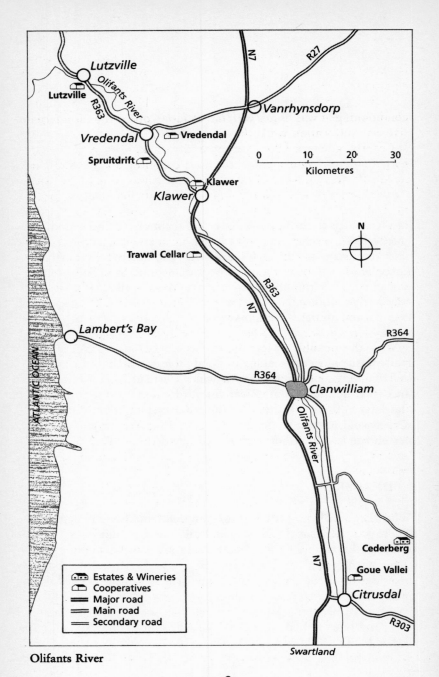

Olifants River

It is a very long drive, first through the endless wheatlands between Malmesbury and Piketburg, and then through more hilly country to Citrusdal. It was one of the hottest and most uncomfortable drives of my life, and I wished I had hired a car with air-conditioning: it was hotter with the windows open, and the alternative was suffocation when they were closed.

Cederberg lies 75 kilometres up a dirt track, high in the Cederberg mountains, and is one of the most beautiful, and certainly the most remote wine farms I have ever seen. Short, tough and wiry, owner Flippie Nieuwoudt is a typical mountain man with a permanent, wry grin and twinkling blue eyes. Self-sufficiency is the order of the day here, as it takes over an hour just to reach the road. As one would expect it is a polycultural farm growing apples, pears and vegetables as well as vines, and there are guest cottages to accommodate mountaineers, walkers, birdwatchers and hunters to provide additional income. The tenants are a good captive market for the fruit and vegetables and, of course, the wine, as there are not many supermarkets up here.

The Nieuwoudt family have been here since 1832, but the first vines were only planted in 1963, when Flippie's father, Oom Pollie, put in a few Barlinka vines for table grapes. They built a small cellar, and their first wine was a *boerwyn*, or farmer's wine, made from the table grapes. Serious winemaking dates from 1977, when they made wine from newly planted wine varieties. The 1978 Cabernet Sauvignon, much to everybody's surprise, won the Distillers Corporation Trophy at the 1979 Olifants River Wine Show, and they now make a range of wines including Pinotage, Merlot, and several white varieties as well.

Transportation is the biggest problem here, particularly as all the wine has to go to Worcester for bottling. Flippie expressed mild distrust of the bottlers: 'I took my tank of Merlot 1992, which I was very pleased with, to Worcester to be bottled, and I am convinced that the bottled stock I collected was a different wine.' My own thoughts are that perhaps it was a different wine, but only because 75 kilometres down a dirt track in boiling heat is quite capable of making any wine different.

Tasting Notes

Blanc Fumé 1995: Pale straw; very oaky nose; there is nice Sauvignon fruit there, but far too much new wood.

Bukettraube 1995: Good, mid-golden colour; spicy fruit bouquet; medium-dry, with loads of ripe, rather Muscatty fruit.

Chenin Blanc 1995: Pale gold; nose of quince and guava; another medium-dry wine with good, clean fruit and the right acidity level.

Weissberger 1995 (semi-sweet from Chenin Blanc): Pale gold; same quincy Chenin bouquet, with more fruit; sweet ripe fruit, no botrytis and good acidity. Long.

Pinotage 1992 (aged in casks of about 10 vintages): Garnet, shading to brown; plummy fruit, with slight acetone; easy fruit, not much tannin showing, and lacks structure, but good for current drinking.

Merlot 1992: Deep red; nose a bit cooked (travel-sickness?); some nice fruit, but lacking balance.

Cabernet Sauvignon 1991 (again aged in old casks): Palish red; nose of summer fruits, ripe strawberries; light and elegant, with blackcurrant fruit and cherries. Good now, but not for laying-down.

Technical Notes

Area under vines: 17 hectares, with 10 newly planted.

Average production: 5,000 cases

Cultivars planted
WHITE: Sauvignon Blanc, Chenin Blanc, Bukettraube
RED: Cabernet Sauvignon, Pinotage, Merlot

Useful Information

Owner/Winemaker: Flippie Nieuwoudt
Address: Cederberg Kelders, Dwarsrivier, PO Cederberg 8136
Telephone: 027.4822827 *Fax*: 027.4822825

Tasting/Sales: 08.30 to 12.00 and 13.30 to 17.30

VREDENDAL WINERY

Established in 1950, this vast co-operative has 158 members, and processes a massive 55,000 tons of grapes a year, more than the entire production of New Zealand. There is currently a team of three winemakers, a necessity in view of the large range and volume of wines. Apart from distilling wine, about 150,000 cases are bottled, a considerable volume goes into 3-litre boxes and most of the rest is sold in 5-litre containers.

In the past the main business of this huge winery was the making of wine for distilling, and although this is still the destination of most of the production, they are moving more and more into the making of table wines. At first it was chiefly white wine, because the plant material for distilling wine consisted of only white varieties like Chenin and Colombard. However there is now a definite shift towards the making of red wines. Newer plantings of white cultivars include Sauvignon Blanc, Weisser Riesling, Chardonnay, Bukettraube, Harslevelu and Fernao Pires; for red wine it was initially mostly Tinta Barocca and Pinotage, but there is now a swing towards Ruby Cabernet, Cabernet Sauvignon and Cabernet Franc. A very small amount of Pinotage and Shiraz are also planted, with Pinotage likely to increase.

From such an unlikely, hot area, the quality of the wines is surprisingly good, and the Cabaret, a blend of cask-aged Ruby Cabernet and Cabernet Franc, has been honoured twice: the 1993 was best Ruby Cabernet in the Young Wine Show, and the 1994 won the General Jan Smuts Trophy for best young South African wine of the year.

Tasting Notes

Sauvignon Blanc 1995: Pale greenish straw: uncomplicated Sauvignon nose; clean and straightforward with the right balance of fruit and acidity.

Goiya Kgeisje 1995 (Bushman Kung language meaning 'First Wine', 50/50 Sauvignon Blanc/Chardonnay, now successful

Tesco blend): Pale greeny gold; quite good fruit bouquet, less fresh than the Sauvignon Blanc; disappointing, as this marriage of blends usually is.

Dry Red 1994 (50% Pinotage, 25% Cabernet Sauvignon, 25% Merlot, oak chips): Light, brilliant red; cherries and tobacco on nose; pleasing fruit, no great pretensions, nice summer wine to drink chilled.

Cabaret 1994 (79% Ruby Cabernet, 21% Cabernet Franc, 6 months in 25% new, 75% used French casks): Deep, bluey red; ripe, minty fruit aromas; delicious, fresh fruit, with a bit of structure and soft tannins. Good.

Technical Notes

Co-operative: 158 members

Average production: 50,000 tons, of which 150,000 cases bottled.

Wines produced
WHITE: Sauvignon Blanc, Chenin Blanc, Chardonnay, Grand Cru, Fernao Pires, Blanc de Noir, Special Late Harvest, Noble Late Harvest, Meisje, Hanepoot Jerepiko
RED: Cabaret, Maskam, Dry Red, Goiya Kgeisje, Hanepoot Jerepiko
SPARKLING: Sec, Semi-Sweet
'PORT'
ALSO (produced under Namaqua label): Medium Sherry, Soet Hanepoot, Rooi Jerepiko, Van Der Hum Liqueur, Three and Five Star Brandy and Witblits

Useful Information

General Manager: Izak Visagie
Winemakers: Louis Nel, François Weich, Danie de Kock
Public Relations: Erline Bester
Address: Vredendal Winery, Box 75, Vredendal 8160
Telephone: 0271.31080 *Fax*: 0271.33476

Tasting/Sales: Weekdays 08.30 to 12.30 and 14.00 to 17.30, Saturday 08.00 to 12.00

Facilities: Large shop selling winery's produce, plus wines from other wineries and international branded spirits

SPRUITDRIFT CO-OPERATIVE

One of the Cape's younger co-operatives, Spruitdrift is situated at one of the very few bridges across the Olifants River: Simon van der Stel crossed the river here on his expedition to find the copper mines of Namaqualand, and a settlement grew here that was to become bigger than Vredendal.

Founded in 1968, with the first wine produced in 1970, there are currently 92 members with around 1,200 hectares of vines, and the well-equipped winery handles an average of 28,000 tons of grapes annually. The farms are widespread, and, although they are all on the low-lying land along the river banks, there is a wide variety of soil types: to the north around Lutzville there is a lot of sand, but nearer to the winery the soil is red Karoo and gravel, with clay and rock subsoil. Irrigation is essential throughout the region, but in the past there was only flood-water to rely on when the river was in spate, so only the land very near the river could be used. It was not until 1976 that electricity came here, making pumping for irrigation far easier, and opening up the possibilities for vine culture where the soil is much better, above the level of the existing irrigation channels.

In view of the extreme heat at harvest time, much of the harvesting is by machine in order to gather the grapes at optimum ripeness, and a lot is done at night. Only 2% of the wines are bottled, the rest going either in bulk to the merchants or for distillation. The co-operative also sells grapes to the Bergkelder, which are transported to Stellenbosch at night in order to avoid oxidation in the heat of the day. The vast majority of the grapes are white: about 9,000 tons of Chenin Blanc and 7,500 tons of Colombard are harvested, whilst there are only some 700 tons of Sauvignon Blanc and 500 tons of Chardonnay. Chenin and Colombard can be huge yielders, and crops of 90 tons to the hectare have been recorded for Colombard, though the wine from such grapes is only fit for distilling. Only around 6% are red, and those mainly Pinotage, though more reds are planned.

The flowers in the grounds of the winery are spectacular and, together with the wines, these attract many visitors.

Tasting Notes

Sauvignon Blanc 1994: Pale straw; faint Sauvignon character on clean fruit bouquet; palate also lacks typicity of grape, but has some nice clean fruit.

Riesling 1994: Mid-gold; strange, rather dusty nose; fruit a bit flat and lifeless, finishes somewhat short.

Chardonnay 1995: Pale straw; citrussy fruit aromas; good fruit in mouth, with some nice Chardonnay fatness.

Merlot 1995: Medium deep colour; strong volatile acidity on nose; some good fruit, but v. a. very noticeable.

Pinotage 1993 (6 months oak): Nice plummy red; nose has green stalkiness, and some game; some jammy fruit, but the wine is fading fast.

Cabernet Sauvignon 1993: Good colour; curious, rather unpleasant wet dog bouquet; in the mouth the wine tastes a bit cooked and tired.

Weisser Riesling 1995: Very pale straw; good spicy Riesling nose; medium dry, with excellent fruit and good length.

Special Late Harvest Chenin Blanc 1994: Nice medium-deep golden colour; rich, ripe and grapey bouquet; luscious, raisiny mouthful, finishes quite dry.

Hanepoot Jerepiko: Yellow gold; rich Muscat aroma; luscious and rich fruit, with good lingering aftertaste.

Technical Notes

Co-operative: 92 members

Area under vines: 1,200 hectares

Average production: 28,000 tons, of which 6% bottled

Wines produced
WHITE: Sauvignon Blanc, Chardonnay, Premier Grand Cru, Riesling, Late Harvest, Special Late Harvest, Weisser Riesling, White Muscadel, Hanepoot
RED: Cabernet Sauvignon, Merlot, Pinotage, Red Muscadel
SPARKLING: Semi-Sweet

Useful Information

Winemaker: Johan Rossouw
Assistant Winemaker: A. B. Krige
Address: Spruitdrift Co-op Wine Cellars, Box 129, Vredendal 8160
Telephone: 0271.33086 *Fax*: 0271.32937

Tasting/Sales: Weekdays 08.00 to 17.30, Saturday 08.00 to 12.00
Facilities: Lunches for groups of 15 or more by prior arrangement

UNVISITED

Co-operatives: Goue Vallei (Citrusdal), Klawer, Lutzville Vineyards, Trawal Wine Cellar

14
Durbanville

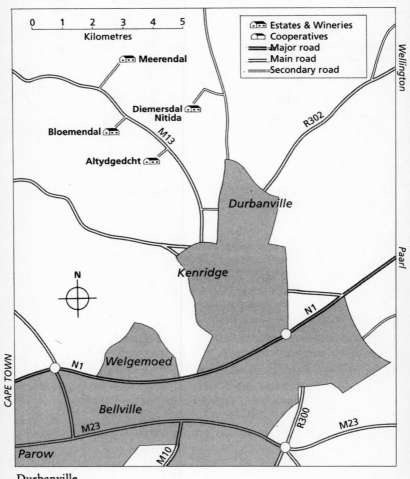

Durbanville

Just to the north-east of Cape Town, the agricultural area of Durbanville is rapidly shrinking beneath urban development. There are
only a handful of wine-producing estates remaining: the best of
these are Meerendal, a member of the Bergkelder, Altydgedacht,
Bloemendal, Diemersdal and Nitida Vineyards.

Sadly time did not allow me to visit any of these properties, but
some good wines are made. The best vineyards lie on the slopes
that benefit from the cooling sea breezes from the Atlantic and False
Bay. The soils are water-retentive, and irrigation is not generally
practised, despite a relatively low annual rainfall.

15
Swartland

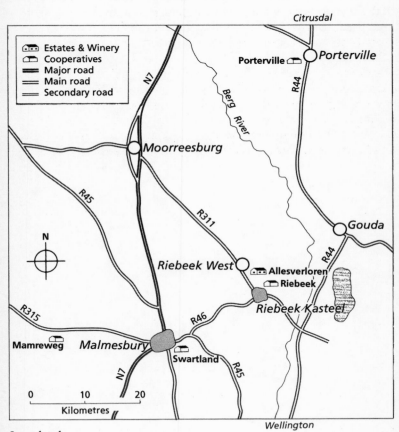

Swartland

Swartland is a large area, about 100 kilometres from north to south, and some 50 kilometres west to east. The Atlantic lies to the west, Durbanville and Paarl to the south and the eastern edge is bounded by mountains, on the western slopes of which lies the valley of Tulbagh. The main crop has always been wheat, and the vine has only been cultivated for a relatively short time. The best vineyards are concentrated at the southern end of the region around Malmesbury. Average annual rainfall is low at around 242 millimetres in the south, and the soils vary, with Malmesbury shale predominant, some isolated pockets of decomposed granite and, in the south, a certain amount of Table Mountain sandstone.

The region is dominated by co-operatives, of which there are four: Swartland Wine Cellar, Riebeeck Wine Cellar, Porterville and Mamreweg, which specializes in Groenkloof wines.

There is just one estate, Allesverloren, which belongs to Fanie Malan and his son Danie. It is situated on the lower slopes of the Kasteelberg, between Riebeeck Kasteel and Riebeeck West. The name, meaning 'all is lost', originates from the eighteenth century, when the then owner returned from church to find that San hunters had burnt his homestead and buildings, and stolen all his cattle. The Malans specialize in 'port' and red wines, especially Shiraz.

Bibliography

━━━━━━

Burman, J. *Wine of Constantia* (Human & Rousseau, Cape Town, 1979)

Hands, P., Hughes, D., & Kench, J. *South African Wine* (Struick Publishers, Cape Town, 1992)

Lichine, A. *New Encyclopedia of Wines & Spirits*, seventh edition (Cassell, London, 1987)

Platter, J. *South African Wines '96* and *South African Wines '95* (Mitchell Beazley, London)

Rudman, C. *A Guide to the Winelands of the Cape* (CGR Wine Enterprises CC, Stellenbosch, 1993)

Simons, P. B. *Nederburg, The First Two Hundred Years* (Struick Publishers, Cape Town, 1992)

Wynboer, KWV's monthly journal (KWV Paarl)

Index

INDEX

von Arnim, Achim, xxvi, 40–2
von Arnim, Hildegard, 40
von Stiernhielm, Baron, 87
von Stiernhielm, Baroness, 87
Vredendal Winery, xix, 281–3
Vriesenhof, 113–18

Wagener, Gerrie, 37, 154
Waitrose, 61
Walker Bay, xx, 151; Bouchard
  Finlayson, 157–60; Hamilton
  Russell Vineyards, 157–8, 160–2
Walker, Jeremy, 85, 97
Warwick Farm, 107–9
Waterside White, 221, 222
Watt, Kevin, 119
weather *see* climate
Webb, Barbara, 78
Webb, Gyles, xxvi, 77, 78
Weisser Riesling (Rhine Riesling), xxi
Welgemeend, 198–200
Wellington, xx, 7, 201
Wellington Wynkelder, 201–3
Welmoed Co-operative, 29
Weltevrede, 243–6
Welz, Stephan, xxvi
Westpeak, 119
wholesaler/producers, xix
Wiehe, Marc, 62–3, 64
Wieser, Johan Jurgen, 14

Wiid, Ronell, 37
Wijnberg, 2
wine auctions, xxvi
wine festivals, xxv–xxvi
'Wine Routes', xxvi
wine shows, xxv
Wine Spectator, 178
Wine Test Match: Australia v. South
  Africa, xxv, 124, 129
winemaking courses, xxv, xxvii
Winshaw, Bill, 53
Winshaw, Jack, 53
Winshaw, William Charles (Oubass),
  52–3
Woolworths (South Africa), 75, 171,
  231
Worcester, xx, xxv, 204–6; Bergsig,
  206–7; De Wet Co-operative,
  207–9; Nuy Co-operative, 210–12;
  Romansrivier Co-operative, 212–14
Wynberg, Lord, 189

yeast, strains of, 119, 180

Zandvliet, 57, 250–3
Zeekoeyenvallei, 13
Zeven Rivieren, 132
Zevenfontein, 132
Zevenwacht, 132–4
Zinfandel, 71, 174